The Geopolitics of Drugs

Translation from the French by Laurent Laniel, Deke Dusinberre, and Charles Hoots

Nikos Passas
Advisor to Northeastern University Press on Transnational Crime

OBSERVATOIRE GÉOPOLITIQUE
OGD
DES DROGUES

The Geopolitics of Drugs

1996 Edition

Observatoire Géopolitique des Drogues

Geopolitical Drug Watch

NORTHEASTERN UNIVERSITY PRESS ✦ BOSTON

Northeastern University Press, 1996

ISBN 1-55553-262-4 (alk. paper)
ISSN 1086-2927

Composed in Fairfield Light by Lisa Diercks.
Printed and bound by Thomson-Shore, Inc., in Dexter, Michigan.
The paper is Glatfelter Opaque.

Designed by Lisa Diercks
Maps by Pascale Perez

This book was translated from the French
thanks to Fondation pour le Progrès de l'Homme (FPH)
38 rue Saint Sabin, Paris, 75011

MANUFACTURED IN THE UNITED STATES OF AMERICA
99 98 97 96 5 4 3 2 1

Contents

Maps

Preface

The Geopolitical Drug Watch—officially known as *Observatoire Géopolitique des Drogues* (OGD)—is an independent organization that analyzes the economic, political, and military aspects of the production, trafficking, and consumption of illicit drugs. It does this by calling on a network of 250 correspondents in 90 countries who are drawn from the academic and legal professions, the media, and nongovernmental organizations. But the OGD is not just a press agency on narcotics. It also sends its own specialists into the field to conduct in-depth investigations. Some of these have been carried out on behalf of national and international organizations, such as the European Union, in regions like Southwest Asia, West Africa, and the Balkans, and on subjects as diverse as cocaine in Europe and a comparison of alternative development projects in Pakistan and Bolivia. This book, the OGD's first English-language publication, is our organization's third annual report. It contains information that was originally published in the OGD monthly newsletter, the *Geopolitical Drug Dispatch,* as well as completely original material arising from our correspondents' and members' investigations on the ground.

In spite of their specialization, OGD staff members often say that their main interest is not drugs. Some people may find this view paradoxical, but in fact it is a way of asserting that concentrating on the *geopolitics* of the illicit drug trade is a highly effective way of analyzing this complex contemporary problem. The manufacture and marketing of drugs are not, in general, the main causes of lawlessness, violence, and injustice. They occur in the context of regional and national entities characterized by underdevelopment and economic inequality, often accompanied by political, ethnic, and social conflicts. They may constitute the economic manifestation of a drive for ideological, nationalistic, or religious control on the part of governments or militias linked to ethnic or religious groups.

Talking about the drug trade also means addressing the issues of human and minority rights, the environment, North-South relations, arms sales, and of course regional conflicts. Illicit drugs generate such substantial profits that they can swiftly become the main stakes of a conflict that they initially merely served to finance. The cases of Afghanistan, Lebanon, and Burma exemplify this process. The recent disintegration of certain nation-states in eastern Europe and Central Asia and the disruption that this has provoked—notably the rise of ethnic nationalism—provide fertile terrain for the growth of illicit financial networks. The fact that the two superpowers have now dropped some of their former client countries simply intensifies those countries' search for alternative financing. Cannabis, coca, poppy, and their derivatives are the only raw materials today whose prices have remained firm on international markets. The increase in surface area devoted to growing such crops is related not only to spiraling national debts but also to the collapse of prices for peanuts, coffee, cacao, and copra. Third World peasants are not, however, getting rich. Taken collectively, it is estimated that they receive less than 1 percent of the estimated US$150 billion in profits generated by the international drug trade. In fact, most of the profits find their way into the economies and banking systems of rich countries.

Developed nations, of course, have set up increasingly sophisticated systems for combating all aspects of drug trafficking and money laundering, notably since the August 1989 assassination of Colombian presidential candidate Luis Carlos Galán. The founding of the Financial Action Task Force (FATF) during a Group of Seven summit held in Paris in July 1989 is an example of such determination.

But it would seem that, on the one hand, the various governments involved and the specialized publications emanating from international institutions possessing information in highly specific areas generally lack a global vision of the phenomena that straddle economic, ethnic, and geostrategic factors. Police departments, for instance, have a thorough knowledge of the mechanisms of drug-trafficking networks, but not necessarily of the social and political phenomena that generate them, nor of the ultimate consequences of police action.

On the other hand, even though the "war on drugs" features prominently in the law-and-order messages that political parties aim at their electorate, it gets short shrift when friendly governments are implicated or when major markets are at stake. The need for independent analysis and assessment, unhindered by diplomatic or economic taboos and free from the sensationalism characteristic of most press reports, is felt by national drug enforcement agencies themselves. But this is not a book for narcotics specialists only. Scholars and students in fields like government, international economic and political relations, development studies, and sociology, to name but a few, will find this book a precious source of information and analysis. The main objective of this publication is to convey in plain language to the public at large, in their capacity as citizens and voters, the hidden stakes of narcotics production and trafficking. It thereby hopes to clarify the debate on one of the greatest threats of our time.

Alain Labrousse
OGD Director

The Geopolitics of Drugs

Introduction

In 1994 and early 1995 the developments observed in illicit drug trafficking since the early 1980s have been reinforced and have even accelerated. The production and marketing of all drugs are growing significantly. "Business connections" and the exchanging of favors between criminal organizations the world over are multiplying. Mafias have penetrated to the very heart of an increasing number of countries. While drug use remains relatively stable in rich nations, it is spreading dramatically in drug-producing countries throughout the Third World.

In Europe, a new method of trafficking has emerged, which the OGD calls "short (or fragmented) networks," greatly complicating the task of law enforcement officials in their fight against the illegal drug trade.

Also for the first time, the growth of synthetic drugs as a proportion of total drug consumption, mainly due to an increase in their production in the former communist countries, confirms fears that a veritable revolution in drug use is taking place all over the world.

Lastly, the globalization of world economies, inspired by the most radical free-trade philosophy, tends to make a mockery of the provisions implemented against money laundering.

Limitations in the Fight Against Money Laundering

The fight against money laundering entered a new stage in 1994. What had been just one of the many weapons available for the "war on drugs" when the Financial Action Task Force (FATF) was set up in 1989 has acquired the status of a panacea, now that it has been acknowledged—implicitly or explicitly—that classic measures based on police repression have been an abject failure. But the unanimous view, voiced at countless international summits, that the fight against drugs will be effective only if major traffickers' wallets are hurt serves to obscure a disturbing reality. In fact, it is increasingly difficult to differentiate, within the international financial system, between the networks used for laundering the money of criminal organizations and those that breathe life into the global, free-trade economy: offshore banks and holding companies; networks of corruption, with their attendant dubious intermediaries feeding on the universal practices of underground funding of political activity; kickbacks or outright bribes; fiddling of consolidated corporate accounts; and tax evasion. It has become glaringly obvious, as demonstrated by this report's section on Switzerland in particular (see Appendix One), that such gestures in the direction of fighting money laundering are intended primarily to avoid a serious diagnosis of the fundamental causes of the disease by pointing to a mere symptom.

Soaring Output

Despite the many warlike declarations and initiatives by officials of the great powers, drug production and trafficking are on the rise virtually everywhere.

In spring 1994, an impressive study by experienced field investigators on behalf of the United Nations Drug Control Program (UNDCP) estimated production of Afghan opium (from which 70 to 80 percent of heroin consumption in Europe originates) at between 3,200 to 3,300 tons, enough to turn out, theoretically, 320 to 330 tons of pure heroin.[1] Such figures prove either that the sophisticated technology (satellite pictures) deployed by the United States is utterly useless or, more likely, that America has been trying to mask the leniency of the Central Intelligence Agency (CIA) toward the activities of its *mujahedeen* allies during ten years of war in Afghanistan. Thus, according to the U.S. Department of State's latest report, 700 tons is the figure for Afghan opium production in the spring of 1993.

Meanwhile, according to American statisticians, which in this case have no reason to underestimate production data for a country supplying 60 percent of the heroin consumed in the United States, Burma's 1994 harvest has remained at about the same level (2,575 tons) as that of 1993, which represented an increase from 1992's 2,280 tons. In Laos and Thai-

---

1. Throughout this text the term *ton* refers to a metric ton (1 metric ton = 2,200 pounds).

land, the other two countries of the Golden Triangle, output is also thought to have remained stable in the past year. By contrast, in other countries in the region—such as China, Vietnam, and Cambodia—numerous clues indicate that production is climbing. To all this must be added the opiates output of countries of the Commonwealth of Independent States (CIS)—Tajikistan, Uzbekistan, and Ukraine in particular—which is also rising fast. So, too, is that of Latin American nations, notably Colombia and Peru (half a ton of opium was seized in Peru in late 1994).

Although 1994 statistics are not yet available, they should confirm increased cocaine production in Latin America. While coca acreage has remained stable in Bolivia and has probably risen somewhat in Peru, all estimates agree that it has more than doubled in Colombia over the last two years. There is good reason to believe that Colombian narcos aim to become self-sufficient in supplies of cocaine-base paste so as to end their dependence on both their traditional suppliers. Despite increasing production and improved yields, prices of cocaine base and cocaine hydrochloride tended to rise during 1994, suggesting that Colombian and other narcos from Latin America have set off to conquer new markets, especially in eastern Europe and Asia. Probably between 1,000 and 1,500 tons of cocaine hydrochloride were manufactured in 1994 (226 tons of this drug were seized throughout the world in 1993).

The world's hashish output, as estimated from seizure statistics and consumption figures, continues at a very high level, with both the Golden Crescent (Afghanistan and Pakistan) and Morocco still vying for world supremacy. While marijuana production remains fairly stable in the Americas, it is expanding all over Africa, stimulated both by the recession and by the adverse effects of structural adjustment programs. Diverted legal drugs and designer drugs come second only to cannabis derivatives as the world's most widely used substances.[2]

Booming drug production worldwide is, among other factors, responsible for a new development in the methods by which the trade is carried out. "Short networks," as the OGD has named the phenomenon, are

---

2. Cannabis (or Indian hemp) is the name of the plant from which marijuana (dried cannabis leaves or flowery tops in smokable or edible form) is obtained. Marijuana is also known as "pot," "weed," and "grass." Hashish (or hash) is cannabis resin and is also smoked or eaten.

also a consequence of the multiplication of local conflicts since the end of the Cold War, as warring parties seek alternative sources of funds.

"Short Networks" and Long Conflicts

Whereas official speeches on the need to fight drugs rely heavily on Manichean vocabulary when evoking "organized crime," observers of criminal activity increasingly face a much more diverse reality in today's fragmented world. Two factors are at play that, although they may sometimes be interconnected, are nonetheless distinct in character. Admittedly, the announced disappearance of the European Union's internal borders and the birth, following the fall of the Berlin Wall, of an economic and financial "Wild East" have offered golden business opportunities to criminal organizations, as well as the possibility of their forming alliances with one another. Some of these—such as the Colombian, Italian, and Chinese organizations—are very old and highly structured. But at the same time, downstream (in the regions where production is actually carried out) as well as upstream (at the transport and marketing stages) the convulsions induced by the collapse of the Soviet Union have compounded the long-standing conflicts of Asia. All along the opium route, where silk was once carried from Asia to Europe, drugs serve as a readily available means of funding guerrilla movements as well as ethnic, religious, or border conflicts. Warring parties use their diasporas and their migrants as a beachhead inside Europe, setting up their own networks for the cause, and sometimes just for profit.

In Latin America different causes have had quite similar effects. In Colombia, the death of Pablo Escobar and the subsequent collapse of the relatively centralized organization of the Medellin cartel have led to the fragmentation of the trade, partly into the hands of small- to medium-scale entrepreneurs who only work together when they have to, as has always been the case with the hundred or so groups wrongly named "the Cali cartel." In Peru, certain organizations called "firms," striving to become independent from Colombian traffickers, are setting up their own cocaine hydrochloride export networks. In Africa, especially in Nigeria, the drug trade wraps itself around ancient smuggling networks that rely on extended family structures.

In Europe, such phenomena trigger market fragmentation. Clans from Kosovo, Chechnya, or Morocco; militants of the Kurdistan Workers' Party (PKK); Afghan or Palestinian fundamentalists; Nigerian "students" and Senegalese immigrant workers; Croat, Serb, or Bosnian fighters; and "businessmen" from Latin America, Israel, Poland, or Russia all create networks of "distributors" (trading in quantities of 1 to 20 kilograms), soon to become "raiders" operating outside classic drug-trading patterns. Political parties, brotherhoods, friends, relatives, former fellow conscripts, or intelligence service colleagues (think of the KGB and its contacts worldwide) provide essential information regarding the size of cities and towns, local dealers, and potential clientele. Raiders stay in a target location for a few weeks, or even just a few days, striking up short-lived relationships, and selling their merchandise—mainly heroin and sometimes cocaine—to local purchasers. Then they leave to stock up again and choose a new target. In reality they are neither "mules" (couriers) nor intermediaries. Most of the time they own the drugs they distribute, having bought them in Albania, Bulgaria, Turkey, Spain, Egypt, Ukraine, or even in Central Asia itself. Europe as a whole is their market, their target. They travel by plane, train, and also by car with their whole family. They avoid friction with local dealers. Except when they are unlucky, as happened in Annecy, France, in late 1994, they are long gone before the local underworld or police even start reacting to their presence.

Whoever manages to look beyond the traditional conception of organized crime—the comfortable idea of centralized, criminal, entrepreneurial hierarchies (the mafia with its long tentacles)—can observe the short networks at work just about everywhere in Europe. In Amsterdam operators have been caught going from restaurant to restaurant, offering fruit juice cans with a false bottom filled with cocaine. In London they hang about in clubs and discos. In France they patronize bars, and in Germany cafes and saunas. They use trains, stations, electronic games arcades, and hotel lobbies as outlets. Or they may lock themselves up in a room at a fancy hotel, working on the phone, waiting for that call. They prefer provincial towns—Annecy, Verona, Karlovy-Vary—and especially sleepy tourist, ski, sea, or spa resorts in low season. Stretching from the Baltic to the Mediterranean, short networks are acquiring something of a name over in Tirane, Sofia, and Istanbul. The drugs from these networks are fairly cheap and very pure. This is because production has boomed in Afghanistan and has started with a vengeance in Central Asia. It is also a consequence of the permeability of the borders of the former Soviet empire, and of the incessant coming and going of refugees and new "businessmen."

Along the increasingly long and varied transit routes, smugglers get their cut and in turn become wholesalers. They consider more and more airports fairly safe: Almaty, Tashkent, Bishkek, and Nairobi are but a few examples. Outboards link the Adriatic and the Black Sea via the Bosphorus with impunity.

Such fragmentation of the western European market is first and foremost the tangible result of the worsening of a series of conflicts, from Asia to the Balkans to Africa. This phenomenon is amply demonstrated by French complacency toward the corrupt regimes of Rwanda, Zaire, or Equatorial Guinea; the Economic Community of West African States getting bogged down in wars in Liberia and Sierra Leone; the European Union's helplessness to put an end to the Bosnian conflict and to Serb oppression of ethnic Albanians in Kosovo; European tolerance of the brakes put on modernization in Albania; acknowledgment in both Europe and America that conflicts in the Caucasus or Central Asia fall within Moscow's competence, or even that they are an internal Russian matter; and silence concerning the Kurdish conflict. All these trends have a bearing on the problems posed by drug trafficking and, in a broader sense, by criminality and drug abuse in Europe.

The Chechen affair is the latest example of this tendency to deterioration. The Russian invasion of this autonomous republic will have three lasting consequences: never-ending guerrilla warfare; the inescapable need for weapons and, therefore, for constant sources of funds; and the subjugation of a peaceful and hardworking civilian population to nationalist militias who will weave closer links with the Chechen criminals' traditional operations within their diaspora in Russia, central Europe, and the Middle East. Chechnya will act as a precedent reinforcing Moscow's attempts to use Slav criminal organizations and minorities for its own ends—and thus reconquer the strategic region from the Caucasus to the Baltic countries.

A New Role for the Balkans and the Caucasus

The extremely fast growth of illicit drug production and trafficking makes the text of the present annual report, the OGD's third,[3] completely original. Traditionally, the OGD report provides an extensive review of

3. *See La Drogue, nouveau désordre mondial,* Hachette, Paris, 1993; and *État des drogues, drogues des États,* Hachette, Paris, 1994.

one particular region of the world. After focusing on the Golden Crescent in 1993 and Morocco in 1994, this year it emphasizes yet another hot area of the world: the region extending from the Balkans to the Caucasus, where conflicts have been front-page news during the past twelve months.

In this region today, the collapse of the Soviet empire has given a new lease of life to ethnic, religious, and national antagonisms, which are feeding on all kinds of illicit activities, including the drug trade. The convulsions of older conflicts, from Cyprus to the Middle East, as well as the downfall of marxist regimes such as those of Albania and Yugoslavia, are leading to the rapid consolidation of the Caucasus and southern Russia on the one hand and the Mediterranean region on the other. Two NATO member-states that are perpetually at odds, Turkey and Greece, have Mediterranean coastlines, as do all the countries of the Balkan Peninsula. This area, currently the scene of a war in Bosnia, may see the start of another in Kosovo (Serbia) that would probably also lead to the involvement of Albania and Macedonia (the former Yugoslav Republic of Macedonia).

In the Caucasus, as has already been stated, Russian intervention in Chechnya will strengthen Chechen mobsters who will be tempted, like ethnic Albanians in the Kosovo today, to expand their networks ever farther toward the West.

The present report differs from the previous edition in one important aspect. Because the international situation is changing so rapidly, especially in the East, the OGD has decided, for this year at least, not to draw up a classification of the relations between states and narcotics, as these relations have become even more complex than in the past. True, some state institutions in numerous countries are linked to drug-trafficking networks, but they also feed on a lot of other illicit activities. Nigeria, Equatorial Guinea, Panama, Paraguay, Albania, Georgia, Azerbaijan, Chechnya, Russia itself, and so on are "trafficker-states" rather than "narco-states."[4]

4. In *État des drogues, drogues des États,* op. cit., the OGD defined a "narco-state" as "a country in which the state or a sector of the state is involved in the drug trade or uses proceeds from the drug trade." The classification also included, to indicate lesser degrees of involvement, "deeply affected states" and "sensitive states" respectively.

Furthermore, since only Third World countries were listed in the classification, the responsibility of rich countries in the development of mafia-style systems appeared to be relegated to the background. And this despite the fact that the OGD's first report described in much detail the recycling of drug money in the economies of the North; the production and export of chemical reagents that the North is perfectly aware will be diverted to manufacture drugs; arms sales to governments with notorious links to the drug trade; leniency toward nations that constitute strategic allies or good investment opportunities; and so forth. However, it is impossible not to note, as the reader will surely do when referring to the relevant chapters, that no significant changes have taken place in the countries classified as "narco-states" and that a certain number of them (for example, Peru, Pakistan, Burma, and Morocco) have become even more deeply involved in narcotics.

Because of the sheer scale of the phenomenon at hand, the present report, like the previous ones, does not aim to be comprehensive, for fear of assuming encyclopedic proportions. Some countries, like those of the Caribbean and Central America, were thoroughly reviewed in 1994. Since no fundamental changes occurred there, they have not been included this year. By contrast, numerous countries that were not reviewed last year are given attention in the present edition: Caucasian countries, Albania, Bulgaria, the Czech Republic, Cyprus, Hungary, Germany, Australia, Laos, the Philippines, and Nepal. Bolivia and Paraguay are back in the section on South America. The review of African countries continues this year and includes South Africa, Rwanda, Burundi, Guinea, Burkina Faso, Mauritania, and Cape Verde. We have not attempted to review all the countries in the same way but have varied our approach so that readers may obtain a better idea of the place of each country in the overall picture of the international drug trade.

In accordance with the OGD's purpose, this report also contains appendices with analytical reviews of subjects not directly related to one particular country: the legalization debate; an overview of the antilaundering fight through a study of the Swiss case; and a review of the production and trade in synthetic drugs. The OGD intends to develop this kind of approach further in coming years.

1. *From the Balkans to the Caucasus*

All types of illicit activities, including the drug trade, are fueling the antagonisms resulting from the collapse of the Soviet empire. Today, from the Ionic Sea to the Gulf of Batumi, conflicts over ethnicity, religion, and borders are worsening or about to break out. The convulsions from older wars, from Cyprus to the Middle East, as well as the downfall of marxist regimes such as those of Albania and Yugoslavia, have caused the Caucasus, southern Russia and Ukraine, and the Mediterranean region to become interconnected. The eastern Mediterranean, extending into the Black Sea, is an inland sea linking regions that have recently become the scene of fighting: the Caucasus, Russia, Ukraine, and the Balkans. Two NATO member-states that are perpetually at odds, Turkey and Greece, have shores on the eastern Mediterranean, as have all the countries of the Balkan Peninsula. This area, currently the scene of a war in Bosnia could soon witness another in Kosovo (Serbia), which would probably then lead to the involvement of Albania and Macedonia as well. Behaviors responding to the most liberally minded market logic have taken root based on what the peoples and states caught up in the current storm must do to survive because they have entered into contact with Western patterns of consumption, because of their geopolitical location, and because of the very wars they are fighting. The result is that new money elites, warlords, and even trafficker-states have arisen to cash in on disorder, embargoes, and conflicts—which they even go as far as cultivating to perpetuate their own existence.

Macedonia and Kosovo[1]

While representatives from the whole mosaic of the ethnic communities inhabiting the Balkans are involved to a greater or lesser extent in the various illicit activities of the Balkan drug routes, ethnic Albanian communities in Albania, the Kosovo province of Serbia, and Macedonia provide most of the players in heroin smuggling and marketing networks. Also using these routes are large quantities of weapons destined not only for the current conflict in Bosnia but also for the brewing war in Kosovo.

Drugs and Arms . . .

On May 18, 1994, as part of a ten-month-old operation code-named "Macedonia," Italian police dismantled a major Italian-Macedonian network and seized 40 kilograms of heroin produced in Turkey and shipped to Italy via the Balkans. This was not the police's first catch: The Macedonian vice minister of the interior announced in late November that law enforcement agents had seized 68 kilograms of heroin since the beginning of the year. The drugs originated in Turkey, passed through Bulgaria, and were headed for Western markets. The largest seizure, 40 kilograms, took place at the border with Albania. Moreover, 16,405 criminal offenses have been registered in Macedonia since the beginning of the year. Most offenders were nationals of Serbia—in fact ethnic Albanians from Kosovo—and Albania. The borders between Serbia and Kosovo and between Kosovo and Albania are currently under heavy guard. Thus, it is likely that networks of Albanian Kosovars, who sell heroin and purchase arms in western Europe—especially in Switzerland, have now chosen to use Macedonia and Albania as transit points.

Arrests of Albanian nationals, Kosovars, and Macedonians are multiplying in Switzerland, Germany, and—since late November 1994—France. In Annecy, a French town close to the Swiss border, twelve people were arrested on heroin-trafficking charges. Five of them were from Kosovo. Equally significant is a recent case involving a Macedonian resident of Switzerland, who was arrested at the Liechtenstein border transporting 30 kilograms of heroin in his car on his way back from Skopje, the capital of Macedonia. In November alone, 120 ethnic Albanians from Albania, Kosovo, and Macedonia were arrested in Switzer-

1. Romania and the former Yugoslavia were reviewed in OGD 1994 report, *État des drogues, drogues des États,* op. cit.

land. In recent months, significant quantities of heroin have been seized in Switzerland, Germany, Italy, and Greece from traffickers who usually hail from Pristina (the capital of Kosovo), Skopje, or Skorda (a large town in northern Albania). Meanwhile, two towns located on opposite sides of the Serbian-Macedonian border—Vratnica on the Macedonian side, Biastica on the Kosovo side—both inhabited by the same Albanian families, allegedly serve as a heroin passage point.

According to an investigation conducted by a special OGD envoy, the real hub of activity in Macedonia is the town of Gostivar, its equivalent in Albania being Tropaja. Sealed tractor-trailers travel between the two hubs with a frequency hard to justify on the grounds of legal commerce alone. The town of Komanovo, right near a highway and a Macedonian military barracks, reportedly shelters a highly sophisticated heroin refinery, which receives chemical reagents from a factory near the Greek border originally built by the Germans. At Skopje's Grand Hotel, an entire floor is reserved for new mafia kingpins who travel ostentatiously in Mercedes automobiles, wear Armani clothes, and are accompanied by discreet bodyguards toting assault rifles and handguns. The Macedonian government officially describes these young Albanians—whose flashy wealth is all the more provocative at a time of unprecedented economic crisis aggravated by the Greek embargo—as "traders" who are obliged to defend themselves in hard times. Notwithstanding, a high official from the Macedonian Ministry of the Interior maintains that a new Balkan route has been opened through his country. In the first nine months of 1994, Macedonian law enforcement agents arrested 189 individuals on drug-trafficking charges. Most of them were ethnic Albanians.

The war in Bosnia guarantees the Albanian mafia an "understanding attitude" on the part of the Macedonian authorities, since Macedonia's Muslim Albanian population now views the struggle as a veritable holy war against Serbia. Across the border, Albanian authorities are equally understanding—Tirane is inherently in favor of an uprising in Kosovo. Harsh Serbian repression in Kosovo, a formerly autonomous province of Yugoslavia whose population is 85 percent ethnic Albanians, is being carried out not only by the army but also by the nationalist Serbian henchmen of a warlord named Arkan, who has his headquarters in another Grand Hotel, this time in Pristina. Kosovo Albanians, who have lost the autonomy they were granted under Tito, have been alienated from all economic and social activity. They manage to survive thanks to help from their compatriots abroad, a diaspora that amounts to fully one-third of the population inside Kosovo. An Albanian teacher who lost his educational post told the OGD's envoy that not a single family in Pristina could survive without what are euphemistically referred to as "Swiss" funds. In fact, given the urgent need for cash and the obligation to use unofficial banking channels, the Albanian communities in Switzerland, the United States, and Germany have swiftly become active in shipping and distributing heroin. In many cases they have even managed to supplant the local Turkish mafia, which had been entrenched there for a long time. Two factors especially are helping the Albanians. First, the rapidly expanding Caucasian heroin industry (refineries and shipment) is run mainly by Georgian and Armenian gangsters, who are extremely hostile to their Turkish competitors. Second, the Albanians are willing to swap drugs directly for weapons. An additional element in their favor is the growing xenophobia directed against Turks in Germany, a major heroin market. Turks are automatically suspected of trafficking, thereby hampering their network's freedom of movement. The Albanian connection in Germany is much more recent and uses Croat dealers, giving it greater scope.

. . . for Greater Albania

It is legitimate to ask why trafficking on such a large scale, openly known at local levels, has not been picked up by the international media. The silence can probably be explained by favorable attitudes toward a "Greater Albania"; the trafficking is basically being judged on its geostrategic implications. Everyone pretends not to see that a large part of the international humanitarian aid shipped to Albania is sent directly to Kosovo despite Albania's own poverty. Officially, Tirane is calling for extensive autonomy for Kosovo, but the Albanians are well aware that Serbian intransigence will make such a solution unworkable.

So everyone is ready for a new conflict. The U.S. State Department claims that the Balkan conflict is an embryonic war that potentially involves far vaster regions, notably the republics of the former Soviet Union populated by Muslim majorities. A crushing defeat of their fellow Muslims in the Balkans, it is argued, could push these republics into Iranian-style fundamentalism. This theory is used to justify unilateral U.S. action in the area. The only U.S. expeditionary force in the region is stationed in Macedonia, where it duplicates the role of the United

Nations Scandinavian troops, all the while remaining under U.S. command. Marines and intelligence agents, almost all of whom are veterans of the "Special Corps" in Lebanon, initially numbered only 300 (who were regularly relieved in order "to allow the greatest number of soldiers to become familiar with the country," according to one officer). In early 1995, there were 2,150 American troops in Macedonia. The U.S. government, which has witnessed the European Union's ineffectiveness in the Balkans, is not ruling out the possibility of supporting a "Greater Albania" that would put a brake on Serbian expansion. Furthermore, the increased autonomy, or even the independence, of Kosovo would be based on a population that is overwhelmingly homogeneous, and such a development could therefore easily be sold to international opinion.

First and foremost, this means the Macedonian government, which has the most to lose from a redrawing of regional borders. It has been hit hard by Greece's economic and political embargo and has to deal with increasingly dangerous opposition from the ultranationalist Macedonian Revolutionary Organization (VMRO). In order to cling to its majority, the government has had to make concessions to the Albanian minority, which means that it has increasingly aligned itself with Tirane's policies despite certain disagreements. As a result, four deputies from the Democratic party, which represents the Albanian minority, were admitted to the cabinet as ministers after the general election of 1994.

In Kosovo the illicit trade in drugs and weapons is feeding on geopolitical hopes and fears. The province's inhabitants are being held hostage not only by the Serbs but also by local godfathers who "protect" them in the finest mafia tradition. As a FORPRONU (the United Nations force in Bosnia) officer declared to the OGD's special envoy, "weapons, heroin and dirty money are transforming this part of the world into a new drug hub." In the face of this perfectly obvious situation, U.S. priorities in Macedonia dictate turning a blind eye to a drug trade that finances the arming of Kosovo Albanians liable to loosen the Serbian yoke, or even to prompt an uprising. This blindness is made all the easier since the heroin in question is destined for Europe rather than North America.

Albania

Hundreds of used Mercedes and other flashy cars permanently fill an empty lot of 5 hectares (12 acres) between the national highway and the docks of Durrës, Albania's leading port. Among them are the "transporters," or "courier-cars" that carry heroin through the Balkans on behalf of the Italian mafia. These cars were purchased in Italy.

Cars Going like a Bomb

Although a daily shipping line operates between Italy's Adriatic ports and Durrës, the cars make a big detour and pass through Slovenia, Austria, Germany, Poland, Slovakia, Hungary, Romania, and Bulgaria, finally entering Albania via Macedonia and crossing Lake Ohrid to Pogradec (see Map 1). At each stage of the journey, the cars deliver drugs and stock up on televisions, video equipment, and other household goods. To avoid identification, a "transporter car" will make only one or two international trips. The car is given as a "bonus" to the courier, who can have its registration changed by making a simple declaration to an Albanian official. It can then be resold for between US$2,500 and $8,000. Operation Mani Pulite (clean hands) in Italy has paradoxically fueled this traffic, since many politicians and businessmen want to get rid of their Mercedes, which have become signs of suspect wealth. Once "sold," these cars are often reported as "stolen," allowing their owners to cash in on insurance payments too. Several months ago, the president of Albania's Central Bank was arrested in Bari, Italy, behind the wheel of a Mercedes bought in Tirane after it was reported stolen in Italy. These illicit activities rely on a vast black market in visas, passports, and registration plates that make identification nearly impossible.

In fact, Albanians do not perceive such activities as illegal trafficking but rather as simple trade—an activity forbidden and described as "trafficking" by the communist regime for fifty years is now presented as valued business. Drugs have thus moved alongside oil, weapons, cigarettes, fruit, vegetables, the notorious "red mercury," and TNT made at a factory in Gramsh, a town not far from Tirane. This was allegedly used during the bombing campaign in Florence, Milan, and Rome that preceded the 1994 election in Italy. Market forces—and the term must be taken at face value—have acquired the upper hand all the more easily given the current geopolitical context. Two of Albania's neighbors are currently under an embargo: The new Yugoslavia is under international embargo, and Macedonia is under Greek embargo. There is an open war in Bosnia and another brewing in Kosovo. Italy, the land of mafias, is right nearby. Goods pass—often under the protection of the Albanian police—into Montenegro via the Albanian border posts of Hani Horti

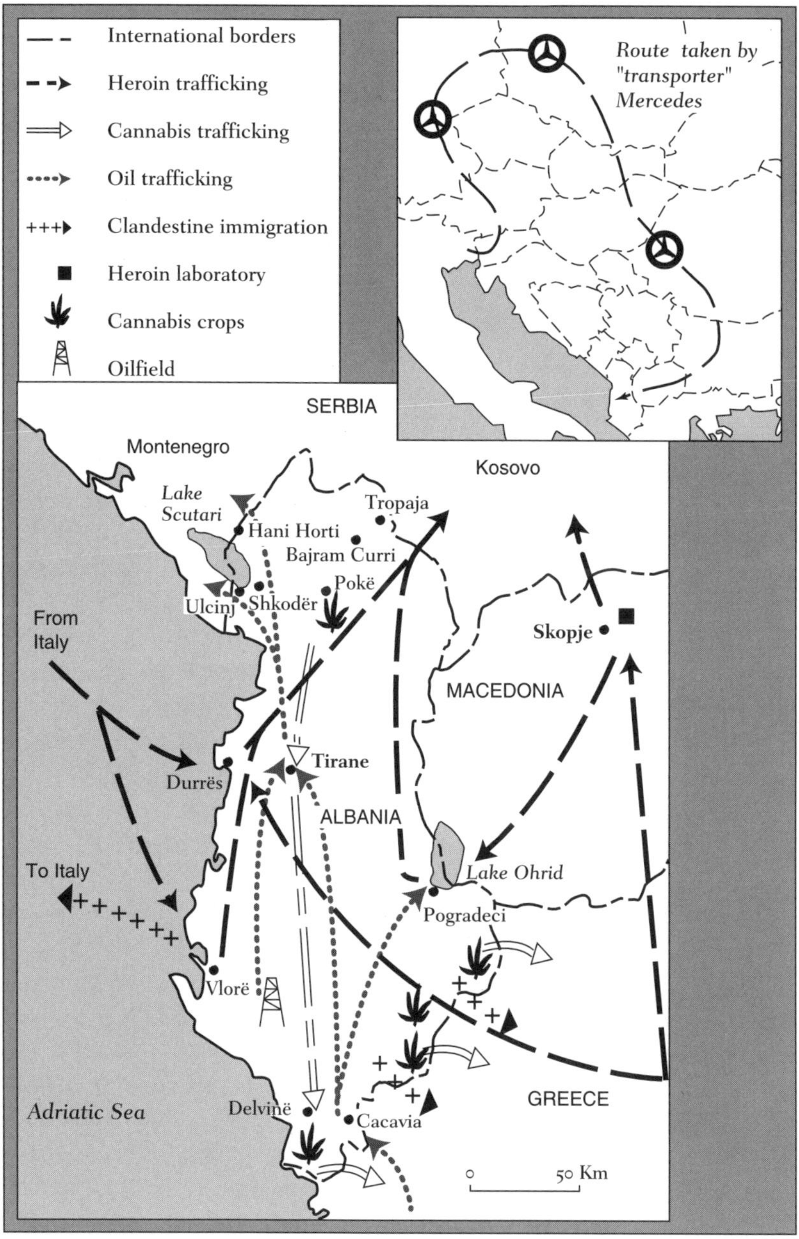

Map 1. Trafficking in Albania

and Ulcinj, into Kosovo via Tropaja, and into Greece via Cacavia. At the port of Vlorë, a fleet of outboards ferries clandestine immigrants to Italian shores and returns with heroin. Thus every Greco-Albanian crisis, every increase in tension in Kosovo, and every hardening of the international community's position on Serbia make for new fortunes in Tirane.

"Family" Government

Local Albanian politicians not only benefit from the ambient disorder, they even seem to count on it. This hardly encourages efforts toward the modernization and restructuring of Albania. All legislative attempts at creating a legal framework acceptable to the international community have been systematically thwarted. Thus, it is quite possible that the latest draft constitution, which under Albanian law could have been submitted to a vote by the Parliament—which would have adopted it—was rejected in the referendum of December 6, 1994, because some dispositions were purposely added that were sure to be opposed by all interest groups. Indeed, Albanian society functions largely on the almost mythical notion of *bessa,* which means absolute respect for verbal promises. Breaking one's word means running the risk of a death penalty or life sentence. In the northern part of the country, towers to hold offenders have been built in villages. If the culprit cannot be punished, then a male descendant must pay for the offense. After fifty years of Stalinism, people are now being punished for breaking promises made before Enver Hoxha came to power. Thus, the "tribal-like" traditional families, known as *fares,* and alliances of mountain clans are effectively governing the country.

The cohesion of the *fares* is far more important than laws, which have remained largely Stalinist. Albania has no investment policy of its own and is making life difficult for foreign investors. It cashes in on crises with its neighbors to such an extent that one type of trafficking may well mask yet another. Thus, deliveries of oil to Macedonia (skirting the Greek embargo) can be used to cover heroin, as are deliveries of kalashnikov rifles to Albanian "brothers" in Kosovo. Heroin arrives not only from Italy in the notorious "transporter" Mercedes but also from Turkey and the Caucasus via the traditional Balkan route, which now crosses through Albania and into Kosovo following the closure of the border between Macedonia and the new Yugoslavia. Furthermore, the presence of a heroin refinery in Skopje fuels trafficking on this route. Albanians trying to escape this situation are obliged to knuckle under if they want to emigrate. Albanian nationals were recently included in drug networks because of pressure from their "brothers" in Kosovo, who are citizens of the new Yugoslavia. For even though ethnic Albanians are united by hatred of Serbs, there remains a strong antagonism between Kosovars and Albanians. Many of the former, who benefited from the autonomy Tito had granted their province—including the opportunity, denied Albanian citizens, to travel abroad and establish communities in Switzerland and the east coast of the United States—now invest in Albania in the guise of rich and envied relatives. Meanwhile, *fares* in northeastern Albania on the border with Kosovo felt Enver Hoxha's yoke all the more heavily, since the regime's top officials all came from the south. Furthermore, Albanians wanting to emigrate to Germany like the Kosovars who settled there long ago are now forbidden to do so by new German immigration laws denying them the status of political refugees, whereas Kosovars—classified as victims of Serbian oppression—are granted that status. Albanians have therefore been reluctantly obliged to seek help from Kosovars in order to obtain false Yugoslav passports. In exchange the Kosovars demand that the Albanians join the heroin trafficking networks, enabling the Kosovars to avoid relying on greedier Czechs and Croatians.

A young Albanian doctor, originally from Shkodër, who had just returned to Albania after having been a dealer in Munich for six months on behalf of a Kosovo network, explained to the OGD envoy.

> Before, an Albanian needed 50,000 German marks to buy a kilo of heroin. Now the Kosovars supply it at 20,000 to 25,000 marks per kilo and, due to their very tight organization, the risks are minimal. I earned 170,000 marks in six months, which I can lend here at a monthly interest rate of 8 percent. That's enough to live on and build a house. Later, when Albania has become a normal country again, I will spend another six months in Germany, so that I can come back and open a private medical practice.

It is estimated that 5,000 false passports—or real passports with forged visas—are in circulation in the German-speaking regions of western Europe (Germany, Austria, certain Swiss cantons). On the black market in Tirane and in Tetovo, the region around Bajram Curri (a hotbed of Albanian nationalism), passports "from Kosovo" now cost as much as those purchased from members of the Greek minority in "northern Epirus" (a region of southern Albania with a large ethnic Greek minority)—an astonishing fact, as the latter almost automatically entitle the holder to a visa to enter Greece, and therefore the European Union, followed by a work permit.

Grass for the Poor

But Albania does not only provide couriers for the heroin trade. It also produces marijuana. In the summer of 1994, at Delvinë in southern Albania, the owners of a 20-hectare (48-acre) field of cannabis were arrested and their crop seized, while to the north, near Pokë, 5 hectares (12 acres) of Indian hemp were destroyed. These operations will not, however, be included in national statistics. Arben Dolafi, the prosecutor in Pokë, provided an explanation to the OGD envoy: "It is strictly forbidden to publicize drug cases until they have resulted in a conviction—and before that happens, a lot of water can pass under the bridge." This situation is confirmed by a young trafficker: "With money and good contacts, you never spend more than 24 hours in jail." When it is pointed out that the media have publicized certain cases, he answers, "Those are the guys who compete unfairly with the godfathers, who haven't respected the *bessa*."

With marijuana crops coming under increasing surveillance in Greece due to international pressure, "pot" is now being grown in the southern half of Albania and then exported into Greece. Since the border between the two countries has been opened, power relations are being worked out between Greeks and Epirotes (residents of the ancient territory of Epirus that straddles Greece and Albania) on the one hand and Albanians on the other. The latter obtain false passports in Greek names (at a cost of US$500 to $1,500) and then blend into the crowd of 300,000 people who cross the border each year, legally or otherwise. The roles are divided as follows: Seeds come from Greece, the couriers are Albanian, the distributors are Epirotes. As political tension mounts between Albania and its neighbors—Montenegro, Kosovo, Macedonia, Greece—prices climb. This mechanism, which applies to oil and cigarettes, also works for marijuana and heroin.

Medical Deal

As a consequence of the country's recent history, drug abuse in Albania has its own particularity. The heroin entering Albania is not aimed at the local market because local abusers take a single drug, pethidine, supplied almost exclusively by local doctors. Until now these doctors have successfully blocked the consumption of other drugs in Albania. Whereas trafficking in heroin and cannabis is handled by the conventional mafias springing from the *fares,* the illegal trade in pethidine (powerful synthetic morphine used medically as a painkiller) is handled by an association of doctors and paramedical workers.

When Albania was hit by an economic crisis at the end of the 1980s, doctors and medical students found that marketing the substance was an efficient way to survive. Enormous stocks of the drug already existed, partly from local production and partly from Chinese imports (considered to be of poorer quality). So it was the doctors themselves who created networks of "hooked" clients all across Albania, making pethidine the national drug. Intravenous pethidine users include high school and college students as well as traders. Recently, female addicts have begun to appear. A doctor's salary varies between US$50 and $70 per month, while a dose of pethidine costs $5. Since stocks long ago fell into private hands, profits are on the order of 100 percent, and can supplement a doctor's income by several hundreds of dollars a day. In Tirane and Shkodër, some addicts inject up to four doses a day.

Because the national health system is based on the principle of local access, there is now no corner of Albania that remains untouched by pethidine abuse. Since the doctors' association functions in a relatively democratic way, no hierarchy has sprung up, as has happened in the case of all other trafficking networks. Each doctor-dealer manages a region determined by the Ministry of Health's administrative division of the country.

Bulgaria

On December 18, 1994, the day after the general election, the resigning interim prime minister, Renata Indzhova, declared: "The election was lost because the state apparatus has not been cleansed." A month earlier, on November 21, she had been even more explicit: "We will not be able to hold an absolutely clean election on December 17 if we do not attack the problem of organized crime today." The red barons, as the former communist *apparatchiks* turned businessmen are known, were the main money sources for the electoral campaign of the up-and-coming young Socialists who easily won the election.

For the population at large, the Socialists, despite the dubious origin of their funds, represent the hope that civil society will be rid of injustice and extortion. Indeed, Bulgarian society as a whole seems threatened by the "security companies" formed by police officials of the old regime, who are accused of racketeering activities aimed at foreign businessmen, Bulgaria's nouveaux riches, and on up to government officials. The "bad cops" now number up to 50,000 and control 50 percent of the country's nightclubs, 70 percent of the casinos, and 80 percent of the cigarette trafficking. They can therefore also be assumed to be the main money launderers in Bulgaria.

Cannabis as Tobacco

In September 1994, Bulgarian police launched a campaign against the country's expanding cannabis crops. Cannabis production is developing fast, and it represents a lot of money for the godfathers who are "protecting" growers. Production is particularly abundant in the wet southern region of the country, where undergrowth combines with marshlands. Six hundred kilograms of cannabis were burned in mid-September in this region, which is currently suffering from a serious economic crisis. Tobacco production, which formerly represented nearly the entire resource base of the region, now finds itself deprived of its traditional outlet, Russia, and must compete with Greece for a share of the European market, which exports the same type of tobacco but has the added advantage of being a member of the European Union. In addition, Bulgarian tobacco farmers supply organized crime groups in Macedonia and Albania, which produce clandestine stocks of cigarettes aimed at supplying an ever-growing market. Cigarette contraband starts out in the border region between Greece, Bulgaria, and Macedonia, passes through Albania, and then floods not only the Balkan countries but Italy as well. The criminal organizations own workshops that reproduce packages of any international brand (to be filled with exactly the same tobacco), undertake mechanized production, coordinate with sea carriers, and so on. As such, these organizations are ready and, more important, able to take charge of the conditioning and distribution of cannabis derivatives should the Bulgarian government succeed in eradicating surplus tobacco production. Up until the Socialists' victory on December 17, observers doubted that the Union of Democratic Forces (UFD), the former ruling party, would risk alienating the farmers. This region, lying on the border with Greece and Turkey, is inhabited by the Pomacs, Muslim Bulgarians, and a Turkish minority. Both groups are represented by the Democratic Liberties Movement (MDL), whose support was crucial if the UFD was to maintain a stable majority in Parliament. But now that the Socialists have an overwhelming majority in Parliament, a political solution could be worked out.

Some farmers also harvested opium poppies in the spring of 1994, particularly in Bulgaria's southwestern regions of Petrich and Melnik. Police spotted some 20 hectares (48 acres) of poppies in this area. Farmers maintained that they were growing poppies to make oil from the seeds. But four persons were arrested while they were making incisions in the poppy capsules (the method by which opium is obtained). According to the head of the National Anti-Crime Service, General Vladimirov, "This is the first time poppies and cannabis have been grown illegally over such a large area." Vladimirov added that the problem is difficult to handle, given that there are only two police officers in all of Bulgaria charged with patrolling illicit crops. On top of this, their helicopter spends most of its time grounded for lack of fuel. Elsewhere, the National Drug Service has revealed the existence of numerous cases of illicit production of psychotropic substances, phenobarbital, or amphetamines by pharmaceutical firms. But lack of regulations in the pharmaceutical industry means that the authorities have little control.

Bulgaria is also an important transit route for heroin coming through the Balkans. In 1993, seizures at the borders with Turkey, Romania, and the former Yugoslavia amounted to 500 kilograms. In 1994, 377 kilograms were seized. On November 7, another 12 kilograms were confiscated on the border with Greece. On November 22, two Bulgarians were arrested at the Greek border in possession of 2 kilograms of heroin, as was another Bulgarian the following day. In both cases the drugs came from Russia via the Balkan route. Seizures show that Bulgarians are working with international organizations, as was illustrated in July when 150 kilograms of heroin was seized in the United Kingdom on a Bulgarian truck that had come through Belgium. Some Bulgarian networks have encouraged farmers to begin poppy growing, which was still legal only a decade ago because it was destined for use in the pharmaceutical industry. But this time it would be for the traffickers' own benefit, eliminating their dependence on deliveries from the Balkan route. The police have an even more difficult task now that the activities of organized crime, particularly in connection with members of the former intelligence service (KDC), are expanding into arms, radioactive materials, currencies, stolen automobiles, and narcotics. "They are trying to turn our country into a well-marked highway for smuggling. But we will resist," declared the outgoing interim prime minister once again, stressing that fighting the mafia groups means above all "purging the state apparatus."

Greece

Official figures suggest that drug use in Greece has skyrocketed since the late 1980s. Marijuana and hashish, both traditionally consumed substances, were never a serious concern for the authorities. Users were supplied mainly by a local output of excellent quality in the Peloponnesus; in growing areas located in the region of Kalamata; in Thrace, due to the initiative of farmers belonging to the Turkish and Pomac minorities; and in Thessaly.

The Little Smoke from Chernobyl

But this domestic production, marketed on a small scale, must today face the stiff competition of imported products sold in the famous Athens flea market of Monastiraki. The market has been expanding constantly for the last four years, and what used to be no more than a picturesque square is today a maze of streets, sprawling over several miles. The "Euxine Greeks" from the Black Sea—traders who come in the hundreds from the countries of the Caucasus, from the Ukraine, and from Russia—have finally hemmed in the area, flooding the sidewalks with an incredible jumble from the countries of the former Soviet Union. But, among the Zenit cameras, the Russian dolls, the chain saws, and the samovars, another product, affectionately known as "the little smoke from Chernobyl," has recently appeared. It is sold at a very low price—about US$8—and its confessed origin does not deter enthusiasts in the least.

Indeed, cannabis and poppies have always been grown in the Ukraine. But in the regions surrounding Chernobyl, because of the administrative no man's land that was created around the crippled nuclear plant, "pot" has thrived. The members of the Greek minority who are longtime inhabitants of the region, some of whose families came during the reign of Catherine the Great, "traditionally" smoked

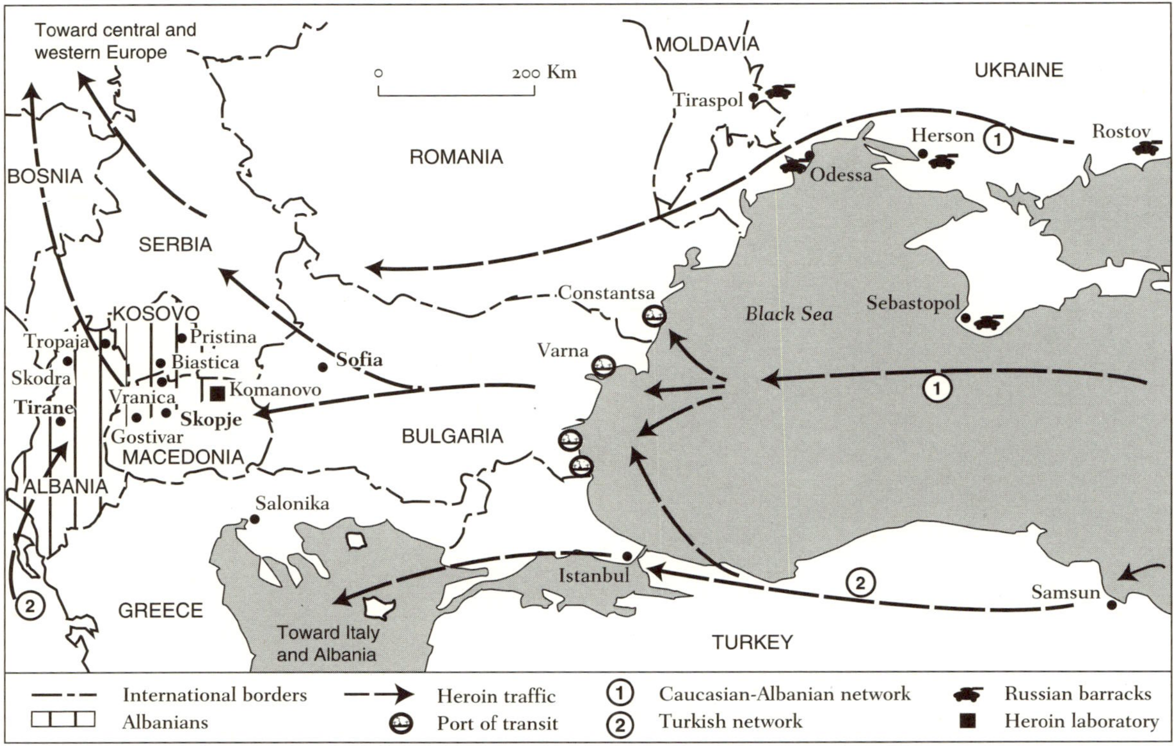

Map 2. Networks in the Balkans

marijuana. Bakers and confectioners also used poppy seeds. Long ago cut off from Greece, they first discovered marijuana's commercial value on returning to their native land. The Greek government let the traders in freely, hoping that they would settle in the north of the country and thus offset the demographic expansion of the Turkish minority. But another product, "Cherno-heroin," also called the "storyteller" or the "contaminated one"—a name later extended to heroin of any origin—soon followed the same route. It reached Greece following the arrival of several hundreds of thousands of Russian Greeks (who are political refugees) and Albanians. The former, refusing to take sides in the conflicts tearing apart the new republics, are often targeted by nationalist "cleansers" of all denominations; the latter merely "accompanied" Greek community members fleeing from the Albanian province of southern Epirus. These Albanians are really economic refugees, often supervised by criminal organizations that the Greek government is unable to control. Furthermore, the proximity of Turkey, Lebanon, and Cyprus, all of them drug hubs, is an added threat to Greece. In 1994, 235 kilograms of heroin were seized, mostly at the post of Kipi, on the border with Turkey. Five hundred kilograms of cocaine, hidden among sacks of rice, were seized between late December 1994 and early January 1995 at Piraeus. The cocaine, from Ecuador, was destined for Albania and Italy. Cocaine seizures in 1994 totaled 654 kilograms.

Mounting Overdoses Complicate Debate

Add a social and economic crisis to these geopolitical factors, and it is little wonder that drug addiction has developed. Indeed, heroin and cocaine seem to have burst successfully into the Greek market. According to high police officials, there are allegedly 80,000 heroin users in Greece, while an official inquiry revealed that one high school pupil out of every ten has allegedly tried drugs (7.5 percent marijuana, 1.7 percent heroin, 2.3 percent cocaine). The government and the opposition seem at a loss regarding this disturbing development, which affects mainly the young and those living outside Athens. Greek narcotics laws are among Europe's most repressive, but they have failed to curb the soaring consumption of drugs. A proposal by the minister of justice in favor of a markedly more liberal law gave rise, within his own party as well as the opposition, to heated controversy, especially as 138 people died of drug overdoses in 1994, double the number of casualties in 1993.

Apart from the Black Sea networks, the biggest problem arises in Albania, where hundreds of clandestine immigrants cross the Greek border each day. In fact, the greatest number of seizures has taken place at the border post of Cacavia, between Albania and Greece. Then comes Chios, an island located near the Turkish coast, on the border between Greece and Turkey. The large-scale smuggling of all types of products is made harder to control by the fact that corruption is also spreading. Thus, after the indictment of customs officers caught in the act of bribery, corrupt practices, and complicity with clandestine immigration networks, Greek Interior Minister Stelios Papathemelis ordered a wave of job transfers affecting customs officials in every region, from the port of Patras (linking Greece to Italy) to the farthest-flung post in the north. Meanwhile, several major traffickers held in Greek prisons got back on the streets either by taking advantage of the liberal parole system instituted by the reformed penal code or by just vanishing. Following this scandal, a number of civil servants and several prison wardens at all levels of the bureaucratic hierarchy have been fired and will soon appear before the courts.

Public opinion, meanwhile, influenced by television reports focusing on the spectacular images of death by drug overdose, tends to associate the increase in drug-related crime with the flow of clandestine immigrants from the north (especially Albania). In a country with nearly 500,000 illegal immigrants and a native population wearying of constant tension with Albania and Macedonia, immigrant workers are in danger of becoming scapegoats. Thus, any debate on adopting a new drug policy tends to veer out of control, and politicians now avoid the topic for fear of losing votes. After working for months on a new drug bill and methadone program, a joint parliamentary committee reported its conclusions to Parliament in August. Party leaders all took the floor to stress the seriousness of the problem, but when the discussion turned to concrete matters, only a dozen members of Parliament remained in the chamber, and even they didn't bother actually to speak out on the issues themselves.

Meanwhile, the international community is more disturbed by the workings of the Greek banking system. The increase in drug consumption, the proximity of the Balkan route, and the privileged links between Athens and Nicosia (especially Nicosia's offshore companies) all make Greece an obvious target for money laundering, particularly since well over half of Greece's gross national product is generated by the underground economy, tourism, and the liquid assets resulting from the existence of a large merchant shipping industry. Thus, a confidential mission of the FATF, which met in Athens on November 15, 1994, revealed the deficiencies of the current Greek banking system and the fact that it is only slowly being converted to European norms. According to the minister of justice, Mr. Couvellakis, a bill is being drafted for the establishment of an official body to monitor dubious banking operations, especially money transfers between tax havens and Greece. Given the sheer volume of liquid assets circulating in Greece, and the fact that tax evasion is a national sport, European experts have doubts about the likely effectiveness of these measures.

Georgia and Chechnya

Trafficking in drugs and weapons takes extremely diverse and complex forms in the CIS. The Balkan routes, in fact, are largely supplied with heroin by mafias from the Caucasus, as are the Baltic and St. Petersburg mafias. Drugs in the CIS are sometimes directly swapped for weapons (notably from Russian army barracks) in order to arm Georgian, Azeri, Armenian, and Kurdish rebel factions.

Networks and Warlords

In Georgia the mafia has infiltrated the highest levels of government: Former Prime Minister Joba Iosseliani is a notorious godfather who heads his own private militia, the "Centurions," as well as gangs of "Gucci boys" (so-called because, like their Albanian counterparts, they go in for expensive Italian stylishness). The Georgian mafia, however, lost its natural port of Batumi, which is now in the hands of a warlord named Abassidje. Abassidje is mayor of Batumi and leader of the Adjares, an Islamic, Turkish-speaking ethnic group that benefits from Turkish sympathies. So it was only when Abkhaz forces (another minority in Georgia) took the port of Sukhumi in Abkhazia (northern Georgia) that an autonomous network could be reestablished to channel traffic into the Balkans.

Thanks to the Abkhaz populations living on both sides of the Russo-Georgian border, the Abkhaz network, which collaborates with the Georgian mafia despite the "war of secession," now controls a major Black Sea port (Sukhumi) as well as a direct junction with Russia and

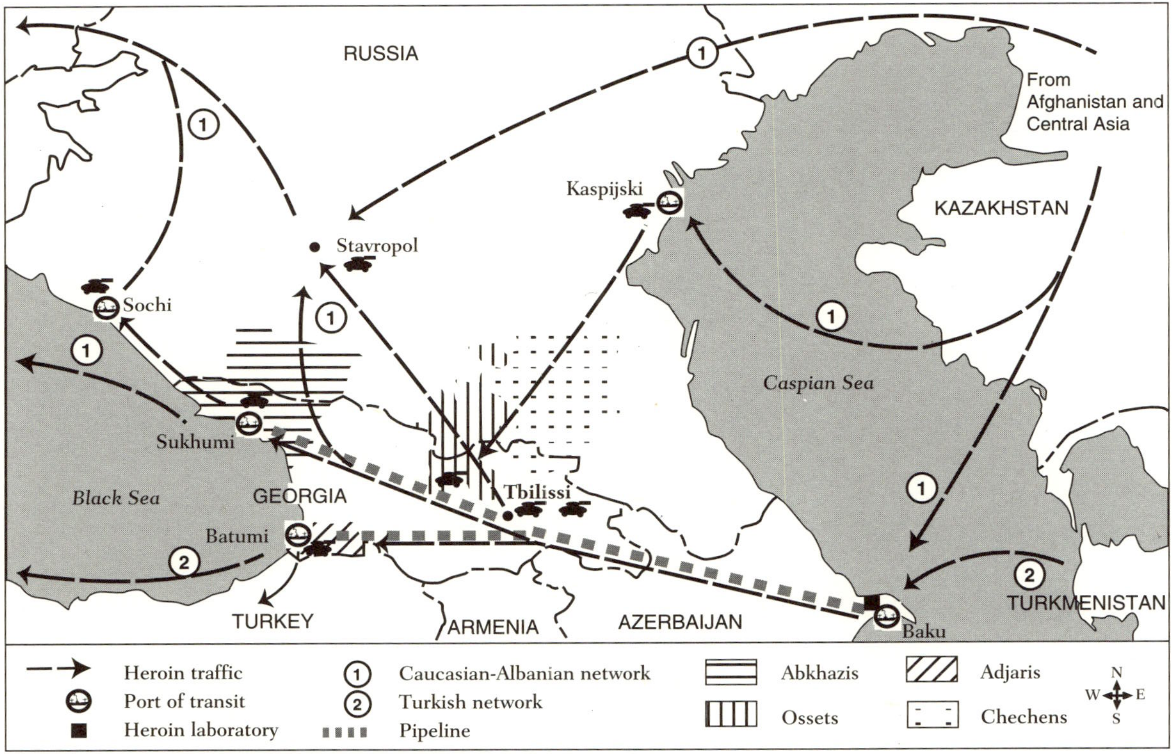

Map 3. Networks in the Caucasus

Ukraine via Abkhazia. Chechen irregulars mobilized during the war are still present in Sukhumi. Drugs (heroin or morphine base from Afghanistan and Caspian countries like Kazakhstan and perhaps Turkmenistan) and weapons are hidden in merchandise loaded onto freighters at Sukhumi and then unloaded on the coast of Bulgaria or Albania. The beneficiaries of such deals are often Kosovo Albanians, since Albanians in Albania and Macedonia are now doing more than merely "enabling their brethren in Prizren to survive"; they are actively preparing an insurrection against the Serbian occupiers of Kosovo.

Russian army barracks along these circuits, especially in Ossetia, provide an almost inexhaustible supply of various products. Left to their own devices by the Russian government, soldiers who have not been paid for years are now selling weapons, rare metals, and fuel at unbeatable prices, often in exchange for heroin. Border posts and barracks in Abkhazia, Ossetia, and Georgia (even Tbilissi), not to mention Russia itself (in the Sochi region and Stavropol), have become enormous wholesale centers distributing all the stocks accumulated during the Soviet regime. Thus, certain shipments of heroin can be exchanged en route for weapons (kalashnikovs, ground-to-air missiles, radio equipment, explosives, mines, etc.), making the trade even more profitable.

From Irregulars to Scapegoats

The Chechens, who initially played the Russian card by supplying support troops during Russia's conflict with the Abkhazis, themselves became Moscow's target on December 12, 1994. Once the Georgian conflict was settled, the Russians conveniently awoke to the fact that, as Yeltsin adviser Vassily Kononesco put it, "Grozny had become a hub for all sorts of clandestine economic activities, a free-wheeling outlaw zone." The Russian offensive in Chechnya nevertheless produced an effect diametrically opposed to the stated goal of "putting an end to the power of criminal gangs." For the two million Chechens dispersed in a diaspora stretching from Central Asia to the Baltic countries and Germany via the Middle East and Turkey (closely linked with organized crime and drug trafficking) have now been joined by veterans of the "battle of Grozny" ready to engage in whatever trafficking is necessary to conduct the inevitable guerrilla war against Russian occupiers. So the war in Chechnya can be added to the list of ongoing conflicts in the Caucasus region. Several geopolitical factors encourage the spread of these conflicts, which in turn spur drug trafficking in the area. Caught between the former Russian and Turkish empires, Caucasian countries have found themselves prey to complicated power struggles after regaining independence. Briefly free of the Russian confederation, they came under pressure from both Moscow and Ankara, neither of which hesitated to inflame ethnic passions, border conflicts, and nationalist factions, thus forcing the fledgling nations either to return to the CIS fold or to make a stand against it. Azerbaijan, Georgia and Armenia live under a constant threat of imminent breakup.

Such a situation inevitably has an impact on drug consumption. Tbilissi, the capital of Georgia, has become a city with hundreds of thousands of refugees crowded everywhere, including hotels in the center of town. Furthermore, organized crime has spread in an unprecedented manner, controlling practically the entire distribution of everyday goods (fuel, bread, foodstuffs, cigarettes, etc.). Gucci boys—young thugs patrolling with kalashnikovs—are responsible for closing most shops and restaurants, driving them into bankruptcy by conducting shakedowns on a vast scale. Nothing escapes gang control, from the foodstalls to the grand hotels in which the gang members live. The Gucci boys are probably part of Iosseliani's backup militia. Having fought in Abkhazia, they treat Tbilissi as war booty. They are heavy drug consumers as well as dealers. Thus, clandestine nightclubs serve not only as meeting places but also as outlets for heroin and cannabis (sold in the form of marijuana). Cannabis oil, amphetamines, and occasionally morphine are also in circulation. But since the usual distribution points (stores, restaurants, etc.) are often closed, drugs can now be found in disused garages and stores, ruined apartments, and various black-market sites.

Part of the population of Tbilissi, including the Gucci boys, fought in Abkhazia and Megrelia during the civil war. In the course of the conflict, combatants found themselves deprived of all military infrastructure and indulged in savage combat practices similar to the ones used in Lebanon, becoming hooked on stimulants taken prior to battle (especially amphetamines) as well as all forms of sedatives (from opium for the wealthy to hashish for the rank and file).

In Ierevan, capital of Armenia, a yellow-brown grade of heroin, probably of local manufacture, is now circulating alongside the traditional hashish and cannabis oil (now taken by the young as well as those over fifty). This phenomenon is marked by the reemergence of the casual use of water pipes. The heroin is sold more or less everywhere, especially in the "secret" nightclubs that stay open all night due to the curfew. In fact, the war in Upper Karabakh is increasingly coming to resemble a "dirty war"—black marketeering and trafficking have spawned a mafia equal to those found in neighboring Georgia. Mafia connections have apparently now affected the highest spheres of both governing and opposition parties. Thus, on December 29, 1994, Armenian President Levon Ter Petrossian suspended the Armenian Revolutionary Federation, the country's grand traditional party founded in Tbilissi a century ago. He accused the party, now in opposition, of shielding a "terrorist organization" that specializes in drug trafficking and was responsible for the December 17 assassination of Ierevan Mayor Ambastur Gualstian. It is not known whether the motives for the killing were primarily political or criminal. Armenia thus finds itself on the brink of implosion just a few months prior to legislative elections.

Across the border in Azerbaijan, stability depends on the vagaries of relations with Russia. The conflict in Upper Karabakh and territorial claims in Dagestan escalate every time Moscow wants to impose its point of view on Baku. The same thing is happening today in regard to Azeri oil contracts and the republic's plan to build a pipeline completely free of Russian control. Baku, a center for oil exports and refineries, has long been an important site for the development of synthetic drugs and, probably, heroin. It serves as a port of entry for opium from Central Asia and the Golden Crescent, sometimes via Iran, and it is a focal point for networks extending into Russia and Europe via the Caucasus or Turkey. The role of Azerbaijan grew during the Upper Karabakh conflict and the Georgian wars because of its proximity to Iran and Turkey, as well as its maritime links with Turkmenistan, Kazakhstan, and the frontier port of Astrachan, a hub of all kinds of trafficking usually based on barter: arms, oil, caviar, and drugs.

Turkey

In 1994 Turkey remained the main transit route for the heroin produced in the Golden Crescent. The country's growing involvement in the transformation of poppy and/or morphine base into heroin has also been confirmed. This phenomenon, together with the implications of the involvement of the PKK in heroin trafficking, is at the root of bloody feuds and the appearance of real "death squads." Besides opiates, in 1994 the police seized 19 metric tons of hashish and close to 17 kilograms of cocaine. Moreover, the domestic market for narcotics is booming. According to Dr. Ayhan Kalyoglu, a member of the Research Center for Drug and Alcohol Abuse (AMATEM), the consumption of illicit substances has grown by 76 percent in the last two years. "Terrorism and the economic crisis in eastern Turkey are the main culprits," he declared, emphasizing the growing role of synthetic drugs and cocaine as well as the development of new consumption habits among Turks.

Drugs in a Dirty War

By the end of 1994, the police had not yet identified a single clue to either the perpetrators or the sponsors of the murders of a dozen persons linked to the heroin trade. The victims were killed in similar fashion throughout Turkey. Among them were Turkish *Maffya* barons (Hussein and Cetin Temuras, Enis Kadamuman, Memdhu Bucak, Vahap Akpinar, Ismail Basaran, Ahmed Oyak); "owners" of heroin laboratories (Fevri and Sahin Arslan); and godfathers and financiers linked to the PKK (Bechet Canturk, nicknamed the "Turkish Escobar," Necded and Savas Buldan, Haci Kaaray, Adanar Yildirim). The first victim in this series of assassinations was Major Cem Ersever, a member of the counterintelligence services. According to the Turkish press, he was murdered on December 23, 1993, because he possessed "devastating information" on the war in southeastern Anatolia and because he had provided cover for drug trafficking by farmers used as auxiliaries against the PKK. The elimination of two civil servants—Ministry of Health Chief Inspector Namik Erdogan (on May 10, 1994) and Prosecutor Mustafa Atesoglu (on September 14)—is allegedly also linked to the drug trade, partly because the latter was killed in the same restaurant where godfather Enis Kadamuman had earlier been murdered.

The slaughter makes observers wonder. Beyond a "classic" settling of accounts among *Maffya* families, the chain of killings could point to the burgeoning activities of death squads originally created to confront the Kurdish independence fighters. Having subsequently targeted those Turkish godfathers partaking in the Kurds' trafficking activities, the squads are now going for the upper echelons of the *Maffya*. They could have emerged from members of the military and police, caught up in the escalation of the war in Anatolia, who might have become involved in trafficking and mafia-style activities. This theory is all the more plausible given that many of them have had firsthand experience, often as military advisers, of similar conflicts in the Caucasus in which drugs are a source of funds for warring parties.

Laboratories for Europe

The year 1994 provided confirmation that Turkey is no longer just the transit country for opiates it has always been but has also become a significant heroin-manufacturing center. Several elements support this conclusion. First, official Iranian statistics list 117 tons (enough to manufacture 11.7 tons of heroin) as the amount of opium seized during 1994, as well as 13 tons of morphine base and a mere 860 kilograms of heroin. The same phenomenon is repeated in Turkey, where 2.7 tons of morphine base were seized as they were entering the country but only 1.6 tons of heroin were intercepted while leaving Turkey. Second, chemical reagents have been the object of record seizures, including one of 21 tons of various chemicals of mainly German origin. Finally, also in 1994, five secret laboratories were discovered housing hundreds of kilograms of sodium carbonate, thousands of gallons of sulphuric acid, acetone, diethylene, hydrochloric acid, acetic anhydride, and so on. Turkey, the world's top opium producer in the 1960s, has cashed in on its existing supply networks, spanning Iran and the Golden Crescent, in order to reach out into Central Asia. Every time local production was curbed by law enforcement, the Turkish *Maffya*'s tentacles reached farther, ever eastward. This expansion was made easier by the Turkish cultural and linguistic area sprawling from Istanbul to faraway Kazakhstan, while in the West, Sicilian networks and Turkish diaspora members provided added support. Furthermore, another 243 kilograms of morphine base, manufactured from legally produced, diverted, local opium, were seized in 1994.

Closer scrutiny of seizure statistics concerning drugs entering the country yields a more detailed analysis of the Turkish opiates situation. Large amounts of heroin, on their way to Europe from the Golden Crescent, continue to cross the country's borders, as is confirmed by the drug squad's annual report. In general, these drugs are controlled by the PKK (see box). Ninety percent of the morphine seized in 1994 was channeled through Iran before being handed over to Kurdish traffickers who, denied access to large-scale facilities in Turkey, processed it into heroin, mainly

The PKK Networks

Seizures carried out in Turkey and Europe—especially in Germany and the Netherlands, where large Kurdish communities live—confirm that drugs contribute to bankrolling the activities (military or otherwise) of the PKK. PKK networks appear to be responsible for 20 to 30 percent of all heroin trafficking via Turkey. From there onward, the networks within the Kurdish diaspora take care of transportation, laundering, and even retailing at street level. However, Ankara clearly exaggerates when it blames the Kurds for the whole of the heroin traffic within its territory. During a European Interpol meeting on "Europe and the Narco-Terrorist Connection" at Antalya, Turkey, in June 1994, the Turkish delegation listed 212 cases arising in Europe over the previous ten years, in which 94.6 percent of the protagonists were alleged to be Kurdish. Interpol's General Secretariat replied that between 1992 and 1994 only seven cases could be attributed to the Kurds. The delegations of most European countries—including France, Sweden, Spain, Denmark, and Switzerland—even stated that they had no information on the PKK's drug activities. Kurds and Turks may also actively collaborate within the same networks, as was revealed by a case in Amsterdam on December 12, 1994.

Interpol-Turkey retorted by publishing a list including the names of 412 PKK members allegedly involved in drug trafficking in Europe. In a recent report, Turkish drug enforcement agencies went as far as stating that the PKK is still having poppies grown in Lebanon's Bekaa Valley, even though this crop has all but disappeared from the area since 1992. While such claims clearly lack objectivity, they also obscure a more disturbing phenomenon: the Anatolian conflict, and the role drugs play in financing a push toward the alliance—tactical, maybe, but nonetheless real—between the PKK and fundamentalist forces in Turkish Anatolia and perhaps beyond.

in the Baku region of Azerbaijan. This information is confirmed by Turkish heroin seizures near the borders of Turkish Kurdistan with other countries: at Esendere (180 kilograms) and Gurbulak (300 kilograms); at the Iranian border; and at Cilvegozu and Oncupinar, near Habur, a town close to the border with the autonomous Kurdish region of Iraq.

As for the drugs—mainly morphine base—controlled by Turkish organized crime, they enter via either Iran or Turkmenistan, Azerbaijan, and Georgia. The 1,200 kilograms of morphine base seized in Uzbekistan on a sealed tractor-trailer (TIR) from Afghanistan in August 1993 were on one of these routes. Sea routes are also still very popular, as suggested by two seizures on ships from Pakistan, both carrying over 2 tons of morphine base. When entering from the south, morphine base always arrives via Syria and Lebanon, supplying Turkish and PKK networks indiscriminately.

The vast increase in seizures of synthetic drugs (ephedrone, amphetamines), mood elevators, and supposed aphrodisiacs from Germany, central Europe, and Azerbaijan constitutes a new development. It confirms Turkey's role as a hub for these drugs as well as opiates. The synthetic drugs are destined for the ruling classes of Saudi Arabia and the United Arab Emirates. In 1994, with 4.57 million tablets intercepted, seizures of synthetic drugs increased twentyfold compared with 1993.

The Balkan Heroin Networks

Heroin trafficking to Europe in partnership with Italian criminal organizations is more than ever a Turkish speciality. The police have identified five major possible routes within the Balkan region: through the Black Sea, especially the ports of Derince, Adapazari, and, closer to the Caucasus, Trabzon; sea routes through the ports of Romania (notably Constantsa) and Bulgaria (notably Varna) but also Italy (Trieste) and Albania (Durrës); sea routes via southern Turkey, used chiefly by the PKK (ports of Karatas, Mersin, and Yumurtalik) to Trieste, Bari, and Brindisi (Italy), often via Patras, Greece; land routes via the border posts of Kapikule, Pazarkule, and Derekoy, linking Greece and Bulgaria; and land routes via Romania and Hungary, Austria, Slovakia, and Switzerland. Routes may also be mixed, with drugs switching back to the sea route in Greece or Albania up to Italy or even Spain. According to the Ankara authorities themselves, Turkish heroin networks control 50 percent of the traffic on the Balkan route and 30 percent of the western European market. Adding heroin seizures in Turkey (1,580 kilograms) to seizures in Europe of drugs from Turkish-controlled routes or Turkish traffickers (1,980 kilograms) yields over 3.5 tons of confiscated "Turkish" heroin in 1994. To these, it will from now on be necessary to add the small weekly interceptions of 5 to 10 kilograms carried out at the Greek and Bulgarian borders (280 kilograms) as well as in the rest of the eastern Mediterranean, including Egypt (360 kilograms). A phenomenon similar to what occurred in "post-Escobar" Colombia can be observed in Turkey: The market, fueled in particular by a record-breaking Afghan opium harvest of 3,200 tons in spring 1994, tends to expand, opening the field to small-scale "entrepreneurs" who are running family businesses using the "short network" technique.

Besides these new developments, Turkey's central role in the heroin trade is fostered by the passage of some 400,000 TIR trucks annually, as well as by the presence of hundreds of ports, twelve international airports, and hundreds of private airstrips. Moreover, the coastlines of the Marmara Sea and the whole of the Black Sea are turning into launching pads allowing, just as in the Caucasus, swift access to the new markets born out of the collapse of the Soviet Union. Regional conflicts involving Georgians, Chechens (over 1.5 million of whom live in Turkey and the Middle East), Azeris, and Armenians have a more direct influence on trafficking routes. Traditional routes are diversifying, as the Caucasian conflicts join up with those of the Balkan Peninsula. Ethnic Albanians from Kosovo and Macedonia trade on the Balkan route and use the Italian ports on the Adriatic Sea. Turkish, Russian, and Caucasian networks pass through Bulgaria and Romania. Thus, Turkish drug traffickers are present not only on the old Mediterranean routes dominated by Italian organized crime but also on the new, more autonomous Balkan routes and the fiefdoms of Russians and Caucasians. Lebanese and Kurds to the south and Serbs and Croats to the north also claim a piece of the action, thereby infinitely multiplying the land and sea variations on the Balkans' illegal trading routes.

2. *The CIS and the Baltic Countries*

The collapse of the Soviet empire and the rise of a market system in its most unregulated form have radically transformed the entire Eurasian continent. A general dismantling of institutions, production mechanisms, and moral and ideological precepts is now under way. Observers have noted the swiftness with which the "CIS subcontinent" has adopted habits and models scarcely known just five years ago, such as drug trafficking and consumption. Conflicts in Central Asia have exacerbated the situation. Islamic fundamentalists, warlords, and former party officials are slugging it out for control of this windfall. Unlike Turkmenistan (which nevertheless seems to have long been host to a heroin lab linked to the Italian mafia), Uzbekistan, Tajikistan, and Kirghizistan have an apparently bright future as poppy and cannabis producers. Their local production is complemented by drugs coming from Afghanistan, Pakistan, and to a lesser extent, India. Drugs now pass through Central Asia on their way to Europe and the United States, not to mention Russia itself.

Russia[1]

It is no exaggeration to say, as have several observers quoted in the English-speaking press in 1994, that close to 3 percent of the population of the CIS is now "hooked" on one or several drugs. Those millions of consumers represent a significant market, a rear base for traffickers, and an important source of funds. "The number of addicts doubles every year," declared Leonid Shpilenia, the head doctor of St. Petersburg's only facility for treating drug abuse, at the end of 1994. St. Petersburg is particularly affected by drug abuse, with 200,000 addicts, 50 percent of whom are under eighteen years old.

A Focal Point for Organized Crime

This domestic demand and the facilities that exist for the passage of all illegal merchandise, including drugs, foster contacts between Italian and Russian mafias, Colombian cartels, certain narco-states, and Far Eastern criminal organizations. Hence new large-scale, intercontinental bartering transactions have appeared, as have new trafficking hubs. The arrest of Colombian citizens who had come to St. Petersburg in order to set up a secret cocaine laboratory was thus mentioned at the International Conference on Organized Crime held in Naples in November 1994.

Chinese ephedrine deliveries in Russia are rising dramatically. Increasing numbers of Nigerians are shifting cocaine between Latin America and Africa by trafficking via Moscow, where 18.05 kilograms were confiscated in four separate seizures. And more and more Poles are passing through, smuggling Nepalese hashish into their country. In the last sixteen "buy and bust" operations, 52.24 kilograms were seized between January and September. These are the most notable trends in the drug traffic in Russia, according to information provided by Russian customs to the OGD correspondent at the end of 1994. The same sources say that border seizures are constantly on the increase. Thus, during the first nine months of 1994, 2.105 tons of various drugs were confiscated, twice as much as during the whole of 1993 (excluding the "exceptional" seizure of 1 ton of cocaine in St. Petersburg). Of 1.5 tons of poppy straw intercepted on the Russia-Ukraine border, 1 ton was found at the Briansk border post.

1. Tajikistan was reviewed in the OGD 1994 report, *État des drogues, drogues des États,* op. cit.

Seizures at the Border with Ukraine

At Briansk, a Russian post on the border with Ukraine, an allergy to poppy straw (used in Russia and eastern European countries to manufacture a brand of unsophisticated heroin) on the part of some customs officers is all it takes to intercept loads being smuggled into Russia. An OGD correspondent was able to verify on the spot how three or four officers, taking turns, sneeze or become red-eyed when they come near poppy bundles. Indeed, a sniffer dog's nose is dulled after it has inspected one or two train carriages from Ukraine loaded with meat products, improperly branded "salami," thereby cashing in on the collapse of the Ukrainian currency. One ton of poppy straw was seized in this area in 1993, and 856 kilograms in early 1994.

But since the end of May, those carrying drugs have become far more prudent. Until then, customs officers could find the straw quite easily in bags or false mattresses, as in the case of the 360 kilograms seized on January 20, 1994, from a group of gypsies. Currently, when traffickers don't bypass customs or use local smugglers, they hide the merchandise with much greater care. Many of the customs officers are scholars or have had other jobs. The chief of customs at the passenger station was formerly a nuclear submarine captain. While newcomers compensate for their lack of experience with their enthusiasm, enforcement is made harder by the fact that members of social strata newly affected by economic hardship have become involved in the traffic. On July 6, the OGD correspondent saw the police arrest an electronics engineer traveling from Kiev on the Odessa-Moscow train who was attempting to sell 2 kilograms of poppy straw. As he could not make a living on his monthly wages of 15,000 rubles (US$3), he first tried to make ends meet moonlighting as a taxi driver, using the car he had purchased under the Communists. However, he could not foot the bill when it broke down.

Customs officers are convinced that Briansk is also on one of the alternative Balkan heroin routes. The drug allegedly comes by rail from Turkey via Sofia, where people called *tchelnaki* (bag carriers) board the train. They pile up merchandise so high that each carriage is transformed into something of a fortified camp, which one enters by crawling underneath the packages. Besides, Briansk is also an important road junction. While they wait for the setting up of a drug squad, which is in the pipeline, customs officers have few means to intervene.

The seizures carried out in the region, which are fairly modest compared with those carried out elsewhere in the world, do not reflect the real scale of the drug traffic. They do, however, shed light on the current inefficiency of the Russian state. True, the state has been deprived of its most effective structure, the Communist party, whose efficiency relied on two self-contained bodies—the Red Army and the KGB—as well as on a population of technocrats acting in the party's name. Soldiers, serving or retired KGB agents, and technocrats are today the main agents of Russia's savage brand of capitalism. In major urban centers, they constitute an unavoidable power base for the "protection" and development of Russian and foreign firms. Those who know how to handle weapons are the "protectors," while technocrats establish contacts both within the nooks and crannies of Russian bureaucracy and abroad. Since until recently "business" in Russia meant "state business," the former agents of the state necessarily hold the connections, the foreign bank accounts, the offshore companies, and the dummy companies in Western countries. According to financial law enforcement officials, illicit revenue from laundering and recycling activities in Russia amounted to 1.5 trillion rubles (over US$1 billion) in 1994 alone. According to Russia's Central Bank, the equivalent of nearly US$10 billion more is currently held by individuals and is awaiting recycling.

The Far Eastern Networks and the Far North

Chinese ephedrine is processed into tablets. For the most part, seizures are made at Blagovechtchensk, in far eastern Russia, from "bag carriers," as the freelance international traders who have been crisscrossing the former communist countries for the last three years are known. They are especially active between Russia and China. While ephedrine has thus far been hidden in passenger luggage, "commercial" cargoes are increasingly numerous. One and a half million tablets of ephedrine were seized in two months, and with the Amur River freezing over during winter, customs officers predict that the number of smugglers will rise sharply. There is every reason to believe that this ephedrine was diverted from the Chinese pharmaceutical industry. Part of it seems to be destined for the Russian market, where it is already easier to obtain than the ephedrone produced from the *Ephedra vulgaris* plant harvested in Kazakhstan and Kirghizistan.

Heroin arrives from Southeast Asia. On June 9, a joint operation by the Department for the Fight against the Illegal Circulation of Drugs

(MVD), the Border Guard Corps, and the Counter-Intelligence Service of the Navy of the Pacific, resulted in the seizure of 8 kilograms of heroin. The drugs were discovered while two North Korean nationals were attempting to sell them. A chemist belonging, according to the MVD, to a "major criminal organization" was also arrested while he was analyzing the heroin at the request of the buyers. According to information obtained from police sources by the OGD correspondent, the North Korean intelligence service was involved in this case.

Although it has not yet assumed catastrophic proportions, another development deserves a mention. Around the Neva and Indighirka river deltas, as well as in the Ob Gulf, there has existed a tradition of growing mushrooms and other hallucinogenic plants—*Hieracium pilocella, Cardamine concatenata,* "arctic grapes," or *Arcostaphilos,* and so on. Nowadays, it seems that the whole of the Russian far north knows about those lichen-mushrooms, which are beginning to be experimented with in Moscow. When they return to the capital, people forced into labor camps, former inmates in penitentiaries, soldiers, and miners from abandoned barracks and mines are all bringing back with them such "exotic" habits, which they propagate among urban dwellers.

UKRAINE The end of 1994 saw the first anniversary of the establishment of a national police in charge of road surveillance, a task hitherto entrusted to totally inefficient regional police services. The national road police's tasks include fighting car theft and trafficking in all sorts of goods, including drugs. At a press conference, high officials of the Ministry of the Interior declared that during the first year of its existence the new force, allegedly numbering 26,000 men, had seized from vehicles 218,000 litres of spirits, 1.2 million tons of contraband sugar, and 440 kilograms of drugs. These amounts of drugs are derisory when compared with the Ministry of the Interior's statistics for all law enforcement services: 9,147 kilograms for the first six months of 1994 (as against 28,230 kilograms for the whole of 1993 and 14,443 kilograms in 1992). The seizures break down into 937 kilograms of cannabis and 57.8 kilograms of opium. The rest, of unspecified nature, was probably poppy straw. The lack of efficiency of the Ukrainian national police was attributed to a shortage of staff and equipment (only 22 percent of police cars are equipped with a radio).

In 1994 there were an estimated 44,000 drug users in the Ukraine (as against 39,000 in 1993 and 33,000 in 1992). During the first half of that year, the police recorded 63 thefts of narcotics (including 12 burglaries in pharmacies), and 10,869 breaches of the antidrug legislation. The police say they intervened 219 times against drug use in public places. But these statistics should be taken with a pinch of salt, as law enforcement agencies are far from equipped to confront new trends in drug consumption. Kiev for instance, a city of 2.5 million inhabitants, has only one hospital ward capable of treating fifteen abusers on a 24-hour basis. A psychiatrist working in the ward told the OGD correspondent that medicines, especially amphetamines, are diverted from the state's stockpiles and increasingly abused. He added that drug addiction exists among all age groups and that people with a long history of abuse are taken into "rehabilitation work camps" (*Lechebno Trudovye Profilaktorii*, or LTPs), where they may be locked up for several months. Three of the LTPs that were set up throughout the Soviet Union in the 1970s allegedly still operate in the Kiev area. Each supposedly has a capacity of 200 people.

Kirghizistan

A small mountainous Central Asian republic, Kirghizistan possesses a significant potential of 60,000 hectares (144,000 acres) of wild marijuana in the Chu Valley, an area of some 138,000 hectares (331,200 acres) straddling Kirghizistan and Kazakhstan. In Bishkek, the republic's capital built by early Russian colonizers, "grass" can be found on roadsides, in gardens, and even in front of the central police station. Cannabis also abounds in the regions of Osh and Jelalbad in the south by the borders with Tajikistan and Uzbekistan. Furthermore, the police recently discovered the existence of a new cannabis variety originating in the Kokang region of China with a THC content (4.6 percent) superior to the local variety. A traditional opium producer, Kirghizistan is above all a transit country for the opium and heroin produced in Afghanistan.

A River of Opium

On average 100 kilograms of opium come into Kirghizistan each day, enough to produce 10 kilograms of heroin. According to information gathered by the OGD correspondent in Badakshan, a region that overlaps Afghanistan and Tajikistan, the opium enters Kirghizistan by the Osh-Chorog route. The flow of opium then follows the Ferghana Valley, near the region of Penjikent. The Ferghana Valley is divided among three countries—Kirghizistan, Uzbekistan, and Tajikistan—and is also a major poppy-growing area. Poppy production has increased there following Iran's implementation of large-scale counternarcotics measures. It seems that half the agricultural work force in the region is employed in poppy growing.

Once in Kirghizistan, the "opium river," which is essentially fueled by Afghanistan's output, divides into two roughly equivalent branches (see Map 4). One goes on toward Osh and the other, negotiated on horseback or by car when conditions permit, leads to Uzbekistan along dry riverbeds, including that of the Ferghana River. This region is a fiefdom of Islamic fundamentalism and a powder keg of interethnic animosities waiting to explode. This route has an obvious advantage. One kilogram of *khanka,* the local slang term for opium, sells for US$40 to $60 in Afghanistan. In Chorog it goes for between $120 and $200. In Osh, the same quantity can be sold for $1,300. In Bishkek, the capital of Kirghizistan, the wholesale price varies between $3,000 and $4,000. Finally, a portion of this opium makes its way to Moscow, where it will fetch $8,000 per kilogram. It is thought that heroin laboratories may already have been set up in Tajikistan, principally with the help of Pakistani know-how.

Police and customs posts are in no way a serious obstacle along the routes. This observation was confirmed by Tokone Kassymbekov, deputy chief of the antinarcotics division of Kirghizistan's Ministry of the Interior. He says that he recently traveled the opium route from Chorog to Osh and even crossed into Afghanistan illegally. According to Kassymbekov, however, the acute lack of resources to police the region is not sufficient to explain the impunity with which traffickers operate. "If, by chance, agents from a checkpoint arrest someone transporting drugs," says Kassymbekov, "they will let him go in return for one-third of the shipment. I myself needed only three days of investigation in Osh in order to get my hands on 52 kilograms of opium. That represents half of all seizures made in Kirghizistan since the beginning of the year." Such widespread corruption can end up discouraging even those with the best intentions. On April 28, 1994, police authorities intercepted a Moskvitch car in Osh. Inside were Hussayn B., head of the local vodka distillery, and Tarass S., a captain in the local police force recently trans-

Map 4. Tajikistan's and Kirghizistan's Opium River

ferred from Bishkek. The trunk of the car was filled with opium. When the police refused to heed their pleas, the passengers finally proposed handing over the entire shipment plus US$25,000 in exchange for letting them go. To the surprise of the local population, the police authorities chose to arrest them anyway. But the judge, who only a few days previously had sentenced to prison a man arrested in possession of 10 grams of opium, acquitted the accused. One of the policemen told the OGD correspondent that he had met Tarass S. in Osh after the trial. "You know, you're really an ass," Tarass told him. "You refused $25,000. The judge made $75,000."

Life and Death of a Godfather

The Chorog-Osh route is the umbilical cord of Badakhshan, its only link with the outside world. Everything passes by Osh, in particular necessities such as flour, gasoline, and medicines, en route for the Russian border guards and their CIS allies who "patrol" the border with Afghanistan. Opium is hidden in Russian army trucks "lent" to Tajik drivers or in trucks belonging to Tajik transportation companies in Osh. Power in Tajikistan is divided among the police, the OMON (local riot police), warlords and/or religious leaders from each area, and opposition leaders. However, the solidarity between Pamiris (inhabitants of Upper Badakhshan) and Ismailis (a Shiite Muslim sect to which a large portion of the population belongs) allows the distribution of profits, including those from drugs, with a minimum of conflict. As a consequence, the region has rapidly become "Central Asia's biggest poppy-growing area," according to General Guennadi Blenov, Tajikistan's interior minister. However, when Tokone Kassymbekov broached the subject of cooperating with Tajik police, who appear to represent a measure of continuity with the former Soviet government, he was rebuked. "We are not going to arrest our own people over opium," was their reply. "There is nothing to eat here. We have only opium and the stones from the mountains."

As for the warlords, they did not wait to divide up control of the border and the revenue resulting from the opium passing through each of their territories. At every corner, opium is offered in exchange for dollars or, better still, food or manufactured goods: flour, canned foods, clothing, and so on. While dealing with small retailers is more profitable, dealing with drug barons is safer, since it brings protection from unlucky encounters on the road with police officers, militia members, bandits, and others that could result in the confiscation of the drugs and sometimes even death. Here as elsewhere, the opium—locally produced or imported from Afghanistan or Pakistan—plays a major role in the economy. For the warlords, it represents a means to control the population, as well as merchandise they can trade for weapons.

Thus, the man who was the most famous opium kingpin in the region until late 1994, Abdul Rakhmon Ajubekov, alias Aliosha the Hunchback, provided important clients with a comprehensive service: two armed guards and, most precious of all, safe-passage papers with Aliosha's round stamp, guaranteeing the courier and his merchandise clear sailing all the way to the border with Kirghizistan. A true warlord, Aliosha controlled the Chorog border region with the help of his 300 to 400 well-armed soldiers, who distributed flour and gasoline to the inhabitants. Aliosha was one of the first to get involved in large-scale opium trafficking back in 1989. His right-hand man is O., a former police officer from Osh, nicknamed *Luch* (the ray). Aliosha's strength resides in his ability to maintain excellent relations with the six narco-clans in Osh, aligned according to ethnicity—Kirghiz, Kurd, Uzbek, Turk-Meskhet, Azeri, and Russian. Numerous former police officers hold positions of responsibility within these groups, giving a very special character to the "confrontations" between them and their "colleagues" in the antinarcotics service.

Aliosha was killed on December 9, 1994, by a bomb placed in his car in front of his headquarters in Chorog. There are several possible explanations for the murder. Tajik intelligence links Aliosha's assassination to the dismissal of local commanders and the wave of executions ordered by Islamic fundamentalist opposition figure Rezvon Sadirov against them in retaliation for their "distancing themselves from God's cause and accepting compromise with *kafirs* (infidels)." The Islamist-Democratic opposition has, of course, denied responsibility for the murder of such a popular figure. Other observers believe that officers within the Russian border guard contingent in Tajikistan were too deeply implicated with Aliosha to let him live. Whatever the truth, one thing is certain—his disappearance will not dry up the opium river that passes through the region. Thus, no increase in opiate prices was noted in Moscow following his death. Indeed, the "states within the state" of regional warlords, of whom Aliosha was the most visible representative, are in the process of creating a vast network, a kind of no-man's-land, in which the production and transfer of opium from the Golden Crescent is becoming the main economic activity. The absence of centralized power in the region is drawing the drug traffic from Asia toward the Russian networks that can guarantee unparalleled safety.

UZBEKISTAN According to information obtained by an OGD correspondent in this region in late 1994, Pakistani narcotics traffickers are making efforts to open drug routes in former Soviet Central Asia. The object of these routes is to establish outlets in addition to those already in place farther south (in India, Baluchistan, the Makran Coast) for the enormous heroin production generated by laboratories located in Pakistan's tribal zones along the border with eastern Afghanistan—and, according to some sources, in northern Afghanistan and southern Tajikistan. The major problem faced by Pakistani traffickers is assuring a regular supply of the competitively priced chemical reagents necessary to refine the heroin. Chemical reagents have become more difficult to obtain in the wake of the tighter restrictions imposed on such products in the West and in India. Pakistani traffickers are looking increasingly to the former Soviet Union, whose technical know-how, industrial equipment (capable of producing in particular acetic anhydride), geographic proximity, and political instability constitute ideal conditions for smuggling networks. The most heavily traveled trafficking routes are through wartorn Tajikistan on the one hand and along the opium river supplied by the late Aliosha the Hunchback on the other (the latter passing through the Pamirs in Upper Badakhshan before reaching Kirghizistan). Two other popular routes, however, pass through Termez, situated on the border between Uzbekistan and Afghanistan, and Merv, in Turkmenistan. According to locals questioned by the OGD correspondent, both of these routes end up in Bokhara. It is from this historic city, once a major stop on the ancient silk road, that narcotics are forwarded to Russia and then Poland before being sent on to western Europe.

KAZAKHSTAN Kazakhstan's role as a major crossroads for opium and heroin trafficking from the Golden Crescent countries was confirmed by several events in 1994. In May, an operation launched jointly with Russian police resulted in the dismantling of a trafficking network supplying the South Korean market. Run from the capital Almaty (formerly Alma-Ata) by South Korean businessmen, the network included seventeen Russians based on Sakhalin Island, north of Japan. Elsewhere, increasingly severe antidrug legislation in Turkey, which now authorizes the payment to informers of half the value of the drugs seized as a result of their information, has led Turkish gangs to use this northeastern route more often. In addition, the villages of Panfilov and Drujba, situated on Kazakhstan's border with China, have experienced increased drug trafficking.

Regarding cannabis production, the Kazakh government gave the go-ahead in early May for the creation of a cannabis farm in the famous Chu Valley, located 300 kilometers west of Almaty. Indian hemp grows wild on an estimated 138,000 hectares (331,200 acres) of this valley's total surface of 4 million hectares (10 million acres). The legal production is in the hands of a joint venture with the Kazakh government called Asia, some of whose partners allegedly include Californians. Asia hopes to obtain some thirty different derivative products from the plants, ranging from textile fibers to paper and from medicinal substances to feed for livestock. Besides the fact that the project will provide the state with revenues from a natural resource hitherto exploited only by traffickers, the cannabis harvest concession will also free 136 police officers currently charged, so far ineffectively, with surveillance of the farm's immense perimeter. This project follows in the footsteps of large-scale fiber hemp farming projects launched in Great Britain in 1993 and in Germany in 1994, with the agreement of the European Union.

The Baltic Countries

The Russian-speaking population of these three countries not only provides fertile soil for all sorts of demagoguery—especially the highly dynamic one of Russian nationalism—but is also heavily affected by the rise in crime, recruitment of outlaw gangs, and consumption of illicit drugs. From Vilnius to Talinn, narcotics trafficking—disguised as trade in nickel, zinc, chrome, and other nonferrous metals—has been the major source of rapid, spectacular fortunes made in the region since 1991. As late as 1994, the drug scene was still dominated by the Soviet system's "alcoholic tradition," but by opening themselves to free trade, the Baltic countries are also leaving themselves wide open to the international drug trade.

Mafias and Geostrategic Interests

On November 5, 1994, a bomb exploded under a railway bridge 30 kilometers outside Vilnius, the capital of Lithuania. A catastrophe was avoided only because two express trains were unexpectedly delayed. The most frequently mentioned explanation, apart from a possible attack by the Polish National Liberation Front against Russian military movements from the enclave of Kaliningrad, is that of a mafia operation. Lithuania, in fact, is a mandatory transit country for all trade, legal or otherwise, between Russia and the former East Prussia (Upper Königsberg) annexed by Stalin. Meanwhile, the Estonian press was speculating on a possible mafia role in the tragedy of the ferryboat *Estonia,* which went down in the Baltic Sea on September 28, 1994; reports alluded to rumors that a truck loaded with contraband cobalt was on the ferry and also cited the existence of fierce competition on this highly profitable sea link.

The only act for which credit has been claimed was a bomb alert in Lithuania's one nuclear power plant, following the death sentence pronounced against Georgian godfather Boris Dekanidze, head of the "Vilnius brigade," one of the country's main gangs. Dekanidze was sentenced to death in October 1994 for masterminding the murder of Vitas Lingys, a journalist who had just published an investigation into organized crime in Lithuania and who had refused, despite threats, to withdraw an article describing the gang's activities.

This situation, in which fact mingles with fantasy, is revealing of two closely linked phenomena. On the one hand, Baltic independence has led to an uncontrolled economic and financial boom that provides fertile ground for mafias and various types of trafficking. On the other hand, the new Baltic states are still coveted by the Russian government, which has not renounced the former Soviet Union's strategic outlets on the Baltic Sea and Scandinavia. The temptation for Russia to exacerbate the first phenomenon in order to favor the second constitutes a major factor behind long-term instability in the region. Obviously, the proximity of Baltic countries to the West via links with neighboring Nordic countries and, more generally, with the European Union gives them temporary shelter from brutal invasion such as occurred in Chechnya (where mafia activities served as a direct excuse for armed intervention), but a number of factors remain worrisome.

Ethnic Russians represent 50 percent of the population in Latvia and roughly 30 percent in Estonia. The Estonian government, worried about the falling birthrate among the Baltic community, is trying (without much success) to take an exact census of the former Russian officers receiving pensions from Moscow and is also prosecuting members of Parliament accused of belonging to the former KGB. Russian nationalist parties more or less overtly appeal to members of these substantial minorities, who have been excluded from jobs and government since independence. On November 2, 1994, a decree issued by Boris Yeltsin conferred full powers on the Russian president to designate "the forces and means necessary to evacuate" Russian citizens residing abroad. These "means" explicitly include carrying out military operations in "countries bordering the country of residence" during unspecified "emergency situations." Formulated two months prior to the attack on Chechnya, this clause—based on the United States' Monroe Doctrine—set the tone for a policy shift inspired by pressure from Vladimir Zhirinovsky's ultranationalist party, whose strength in the Russian Parliament makes it the linchpin of an alliance that may soon evolve from tactical to strategic. In the same vein, several days after issuing the decree, Yeltsin inspected reinforced frontier posts on the Estonian border established by the 1920 Tartu Treaty but contested by the Russians. Similarly, in mid-November Alexis Zybin, leader of an anti-independence movement in the late 1980s, founded a third Russian party in Tallinn.

Transit and Consumption

Lithuania has become a notable transit corridor between eastern and western Europe since the fall of the Berlin Wall and is therefore most heavily affected by trafficking. At the heart of major air, road, and river networks, the country boasts over 14,000 freight companies handling an annual total of 72 million tons of merchandise. Drug consumption, following the pattern of neighboring Poland, is dominated by homemade heroin (in the form of *kompot*) supplied mainly by local poppy production. Although local cannabis crops have also been reported (and several destroyed), the rapid growth in demand has spurred the importation of cannabis by-products from Ukraine, Armenia, Georgia, Kazakhstan, and Uzbekistan.

Ephedrine, obtained from the *Ephedra vulgaris* plant that grows on the vast stretches of Kazakhstan, arrives in the form of vials or crystals of hydrochloride via St. Petersburg or Kaliningrad (which has become a real hub of drug trafficking in the eastern Baltic). The very simple process of adding potassium permanganate and acid vinegar to ephedrine yields ephedrone, which addicts inject. Other synthetic drugs in circulation include Teofedrin, Metandestronolon, Relanium, and Radedorm. The Chinese triads, which control the clandestine immigration networks that now constitute a major phenomenon in eastern Europe (209 arrests in 1993, representing 21 percent of Lithuanian border infractions), have also invested in the ephedrine trade. In China, one of the major producers of this precursor chemical, ephedrine can be sold legally.

While their role in such trafficking cannot be accurately determined, Pakistanis, Lebanese, Turks, Iraqi Kurds, and Sri Lankan Tamils are also "regular" clandestine travelers. But Russians, Azeris, Ukrainians, Georgians, and Uzbeks were the nationalities most heavily implicated in contraband drugs in 1994. Many addicts in Latvia and the Russian district of Kaliningrad go to Lithuania to buy their precursor chemicals (acetone, acetic acid). Amateurish beginnings are now giving way to much more sophisticated methods, for which the overstretched police force is little prepared; increasingly common use is made of special couriers and vehicles with special hiding places.

The situation is less marked in the other Baltic countries, which are less implicated in central European trade routes; yet consumption follows similar lines. In Latvia, where a monitored shipment led to a first seizure of cocaine in 1994, the most commonly consumed drugs remain *kompot,* ephedrine, barbiturates, and cannabis derivatives. A glass or matchbox is the most common unit of measurement during sale. The prices in Riga in the fall of 1994 were US$6 to $7 for a glass of poppy straw, $5 for a gram of ephedrine, $25 for a matchbox of marijuana, and double that price for a box of good quality "Caucasian" hashish. As in Estonia, needles are sold very cheaply over the counter, and addicts who inject therefore now make strictly personal use of them. But health authorities are worried that consumption of imported heroin may grow along with the rapid increase in prostitution, which already represents the single most important cause of the spread of the HIV virus.

Drug seizures in Latvia and Estonia remain rare and, apart from the "historic" discovery of 3.5 tons of MDA in Latvia in 1992, are of modest quantities that probably bear no relation to the real extent of trafficking. According to authorities in Riga and Tallinn, the infrequency of seizures is due less to corruption than to a crucial lack of surveillance resources. Thus, only ten of Latvia's newly created twenty-six customs zones (replacing the former eight zones) are supplied with basic computer equipment. Furthermore, the transfer of some of the Customs Department's functions to the Tax Office has severely disrupted an organization that has a mere four years of experience. The priority given to tax collection is even more flagrant in the case of border guards, a force that only recently cut its ties to the Russian army and therefore is given only minimal attention by the central government. A similar problem exists on the border between Estonia and Russia, where the border guards—most of whom are draftees—have neither the training nor the motivation to put a halt to booming contraband activities.

3. *Eastern, Central, and Northern Europe*

Eastern and central Europe, situated between the CIS and the Atlantic Ocean, are bearing the full brunt of the collapse of the USSR and the subsequent outbreak of Balkan conflicts. This instability has led to trafficking in all sorts of commodities (weapons, drugs, plutonium), uncontrolled migration, the circulation of dirty money, and so on. The European Union is cooperating with Hungarian authorities in an effort to establish a first line of defense against the Balkan route, as witnessed by the record number of heroin seizures in Hungary. Kosovar, Lebanese, Moroccan, and Russian traffickers are now competing with their Turkish and Italian counterparts for control of markets in Germany and Switzerland. The Russian mafias have made Belgium one of their favorite fields of operation. Holland, meanwhile, is seeing its very liberal drug policy perverted by locally based "short networks" that extend throughout Europe. The governments of these countries nevertheless seem in no hurry to intervene "at the source," that is, directly with the relevant authorities in Pakistan, the CIS, or even Turkey and Morocco.

Hungary[1]

In 1994, 812 kilograms of heroin were seized in Hungary, as against 350 kilograms in 1993 and less than 100 kilograms in 1992. Nearly all seizures were made on the border with Romania, from trucks from Turkey traveling along the Balkan route. The most significant seizures include 211 kilograms at Artand on April 20 and 90 kilograms at the Nagylak border post on August 6. Because of the war in the former Yugoslavia, one of the main variations on the Balkan route has been a diversion into Hungary, taking advantage of the country's role as a hub of intense road and rail traffic.

Outpost on the Balkan Route

In 1993 some 50,000 trucks rolled through the customs post at Gyula, also on the Romanian border, where several other seizures have been made. Searching one of these vehicles takes between eight and sixteen hours. Heroin also moved along the Danube-Main-Rhine waterway, which links the Black Sea to the countries of the European Union. The United Nations has declared a total embargo on all river traffic with Serbia, but this ban is being skirted by roll on–roll off traffic (trucks transported on boats): Trucks hauling containers are unloaded from the boats at the beginning of the forbidden section of the Danube, driven overland, and then reloaded on other boats beyond the part of the river that crosses Serbian territory, under U.N. control, at the Serbia-Romania and Serbia-Hungary borders.

The networks of Kosovo Albanians that were broken up by Hungarian police in 1992 have gradually reorganized themselves. Thirteen Kosovan smugglers were arrested in 1994. On June 11, Albanian godfather Hyseni Luan was arrested in the suburbs of Pecs, a city in southern Hungary, not far from the border with Croatia, for the murder of another Albanian. Turkish traffickers are also highly active, and it is difficult to pick them out from the flow of genuine Turkish immigrant workers who cross Hungary on their way west. Twenty Turkish traffickers and couriers were arrested in 1993, and thirteen in 1994. Despite these enforcement measures, the heroin seized represents just a minute part of the estimated 20 tons that traverse the country every year, according to a declaration made to the OGD correspondent by a Hungarian drug

1. Poland was reviewed in OGD 1994 report, *État des drogues, drogues des États,* op. cit.

squad official. Furthermore, half a dozen Hungarians were named as participants in the network of Turkish trafficker Yilmaz Aliz, who was arrested in Madrid, Spain. Transit trafficking is beginning to have local fallout; for the first time in 1994, heroin was to blame for four deaths by overdose.

Domestic Production and Consumption

Several cases suggest that Hungary is on the way to becoming a producer and exporter of marijuana. On July 7, at Vasad, a town 36 kilometers south of Budapest, a police raid on an isolated farm resulted in the seizure of 500 kilograms of marijuana. The plants had only just been harvested from 27 greenhouses equipped with the latest in Dutch technology. The owner was a Dutch national of Hungarian origin with a long criminal record. The seeds came from the Netherlands, and the cannabis had a THC content of 12 to 14 percent, compared with 0.5 percent for the "improved" forest variety found in Hungary. The trafficker, who exported his entire production to the Netherlands, took care to hire illegal Romanian laborers who spoke no Hungarian, all cautiously confined within the farm perimeter by barbed wire. One week later, more than 727 kilograms of marijuana, again grown in greenhouses, were seized in Zalatarnok, between Lake Balaton and the Austrian border. This time the owner was a U.S. citizen of Hungarian origin who had fled to exile in the United States following the 1956 uprising in Hungary. Under the program to return private property seized under the communist regime, he had recently recovered several houses and land that belonged to his family and on which he was now cultivating cannabis. In this case too, the seeds came from the Netherlands. Part of the production was to be exported to the Netherlands and Austria. However, it was the sale of marijuana to the tourists, both Hungarian and foreign, who fill the beaches of Lake Balaton in summer that allowed authorities to trace the drug back to its source. Antinarcotics police believe that these two discoveries are not isolated cases, given that plants under opaque greenhouse glass are not easily recognizable in a rural country with a number of relatively sparsely populated regions. In 1994 a dozen other plantations, the output of which was meant for the domestic market, were destroyed and facilities with a capacity to produce 800 kilograms of marijuana were seized.

The privatization of the Hungarian pharmaceutical industry is also having negative consequences. In Biatorbagy the police discovered a synthetic drug laboratory in a house and seized 15 kilograms of amphetamines and 30 kilograms of semimanufactured products awaiting refinement. The amphetamines were destined for Scandinavian markets. The house had been rented by a Greek national and a Hungarian citizen resident in Sweden. The laboratory, which officially produced cosmetics, was discovered after the Swedish police tipped off their Hungarian counterparts about its existence.

Cocaine, which was hitherto considered in transit in Hungary, is now the object of mounting consumption. Seizures in 1994 increased tenfold compared with 1993, with 26.543 kilograms confiscated. Cocaine is especially popular with the new "businessmen"—traders in adulterated gasoline, stolen car dealers, and other specialists in financial scams. Domestic cocaine trafficking has resulted in some spectacular shoot-outs: Three people died in Budapest on December 26 and 27, 1994. Hashish and even LSD are enjoying a new vogue among high school students.

Western Participation in Money Laundering

A new antilaundering law, based on the model proposed by the European Union, was passed in Hungary in July 1994. But there are still doubts about its scope. Indeed, while the law was passed, the exception status granted to the Central European International Bank (CIB) was reaffirmed. The bank was set up on November 9, 1979, in order to operate in U.S. dollars outside Hungary. Following the end of the communist regime, some major international banks bought into CIB, each acquiring shares worth 13 percent of CIB's capital. The banks were Banca Comerciale Italiana, Bayerische Vereinsbank AG, the Long Term Credit Bank of Japan, the Sakura Bank and Société Générale. Hungary's Central Bank kept 30 percent of the bank's total shares. The representatives from the shareholding banks rotated as chairpersons of CIB. Proof that the Cali cartel had deposited money in CIB was given during the trial in Luxembourg in 1992 of three Colombians: Ricardo Mahecha (eventually acquitted on grounds of insufficient evidence), Edgar García Mantillo (sentenced to five years in prison), and Franklin Jurado (four and a half years in prison). In a memo addressed to García, Jurado described his laundering method, which consisted of five steps from 0 to 4. As the funds progressed from step 0 to step 4, the risk of their origin being uncovered diminished. In a report on "transactions carried out in Europe between May 15 and June 21, 1988," Jurado, when mentioning among others the CIB, recommended using Hungarian financial markets during steps 3 and 4 because of "the geographic, economic, and political situation" of the country. Accounts opened under false identities by Jurado's network were indeed identified at the bank.

CZECH REPUBLIC Czech police seized 500 kilograms of Afghan hashish from a truck on August 15, 1994. The drugs' ultimate destination was the Netherlands. Again in August, two Czech truck drivers were convicted in Morocco of transporting 2.7 tons of hashish. In late July, the assistant director of the Anti-Narcotics Brigade, Jiri Komorous, announced that in "... a little more than one year, [the Czech Republic] has moved from being a transit country for heroin to being a target country. In Prague, demand has outstripped supply, and prices are lower than in Western countries." There are three explanations: The Czech Republic is one of the last stops on the Balkan route; numerous immigrants from the former Yugoslavia and former Soviet Union have come to reside there during the past years; and turbulent Czech youth and the hordes of tourists from western Europe and the United States constitute a potentially enormous market. According to Komorous, former intelligence operatives from former Soviet bloc countries have now formed well-armed and organized gangs. The country is also on a cocaine route. Thus, on January 20, 1994, a regional court sentenced Alonso Delgado Martínez of Colombia to ten years imprisonment for importing 100 kilograms of cocaine through his company, Yaros Prague, in 1991. The drugs were seized at Nachod, on the border with Poland, and were destined for the western European market. Most narcotics, from heroin to cocaine to LSD and Pervitine, are sold in the bars of the Formanka neighborhood. Pervitine, a locally produced amphetamine, is still consumed more than "natural" drugs in the Czech Republic. One gram of heroin, whose price has fallen by two-thirds over the past year, costs only US$35, compared with $110 in Vienna, just 150 kilometers away. Heroin purity varies between 55 and 60 percent. According to Dr. Jiri Presl, director of Prague's first drug treatment center, the number of drug addicts could soon reach 10,000, though heroin consumption was nearly unheard of only two years ago.

Germany

Caught between western Europe's great drug markets and the disorders prevailing in the former Soviet empire, Germany is a border-post country. Still recovering from the shock of reunification, it receives a large share of the narcotics traveling along the Balkan route. It is a meeting place for immigrants from all the states "sensitive" to narcotics—Turkey, Italy, Poland, the former Yugoslavia, the Caucasian countries, and so on—and the scene of confrontation between various diasporas. It is therefore little wonder that in the past three years Germany has experienced an unprecedented boom in all types of crime. Drug trafficking is no exception, especially as 190,000 hard drug users live in the country. In a Germany where xenophobia and racism are already in ample supply, the pictures of the bullet-ridden bodies of Russian, Chechen, Kosovo Albanian, and Turkish gangsters that are regularly splashed across the sensational press (there were 122 drug-related murders in 1993) are perhaps part of a campaign aimed at substituting the communist bogeyman with the threat of organized crime. In such circumstances, discussions about the criminalization of German society, together with a national debate on the decriminalization of cannabis consumption (see box), have climbed to the top of the political agenda.

A Juicy Market for Organized Crime

Heroin seizures in Germany are continually rising. In most cases the drug enters via the northern branch of the Balkan route after passing through Bulgaria, Romania, the Czech Republic, or Switzerland. During June and July 1994, about 560 kilograms of heroin were seized, including 60 kilograms in Kassel on July 7, after the Swiss and German authorities collaborated to break up an international network of Turkish traffickers established in all German-speaking countries. In August, seizures reached 150 kilograms, including 30 kilograms transported by Kurds on a highway near Frankfurt, where Moroccan "short networks," which are especially active on the Belgian and Dutch borders, now control up to 60 percent of the heroin market. Between June 1993 and March 1994, 32 kilograms of heroin were seized, together with 330 kilograms of hashish and 6 kilograms of cocaine. The chief of Frankfurt's drug squad, Norbert Ditt, declared in July 1994 that "Moroccan families have transferred 4.5 million deutschmarks to bank accounts in Melilla [a Spanish enclave in Moroccan territory], which were then invested in real estate." The

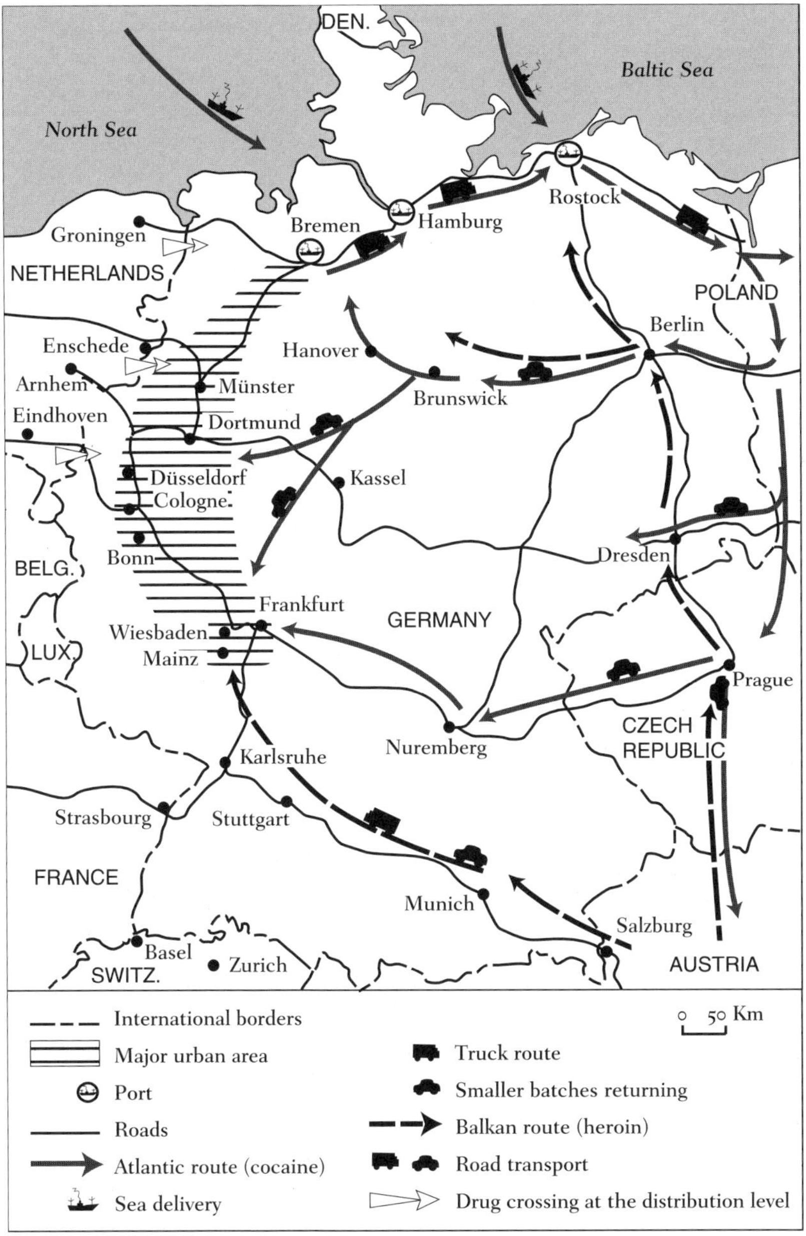

Map 5. Main Drug Routes into Germany

German consulate in Melilla has started legal proceedings to obtain the seizure of such property.

The trial of the members of a vast trafficking network headed by Oscar García Escobar, a Colombian national linked to the Cali cartel, took place during the summer of 1994. The organization was infiltrated and destroyed by the Bundeskriminalamt (BKA), the German criminal police, in 1993. Working with German, French, and Italian traffickers, the network had allegedly smuggled close to 2 tons of cocaine and 8 tons of marijuana into Germany since 1990. Using the controlled delivery technique, the BKA was able to seize 1,050 kilograms of cocaine throughout 1993. The BKA's investigation shed light on the method used by the Cali cartel in Germany: The cocaine is delivered to the harbors of Bremen, Hamburg, or Rostock in containers. These are then loaded on to TIR trucks (such trucks are subjected to customs inspection only at the countries of pickup and delivery) bound for the Czech Republic, Poland, and the Netherlands. In all three countries, but especially in the Czech Republic, the drugs are repackaged into smaller batches before being sent back, along various routes, to Germany and other European countries. This explains why most cocaine seizures within Germany average 5 to 20 kilograms in size, the latest being of 18 kilograms in September 1994. Provisional figures for 1994 indicate a total of over 2 tons of cocaine seized.

About half of the 5 percent of all crime in Germany directly related to narcotics is attributable to foreigners. According to BKA statistics, Bosnians, Croats, Macedonians, Kosovars, Slovenians, Russians, and Moroccans are now fighting over a market hitherto controlled by Turks (over 32 percent of drug-related crimes were still attributed to Turks in 1993). But the authorities' main concern is the significant rise in "white collar" drug-related crime—fraud, dummy companies, and large-scale investment in real estate (currently experiencing an unprecedented boom due to German reunification). Nowadays, these are the privileged laundering methods of Turkish and Russian mobsters. Russian "sports clubs" (those of the Dolgoprudny area of Moscow are often mentioned) have started investing in real estate with the profits from extortion, the drug trade, and trafficking in works of art.

The latest BKA report on the drug situation states that "the flexibility of organized crime and its ability to adapt to the German legal framework constitute a real threat." In plain language, this means that numer-

The German Chemical Industry Under Close Surveillance

While the debates on the legalization of soft drugs and money laundering have been widely publicized in the media, another subject, where the stakes are at least as high, has been evaded: the German "Law on the monitoring of chemical reagents production and export," which was enacted in October 1994. In 1990, when the U.S. Drug Enforcement Administration (DEA) accused the German pharmaceutical industry of supplying chemical reagents to Colombia and Turkey without any form of control, the government in Bonn rejected the accusation, arguing that it was ill founded. However, several developments forced the German authorities to revise their position. Large seizures of chemical reagents in Turkey and in several central European states have made it obvious that Germany was supplying these countries' chemical industries. Before the law was voted, the German government had called for the "self-regulation" of chemical manufacturers for a whole year—to no avail. Now, German chemical manufacturers and traders are legally responsible for the destination of their products. Moreover, exports are submitted for prior authorization to the Federal Bureau for Pharmaceutical Production (BAM), and would-be exporters have to inform the BKA and the Federal Customs Service. It is nevertheless probable that the law could be circumvented without too much trouble, as is suggested by a recent case involving Sopharma in Bulgaria. Spokespersons for this pharmaceutical company stated on December 8, 1994, that the 16 tons of "psychotropic substances" seized by the Bulgarian police were in fact a pharmaceutical thinner supplied by the German multinational AEG. According to the Bulgarian police, Sopharma, thanks to fake German end-user certificates, was serving as a front for the supply of German chemical reagents to Dutch secret laboratories.

ous German civil servants are being corrupted by Russian criminals; in 1994, courts heard thirty cases of active or passive corruption involving politicians, officials of the judiciary, businessmen, and even media personalities. After being present in Germany for four years, the mafias from the CIS seem to be particularly well organized. BKA statistics may already ascribe predominance in particular sectors of criminal activity to particular nationalities within the CIS.

Besides prostitution, Russians (13,151 arrests) specialize in money

Decriminalization: Constitutional Court Creates Confusion

In April 1994, a surprise ruling by the Constitutional Court advised Germany's *Länder* (states) to cease prosecuting the purchase and possession of marijuana for personal use. After fifty years of prohibition, Germany's highest court thus decriminalized the consumption of cannabis derivatives without modifying drug enforcement laws or penal procedures.

There are several reasons for the ruling. For one thing, the great number of users (five to six million) had progressively led police forces, overwhelmed with trafficking in other drugs and criminality in general, to abandon prosecution for this category of users. Furthermore, judges wanted to free up courts submerged by a flood of minor infractions (30,000 per year). But by not explicitly establishing the quantity of cannabis concerned, the Constitutional Court's ruling left the *Länder* a freedom of interpretation that immediately became an electoral issue, sparking heated debate over legislation. The Social-Democratic party (SPD) and the *Länder* it governs interpreted the ruling in the most liberal way. The state of Nordrhein-Westfalen (where the SPD leader is governor) even went so far as to authorize not only 10 grams of cannabis but also 0.5 grams of cocaine, heroin, morphine, amphetamines, and LSD.

In Bavaria, on the other hand, the extremely conservative CSU party lowered the cannabis threshold to 0.5 grams and passed a law that inflicts a life sentence on drug dealers belonging to "organized networks." Mecklemburg went Bavaria one better by setting the limit at 0.1 grams. As for the very liberal state of Schleswig-Holstein, it raised the threshold to 30 grams. But most of the *Länder* found an easier way to deal with the Court's recommendation: They simply leave the decision up to the police.

laundering, fraud, and other financial crime; Chechens (1,032 arrests) specialize in murders and extortion; Georgians (1,091 arrests) in counterfeit money; and Ukrainians (5,106 arrests) in smuggling in illegal immigrants and forging documents, both booming sectors. Kosovan "families," or *fares,* Macedonians, Serbs, and Croats are involved in drug trafficking on the Balkan route (950 arrests) and theft of high-powered cars (240 arrests). In 40.4 percent of all cases reaching the courts, car theft, prostitution, the trade in illegal workers, and economic crime are related in some way to the narcotics trade. Thus, Herr Schmidbauer, Chancellor Kohl's minister for regional coordination, could write in a report published as early as 1993 that "laundering networks move funds worth some DM320 billion" (about US$250 billion). He thinks that this money originated mainly from the Balkan route and the activities of the Russian mafia.

Neo-Nazis and Fundamentalists

On June 7, 1994, a municipal councillor of the Dutch city of Arnhem for the neo-Nazi Centrumdemocraten party was accused by the German authorities of heroin and cocaine trafficking. Charlie Sergeant, a member of the British "88" (the sum of the figures making up Hitler's birthdate) neo-Nazi group, was convicted of drug trafficking in England. He traded in drugs between the Netherlands, Germany, and Northern Ireland. Although they rant and rave against "foreign traffickers," some neo-Nazi activists seem nonetheless to copy their methods, thereby adding their own names to the long list of "ideological traffickers," alongside the Turkish "Grey Wolves," the PKK, and North African fundamentalists. Cases of such militant traffickers are multiplying: On May 10, 1994, a score of Kurdish PKK members were arrested in Cologne, where they had marketed 40 kilograms of heroin. On December 3, 1994, 292 kilograms of the same drugs were seized in Schirnding, on the German-Czech border, from a Kurdish network. In large German cities, feuds between the Grey Wolves and the PKK are often related to street dealing. To avoid arrests, both communities use underage children, including twelve- to fourteen-year-olds. The same method is also used by North African smuggling and retailing networks. Police sources say they employ children and teenagers (third-generation immigrants as well as children secretly smuggled from Berber villages back home) in street dealing. According to Wolfram Ritter of the drug squad, the North Africans now seem to be the masters of the drug market in southwestern Germany.

According to Karl-Heinz Reinstät, a police spokesman, Moroccans and Algerians have agreed to share the market of the Frankfurt-am-Main area, and some of their profits help fund Algerian fundamentalists. The German police have already arrested 298 Moroccans and 272 Algerians (including 253 political asylum seekers) on drug charges. The police think that they belong to small, independent groups that have "federated" to total over 1,000 members. Moroccans have already set up networks to import cannabis derivatives from their country. But most of the hashish they put on the market arrives via the Netherlands. Cocaine and heroin are now part of the mixed batches offered to purchasers. Anti-drug services in Wiesbaden report an increase in the passage of "mules" between the Netherlands and Germany. Indeed, Amsterdam's more than attractive prices allow just about anyone to become a dealer (in Amsterdam, the street price for 1 gram of hard drugs hovers around 80 guilders, or about US$50, while the same quantity fetches DM300, or about $200, in Stuttgart). On the Dutch-German border, at least 700 kilograms of hashish destined for a booming German market were seized in 1994, along with several kilograms of cocaine and heroin. Finally, across the border in the German province of Bavaria, over 400 kilograms of heroin were seized from members of communities at war in the Balkans.

The Netherlands

The Netherlands' role as a transit country for drugs on their way to other European countries was reinforced in 1994. Cocaine seizures by customs soared from 2.605 tons in 1993 to 6.171 tons in 1994, while seizures of cannabis derivatives grew from 92 tons to 149 tons during the same period. Only heroin seizures went down—from 110 kilograms to 99 kilograms. The country's domestic drug policy is the object of a national debate. "How can the Netherlands carry on down a schizophrenic path where consumption is legal but trade remains prohibited?" Thus, in late October, the newspaper *De Volksrant* expressed the increasingly widespread demands of Dutch citizens that the state make a clear choice: Either directly market drugs itself, or follow the more repressive policies of other European Union member-states. The liberal policies that have been around for the last twenty-five years are being challenged as a result of pressure from two sources: the Netherlands' European Union partners and the increasingly diverse networks of immigrants who are casting the "Dutch model" adrift.

The Rail Networks

In fact, a new drug-trading level has appeared in Amsterdam: "distribution." Previously, there existed the "wholesale" level (around 1 kilogram of cocaine or heroin) and the "retail" level in the neighborhoods, operated either by dealers in a wide range of places (tourist boats, hotels, nightclubs, amusement arcades, and of course the renowned "coffee shops") or by sellers who attended to their clients in apartments by appointment. The latter arrangement is the most widespread, especially for cocaine trading. A top drug squad official explained to the OGD special envoy that the various programs set up by the city or the state, including tight police surveillance, were aimed not at suppressing the traffic but rather at monitoring it and keeping buyers within fairly well-defined boundaries, thus avoiding excesses. Narco-tourists therefore purchased their drugs at coffee shops, dropouts bought them on the streets, and residents did so by appointment. It was fairly common for the police to "ask" certain "wholesalers" to be less visible by diversifying their outlets or by selling only to "regulars." The police thereby gave priority to intelligence gathering and were able to intervene in major deals so as to regulate the market, which would otherwise have spiraled out of control. But the rather sudden appearance of a new trading level is jeopardizing the system.

The "Amsterdam model," which is applied in other urban areas (see Map 6), has gone adrift. This is not so much the case in The Hague or Utrecht, both major urban centers, but rather in the small Catholic towns in the south (Heerlen, Maastricht); in Tilburg, Breda, Hazeldonk, and Dordrecht (north of Antwerp); and in Almedo, Hengelo, and Enschede (near the German border). These towns, located along the railroads linking the Netherlands to Germany or France via Belgium, are turning into "distribution" centers. The networks are run mainly by Turks in the east and Moroccans in the south. Every morning in the border towns, underage children, who do not risk heavy sentences, hop on trains bound for Amsterdam or Rotterdam. They offer their merchandise to foreign tourists at unbeatable prices (about US$15 for a gram of heroin whose purity is said to be "acceptable" and around $20 for cocaine with an "excellent" level of purity). At every station, the youths are met by another member of the family, who indicates with predetermined signals how much merchandise they are going to be entrusted with.

From Retail to Distribution

This system, which has long existed for retailing, has suddenly turned into large-scale trade. Indeed, narco-tourists have become traders, buying quantities of between 50 and 250 grams of hard drugs, which they will subsequently retail. For the purchase of quantities of over 30 grams of any drug, the price hovers between US$10 and $17 a gram. Certain Moroccans on both sides of the Belgium-Netherlands border thus seem

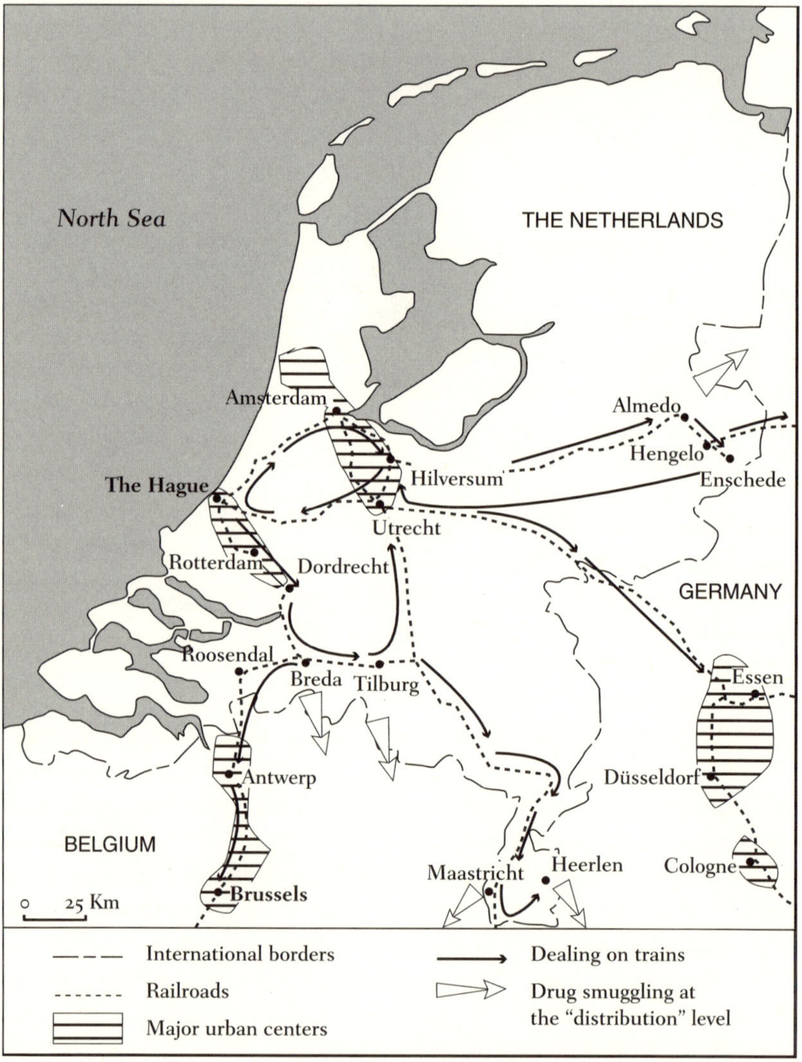

Map 6. The Netherlands: Trafficking Networks Expand

to be working completely independently of the Dutch (heroin and cocaine) or Colombian (cocaine) wholesalers, the latter being represented since the mid-1980s by two well-established families. It seems that the Moroccans, who settled in Belgium and the Netherlands some ten years ago, belong to freelance networks originating in Morocco or work hand in hand with Antwerp Chinese. One of those young dealers, born in Morocco and working "in the family business," told the OGD special envoy that he was making between US$700 and $1,400 per day. Aged sixteen, he negotiates deals of anything between 1 gram and 200 grams of any drug. This diversification is new, as up until now dealers have tended to specialize in one product only.

A similar phenomenon on the German border, but with Turkish families operating with the same independence from "classic" suppliers, appears to have taken off following the pressure applied on the Netherlands by its European neighbors. The police presence and the roundups they have carried out, especially in the Moluccan, Surinamian, Indonesian, Turkish, and other neighborhoods, have combined to make Amsterdam feel more "secure." The authorities' ultimate objective is to restrict the market to a minimum, as is illustrated by the fact that they are planning to close 80 percent of the country's 2,000 coffee shops. The market has consequently expanded along railroad tracks and roads, with the towns beyond the Dutch border having special appeal. Close to 800 people were arrested during the last three months on the Antwerp-Rotterdam route. Local Dutch operators have lost a share of the market to the immigrant competition, and they are trying to compensate by specializing in upmarket clients, who are always ready to buy cocaine at an expensive price—between US$30 and $45 a gram, twice that charged by the Turks and Moroccans, albeit for a lesser-quality product. The seizure of 500 kilograms of cocaine in Amsterdam on October 25, 1994, illustrates how the Colombian exporters go above the head of the former Dutch wholesalers—who as a result sometimes find themselves out of merchandise—to deal directly with the immigrants. In the aforementioned case, the cocaine had been hidden inside 1,200 fruit juice containers sent to the owner of an importing business. The following day the owner started distributing the cocaine-filled containers to traditional Surinamian food stores, called *tokos,* throughout the city. Some cocaine users—especially those who work in the media and have to commute daily between Amsterdam and Hilversum by rail—in this way suddenly came in contact with new suppliers offering various types of drugs, bringing prices down and destroying the cocaine "monopoly." Drugs like Ecstasy, LSD, and other psychedelic substances are thus being traded on an increasingly large scale. It is now nearly impossible for the police to monitor the trade, due to the increasing number of nonspecialized "distributors." An added difficulty for the authorities is that while "distributors" operate within international networks, they still run their business as a family concern. As a result, an absolutely new process has emerged, whereby scores of those trader-smugglers can collaborate to accumulate stocks of several kilograms, making deliveries of 200 grams at a time. The stocks can then be renegotiated in Brussels, Paris, or Frankfurt with comfortable profit margins. In this case, the direction of the trade, which used to go from the kilogram to the gram, is reversed. Faced with an individual carrying about 50 grams, a police officer may now wonder whether that person is a dealer, a "distributor," or a "stock maker."

The End of a Model?

The system known and monitored by the police is consequently being destroyed. Attempts to suppress the "Amsterdam model" are diversifying trafficking methods for all drugs, now making targets of countries that, as early as the beginning of the 1970s, tried to cordon themselves off from a sore deemed intolerable in Europe. This option is much less viable today as, after Turks, Moroccans have become major international traffickers. The deals struck between the Colombian cartels and eastern European mafias gave birth to new hubs. These hubs, be they in North Africa or in the Balkans, aim at using the infrastructure developed long ago by immigrant communities when they settled in northern Europe.

At the local level, this situation presents an added danger for the Netherlands. Far away from permissive Amsterdam, small, Catholic, right-minded towns in the south react with xenophobia and support a hard-line stance when faced with the drug phenomenon. As demonstrated in the recent Antwerp municipal election, the Flemish "ultra" phenomenon in northern Belgium is a manifestation of similar reactions. More than ever, the division between Amsterdam and the rest of the country is threatening the Netherlands' political balance. "As long as neighboring countries cannot get used to the idea of legalization, any decision whatsoever will carry a heavy political price," concluded a top health ministry official. In spite of demands for more repressive policies, the steps taken most recently point toward increased liberalization. Hans van Mierlo, the foreign affairs minister, when asked at the end of talks with a French delegation if he could predict any radical change in Dutch drug policy, replied quoting a famous Edith Piaf song: *"Non, je ne regrette rien"* (no, I regret nothing). Occasionally, original proposals are made. Thus, at a conference organized by the police on October 18, 1994, among guests including businesspeople, lawyers, and Ministry of

Money Laundering: Central Bank Anxiety

Thousands of tourists are drawn daily to Amsterdam's casinos and slot machines in Rembrandtsplein, its red-light district and shop-window prostitutes in Nieuwmark, and its coffee shops in Leidesplein. To cater to this clientele, the Dutch government authorized the installation of independent currency exchange houses in the early 1970s. Now it may be obliged to outlaw them, for Holland's central bank is becoming seriously worried about the laundering of drug money by exchange agencies. "We feel that over a third of these agencies should go," declared a bank spokesperson on January 8, 1995. Tom de Swann, the bank's governor, added, "In no way does the number of these agencies correspond to the needs of tourists."

The central bank has thus ordered financial monitoring of 110 of these agencies, which have until March 1, 1995, to justify every transaction exceeding US$12,000. A former economics minister declared that over 10 percent of the money circulating in the Netherlands—that is, nearly 15 billion guilders (US$8 million)—is recycled money. Of course, laundering is not done by exchange houses alone, and the banks bear their own share of responsibility. On January 10, 1995, Holland's most prestigious bank, ABN-AMRO, announced that it had been "deceived" by a cocaine cartel from Surinam into laundering tens of millions of guilders. All Dutch banks have agreed to adopt antilaundering measures and to investigate "suspect" clients. But the extent of the cash flowing into Amsterdam makes certain banking institutions—notably those dealing with *deelnemings-vrijstellung* (holding companies in which foreign investors hold at least a 30 percent stake)—reluctant to take overly strict measures, especially as the Dutch see the neighboring countries of Luxembourg and (to a lesser extent) Belgium as "tax havens" ready to provide fleeing capital with a new refuge.

Health officials, sociologist Raymond Dufour suggested, "We have to get rid of the coffee shops and replace them with outlets managed jointly by the state and the producers." Along similar lines, the city of Arnhem plans to open a coffee shop in an unused gas station on the highway to Germany to supply the 800 narco-tourists who drive on it every week.

Meanwhile, it was learned on October 23 that the new health minister, Els Borst, approved a project aiming at supplying heroin to 100 of Amsterdam's 7,000 users, those for whom all attempts at rehabilitation have failed. Rotterdam is due to launch a similar experiment. Such initiatives seem in tune with the authorities' current policy: intervening in the market, lowering prices to prevent the arrival of new dealers, cooperating with neighboring countries to limit the development of narcotourism, and above all seizing drugs at the source. Reacting to a declaration by his minister, one Ministry of Justice official declared on January 22, 1995: "We have to stop being hypocrites and tolerate indoors [that is, in the coffee shops] what we forbid outdoors. It might have worked in the 1970s, but today we are overwhelmed."

Cooperation with British police permitted the seizure of 500 kilograms of cocaine from Curaçao in the port of Amsterdam (Hoek van Holland) on November 10. One of the biggest Ecstasy laboratories ever to be discovered in the Netherlands was destroyed by police in Amsterdam in late September. It had been set up by an Israeli network and was given away by a cloud of smoke that disturbed passersby, who alerted the police. Five people were arrested in the Netherlands and Belgium. The Israeli police, who apprehended another nine people, had been supplying information about the network to their Dutch counterparts since last April.

Belgium

The year 1994 was marked by the discovery in Antwerp of several Russian mafia networks with links to the drug trade. The first such organization, revolving around a big Antwerp transport firm, was supposed to receive the ton of cocaine seized at Vyborg, in the CIS, in February 1993. Analysts from the BKA and the Antwerp *gendarmerie* could confirm that the containers concealing the drugs, which were prematurely seized by Russian law enforcement officers, should in fact have had their "identity" changed through a chain of dummy companies based in Moscow and St. Petersburg and then delivered to a network of Israeli traffickers established in the Netherlands via an Antwerp firm linked to the Russian mafia. Elsewhere, the authorities have reviewed the operations of recently created antilaundering services.

The Russian Networks

After the Vyborg case, the second network to be uncovered was that led by one of the godfathers of the Brooklyn Russian mafia, Boris Nayfeld, known as "Beeba." A former bodyguard for New York gangster Evsei Agron, Nayfeld was arrested in New York in January 1994 on charges of racketeering, narcotics trafficking, conspiracy to murder, and association (since 1979) with Russian-Jewish criminal organizations. From at least 1989 to 1993, Nayfeld's sphere of operations was based on companies owned by the Russian community in Antwerp, as well as on their affiliates in Moscow, Berlin, Odessa, Warsaw, and so on. Through these companies, television sets were shipped from Singapore to Copenhagen or Warsaw. The sets' cathode tubes were filled with heroin from Thailand. The drugs were then handed over to Ukrainian "mules" for the onward journey to Kennedy Airport, New York City. As managing director and chairman of the board of various import-export companies located in Antwerp, Nayfeld also provided services on behalf of a Russian-Belgian company, M&S International, controlled by the Georgian mafia in Moscow. The company, which also has offices in Vilnius, Lithuania, was named in the investigation into the murder of the Lithuanian journalist Vytas Lingis by a criminal group named "the Vilnius Brigade." M&S International is also under investigation by the Russian defense ministry for alcohol and cigarette smuggling in collaboration with former Russian military forces stationed in Germany. Before it went bankrupt, M&S International had set up a British laundering sanctuary in the Channel Island of Jersey. This very sophisticated system of dummy companies is currently under thorough investigation. A third Russian network, based in Antwerp, is responsible for smuggling at least one Russian ground-to-air missile from Belarus to Belgium—and probably on to the Middle East if it had not been confiscated. The missile was discovered in an Antwerp warehouse in early 1995.

Faced with the first murders of Russian gangsters on their patch—notably that of a launderer, presumed to be Russian, on his way to Venezuela—Belgian investigators no doubt remembered that ten years before Mossad (the Israeli secret service) had predicted the development of Ukrainian, then Russian, organized crime, starting from Antwerp, that would turn Belgium into a major location for the illicit activities of their *Organizatsiya*. At the same time, Colombian traffickers in Antwerp lost Marco González-Nuñez, one of the bosses of their European organization who, along with his brothers Guillermo and Henri—based in Germany and Colombia respectively—was working for José Santacruz Londoño, one of the top bosses of the Cali cartel. Starting from a seizure carried out in Antwerp in 1991, the Belgian authorities were able for the first time to destroy the Colombians' integrated drug trading network by following the trail from a street dealer all the way up to the cartel's leadership.

Antilaundering Legislation

Like France with its TRACFIN/OCRGDF system, Belgium set up two institutions dedicated to uncovering and investigating presumed laundering networks: CTIF (Department of Financial Affairs) and OCDEFO (Central Office for the Fight Against Financial and Economic Organized Crime). They started operating on July 1, 1993, and January 1, 1994, respectively. At the end of 1994, the Belgians were thus able for the first time to provide an annual estimate of the scale of money laundering inside their borders. From December 1993 to November 1994, CTIF recorded 2,031 declarations of suspect activity in the financial sector, resulting in 597 different files, 108 of which were transmitted to the prosecutor's office. The suspect funds total more than 12 billion Belgian francs (US$400 million).

OCDEFO, which investigates the cases resulting from CTIF's detection activity, maintains that most of the files it receives from CTIF turn out to be effective laundering cases. Notable cases include investigations into the Belgian affiliates of Turkish banks, laundering for southern European mafia organizations, and one financial file directly linked to the Naples Camorra. However, the Belgians have not yet determined whether the Camorra file is a genuine laundering network or a mafia swindle.

4. *Europe's Atlantic Coast*

In late January 1995, people walking along a beach in southwestern France found several sacks washed up by the sea containing a total of over 100 kilograms of cocaine. This incident shows that the dramatic rise in drug seizures carried out in France, Portugal, and Britain in 1994 has not discouraged Latin American traffickers from using the Atlantic coasts of European Union countries. While French seizure statistics were inflated by the quantities confiscated in the French Caribbean, the record British and Portuguese seizures essentially took place in ports and at sea. The coasts of all these countries also seem to attract traffickers in Moroccan hashish, although that drug is also transported by road. Pakistani hashish seems to be destined mainly for Great Britain. Only heroin, which remains Europe's main cause of drug addiction (even though crack is beginning to wreak havoc in Britain) reaches the region via the Balkan route. While Portugal, which is hard hit by narcotics, is looking for its own solution to the problems posed by drug use, France remains one of Europe's most conservative countries, even though advances have been made there in methadone treatment programs. Britain, which in the past implemented pioneering drug treatment programs, seems to be reverting to more conservative policies.

France

In March 1994, the French government set up what became known as the Henrion Commission to make recommendations concerning national drug policy. Its report was due to be delivered to Minister of Health Simone Veil by November of that year. As late as January 1995, however, commission members still had not come to an agreement on the final report, thought by some to be "overly liberal." The final text, submitted on February 3, made only the timid recommendation that use of cannabis be decriminalized. Such tentativeness reveals France's difficulty in coming up with an alternative to harsh enforcement. Yet a spectacular increase in seizures during 1994 confirms the need to adapt national policy to the new situation.

Record-Breaking Year

Drug enforcement squads (including *gendarmes,* national police, and customs officers) broke all seizure records in 1994. Total cocaine seizures equaled 4.5 tons, compared with 1.7 tons in 1993. Crack took root in the Greater Paris region, where distribution shifted from Caribbean groups to Senegalese, Zairean, and Mauritanian nationals who either import what the French call *caillou* ("rock") from Africa—notably Ghana, where a lab was uncovered in 1993—or produce it locally. Veil announced the formation of a working group to study the phenomenon. It will rely particularly on the experience of crack specialists from the Caribbean, where production in clandestine labs (set up on the nearby isles of St. Vincent, Dominica, or St. Martin) is ravaging the French islands of Martinique and Guadeloupe.

Seizures of cannabis derivatives are also on the rise: 54 tons in 1994 (mainly hashish from Morocco) compared with 45.8 tons the previous year. Furthermore, 630 kilograms of heroin were seized (as against 386 in 1993). Among synthetic drugs, seizures of Ecstasy and similar narcotics continue to rise; according to the annual customs report, these not only increased by 41 percent in number (166 as against 118 in 1993) but also by 72 percent in terms of quantity (220,000 pills compared with 128,446). For the first time, the lion's share of Ecstasy seized in 1994 (32 percent of the total) was destined for the French market. Two incidents confirmed the growth of a local market, especially among adolescent ravers: first, the March breakup of a distribution network based in Nanterre, outside

Paris, which imported batches of 1,000 pills at a cost of 30 francs per unit in Holland and sold them for 150 to 250 francs in nightclubs from Paris to Troyes; and second, the June dismantling of another network that distributed Dutch and Thai Ecstasy and LSD in southern France. Ecstasy produced mainly in Holland still passes through France on its way to markets in Britain (27,560 doses seized in northern France on November 12 were destined for British shores), the Iberian Peninsula (2,000 pills and 10 kilograms of amphetamine sulphate were found in a German car near Bordeaux on January 13), and Italy (1,300 tablets were seized on the Franco-Belgian border on November 16 from Italian nationals returning from the Netherlands).

Avoiding excessive self-congratulation, French Minister of the Interior Charles Pasqua cautiously acknowledges that the increase in seizures was "as much a reflection of intensified security measures in general as of a trend in the criminal phenomenon itself." It is, in fact, difficult to deduce market trends from these statistics. Thus, the spectacular upturn in figures concerning cocaine is largely due to the January 1994 seizure in Toulouse of 1.2 tons of cocaine bound for Italy (part of a delivery under surveillance) and from the discovery that same summer of an equivalent amount (in two batches), probably bound for the North American market, abandoned by dealers on the beaches of the French Antilles. As to the "intensified security measures" mentioned by the minister, they induce skepticism when it is realized that, although drug law violations increased by 7.38 percent, arrests of dealers dropped by 7.16 percent. These figures show, and a Ministry of Justice study published in September confirms, that addicts continue to be the main targets of enforcement. In 1991, one-third of all those convicted of drug legislation violations were simple users.

As far as drug squad organization goes, a struggle between the Interior Ministry and the Customs Department since the early 1990s has resulted in a redeployment of customs officers to conventional antifraud missions. The special customs squad operating under the Finance Ministry has therefore put a de facto hold on all infiltration of international drug networks—monitoring deliveries is no longer "à la mode." The new enforcement philosophy, long advocated by Jacques Franquet, former head of OCRTIS (Central Enforcement Office for Illicit Narcotics Traffic) and until February 20, 1995, director of France's Police Judiciaire, was summed up by Interior Minister Pasqua: "The police don't wait to reach the top of the networks before taking action. Now they often arrest dealers as soon as they flush them out." Gilles Leclair, the current head of OCRTIS, confirms that "it's impossible to choke off supplies by monitoring big deliveries, however spectacular they may be. That's why we intend to favor action against networks operating in this country on an daily basis."

Colombians Move In

The major enforcement event of 1994 in terms of trafficking was the success of Operation Margarita, conducted in June. Following a U.S. tip-off, French police broke up a Medellin cartel bridgehead for the first time. This episode demonstrates that France is not merely a transit country for hard drugs, despite the authorities' repeated claims. The network was run from a lavish Paris apartment by Jaime Zuluaga-Botero, alias José, a twenty-nine-year-old member of the Botero family, one of the main clans of the Colombian cartel. The cocaine entered France via the southwest, in shipments of 1 to 6 tons, hidden on sailboats (three of which were seized). The sailboats recovered bundles dropped into the Atlantic by private aircraft. When the police intervened, the traffickers were preparing to spend US$4 million on a ten-passenger pocket submarine to enable them to approach the southwest coast of France in maximum secrecy.

The logistics of the French operation were confided to another Colombian, nicknamed El Turco, whose residence was found to contain 45 kilograms of cocaine and two million francs' worth of foreign currency. For US$40,000 per month, El Turco managed the distribution of cocaine and the collection of funds, relying on three French subordinates (one based in a village near Limoges, another who raised goats near Béziers, and a third living in a hamlet in the Creuse region). Dozens of couriers, transporters, and dealers—often in financial straits—were recruited in nightclubs and arcades. They were paid US$4,000 per month, or by commission. The money was "prelaundered" through ninety-six bank accounts, then shunted through two exchange houses in Marseilles prior to being shipped out to tax havens and on to Colombia. According to police, profits on the sale of 250 kilograms of pure cocaine reportedly reached over US$4 million in six months. Documents seized by investigators recorded wholesale prices set by the network at US$22,000 to $24,000 per kilogram of pure hydrochloride, less than one-third the usual Paris prices, which demonstrates the Colombian dealers' determination to increase their presence on the French market.

The other major event concerns heroin trafficking. On November 25 and 26, the Police Judiciaire in Annecy seized 18 kilograms of heroin imported by a "short network" of Kosovo Albanians. The arrest of six of them confirmed that France is now an active base for these groups, which already operate in Germany and Switzerland. In all probability, the extremely pure heroin was to have been redistributed throughout Europe.

Drugs and Islamic Fundamentalists: Suspicions Confirmed

Various operations conducted against networks supporting Algerian activists of the Islamic Salvation Front (FIS) and Armed Islamic Group (GIA) have provided new proof of the contribution made by drug money to the financing of Algeria's civil war. In March 1994, two different police squads in Lille broke up the same network in northern France following two separate investigations, arresting some twenty suspects. This operation shed light on a heroin distribution network based in Rotterdam that sold 3 to 4 kilograms per month. Several members were implicated in a major ring that forged Algerian documents, notably identification papers for GIA activists. In the same region of northern France, police and magistrates have been overwhelmed by the proliferation of "short networks" set up by clandestine Algerian immigrants who have colonized the local heroin market. "The question is whether the FIS deliberately organizes the arrival of the clandestine immigrants to deal drugs and undermine French youth, or whether it is merely demanding its tithe," mused the assistant district attorney for Lille in the weekly magazine *VSD*. These networks are highly unstructured and disappear after just a few months of activity, making them excessively difficult to dismantle.

On November 8, a vast dragnet in Paris and the surrounding region led to the arrest of seventy-eight persons suspected of having formed a network to support the GIA. The network's main leaders were the four Chalabi brothers, French nationals of Algerian stock who ran an Islamic school in Orly, south of Paris, and were known to police for theft and narcotics dealing. They reportedly organized a heroin supply chain between the Netherlands and France, the drugs being hidden in rented cars and the money laundered through several restaurants. At the same time the brothers set up networks for handling forged papers and weapons (assault rifles, submachine guns, handguns, explosives, and detonators) on behalf of Islamic militia. In an interview published in *Paris-Match,* the chief investigating magistrate Jean-Louis Bruguière remained cautious: "Did the French support network deal in drugs to finance itself? Probably, even though we still have no concrete proof of that; the groups we have dismantled were awash in cash, coming from criminal activities, among others."

On July 24, 1994, French border police, alerted by their German counterparts, uncovered an arsenal in Perpignan destined for Algeria. The investigation led to the breakup of a weapons-dealing network run by FIS Algerians, Moroccans, Egyptians, and a Tunisian from the outlawed Islamic party Ennahdah. In this network weapons purchased in eastern Europe left Germany and crossed France, Spain, and northern Morocco, following local hashish routes. Thus, even when Islamic fundamentalists are not directly financed by the drug trade, they apparently take advantage of the logistics implemented by contraband networks. This theory would seem to be borne out by the Loucini affair. In November 1994, Djamel Loucini, an Algerian businessman suspected of being the main supplier of arms to Islamic resistance fighters, was arrested in Italy at the request of Moroccan authorities and then swiftly freed. According to information published by *VSD* and the daily newspaper *Le Monde,* Loucini was backed in Germany by Algerian drug dealers, who supplied him with the necessary means for transporting weapons. In exchange, Loucini provided the traffickers with access to his laundering operations, used for the funds—basically originating in the Arabian Peninsula—with which he purchased weapons. Similarly, in Italy Loucini has reportedly hooked up with several drug networks organized by the Camorra.

Finally, on January 1, 1995, the British *Sunday Times* newspaper revealed that the British secret service was investigating the activities of Algerian Islamic fundamentalists suspected of collecting funds in London on behalf of the GIA. These activists, who specialize in extorting money from illegal Algerian immigrants, reportedly also force their compatriots to sell drugs on their behalf.

Great Britain

The British all-time record seizures of synthetic drugs (1 ton) and cannabis (47 tons, as against 6 tons in 1993) were broken in 1994. Cocaine seizures of 2.2 tons (as against 700 kilograms in 1993), almost equaled the record level of 1992 (2.25 tons). Following a renewal—noted in last year's report—of the activities in Britain of Italian, Chinese, and Turkish-Cypriot mobsters in 1993, Russian organized crime also became conspicuous in Britain in 1994. Russian gangsters, for whom drug trafficking and money laundering are just two among many "businesses," were involved in several shoot-outs in London. British police officers were dispatched to Moscow in July 1994 to improve collaboration with their Russian counterparts against organized crime.

Cocaine Yuppies and Crack Babies

On January 12, 1995, 250 kilograms of cocaine were seized on a British catamaran off the coast of Sussex in southern England. On November 12, 1994, a joint operation by British and Dutch police led to the seizure in Amsterdam of over 500 kilograms of cocaine that had been shipped over from England. Cocaine purity at street level in Britain is on the rise. Crack seizures, which unlike cocaine seizures are almost always carried out at street level, have increased by 712 percent compared with the same period in 1993, according to National Criminal Intelligence Service (NCIS) statistics for the first three months of 1994. The spread of cocaine trafficking in Great Britain, which the OGD announced last year, has been confirmed and is accelerating. Cocaine hydrochloride (cocaine powder) is mostly consumed in well-off circles and notably by City of London financiers. By contrast, crack cocaine—manufactured from illegally imported hydrochloride by West Indian, in particular Jamaican, networks—is the drug of deprived suburban areas, especially around London. Peckham, one such district in south London with a large immigrant community, has been nicknamed "the British capital of crack" by the media, but it is just one example of the well-known effect of crack on crime and violence statistics.

A *Sunday Times* article published in July 1994 revealed that 160 "crack babies," as children who are born addicted to crack are known, were born in Great Britain in 1994. "Crack babies"—at least those lucky enough to be diagnosed, as doctors are not yet generally familiar with the symptoms of crack addiction—must undergo special treatment as soon as they are born. Doctors could soon become experts: A pediatrician told the *Sunday Times* that a sharp increase in births of crack-addicted babies was noted in the first six months of 1994.

Cannabis Out, Khat In

Seizures of cannabis derivatives soared in 1994. The coast of Cornwall, in southwest England, is one of the privileged areas for cannabis trafficking by pleasure boats, which are numerous in this tourist area. Thus, in August 1994, close to 1 ton of cannabis was seized on land near Launceston. In early September, 3 tons of hashish were intercepted on a schooner near Durgan. Also in September, the police seized over 1 ton of hashish on a private yacht at sea. In November, 10 tons of high-quality Pakistani hashish were discovered in a container from Zambia in Felixstowe, Britain's busiest freight harbor, where seizures of all drugs are frequent. Before reaching the east coast of England, the container passed through the port of Dar-es-Salaam, Tanzania.

Fairly significant amounts of marijuana are also grown intensively on British soil. A debate on the decriminalization of cannabis use, echoed in the press, has been taking place in the country since early 1994. Even though high police officials have declared that they support decriminalization, the law is unlikely to be changed. Indeed, the leaders of all three major political parties have made it clear that they are opposed to decriminalization, notwithstanding the well-known fact that possession of a small amount of cannabis is rarely the object of prosecution; more often than not police merely caution offenders before letting them off.

The faintheartedness of British politicians (with few exceptions) concerning cannabis is surprising in a country with highly developed local programs of heroin and methadone distribution under medical supervision. But it seems that rather than opening a parliamentary debate that could prove costly in terms of votes, politicians prefer to leave things as they are, or even to backpedal. Thus, the government has announced in a roundabout way that it will put an end to the heroin distribution program operated by Dr. Marks in Liverpool for over ten years. Methadone distribution will continue. Although the reasons given for the suppression of heroin distribution were of a purely administrative nature, the government's real motive is probably to align itself with the United

States, which is traditionally opposed to providing abusers with the drug of their choice.

British law does not prohibit the importation or consumption of khat. Great Britain has therefore become a hub for trade in this plant, 7 tons of which allegedly pass through London's Heathrow Airport every day. At first, the imported khat was destined either for traditional consumption by Yemeni and Somali refugees living in Britain or for reexport to such communities in other European countries. But khat's mildly stimulating effect has won over some enthusiasts among the London and Manchester nightclubbing crowd. While the Somalis and Yemenis prefer khat imported from Ethiopia, British users favor the Kenyan variety, which is more potent. According to the weekly newspaper *The Observer,* some 7 tons are sold to users in Britain every week. Thus, the khat trade allegedly generates some £50 million per year, a fair share of which benefits the British economy. The appearance of tablets of methcathinone (a synthetic drug, a khat and Russian ephedrone analog), which are imported from the United States, is of more concern even though the drug is still confined to a few who are "in the know." Methcathinone was described by a user from Manchester as "very, very powerful."

A recent survey indicates that drug-related deaths more than doubled in the United Kingdom between 1984 and 1992. Apart from the "classic" deaths from overdoses of heroin (100 kilograms of which were seized in Kent in October), numerous young people died in England and Scotland after taking Ecstasy at rave parties. Seizures of the various varieties of Ecstasy, which is mostly imported from the Netherlands, have increased very significantly in 1994, and methamphetamines continue to be extremely popular in Great Britain. Moreover, LSD is coming back into fashion, as evidenced by a 93 percent rise in seizures during the first three months of 1994.

The economic policies of the Conservative party, which has been in power since 1979, are considered by its opponents to have contributed to the impoverishment of a large share of the population. They are also partly responsible for the worsening of drug abuse in Great Britain. While the government has made the war on drugs one of its priorities, it has announced a large cut in the budget of the Customs Service (600 jobs could go), one of the key institutions in the fight against narcotics. In this context the prime minister, John Major, and the home secretary,

Michael Howard, have urged their European partners on several occasions to increase funding for the suppression of the drug trade. Have the Conservatives finally found some use for the European Union—making up for their own deficiencies?

Portugal

The newly formed European Monitoring Center for Drugs and Drug Addiction (EMCDDA), which is headquartered in Portugal and has a budget of 4.8 million ECUs (US$5.5 million), elected Georges Estievenart, a Frenchman, as its first director in late July 1994. Lisbon offers the EMCDDA, which was inaugurated on April 26, a prime location for studying the various aspects of the drug problem in the European Union. A transit country for all types of drugs, Portugal also has to contend with rising addiction rates. Furthermore, there are indications that Portugal is in the process of becoming a large money-laundering center. The following quantities were seized in 1994: 1.7 tons of cocaine (200 kilograms in 1993); 40.4 tons of hashish (52.7 in 1993); and 88.4 kilograms of heroin (92 kilograms in 1993).

Drugs in the Cities and in the Country

Drug consumption among Portugal's working class began with the return of colonial expeditionary troops from Angola and Mozambique between 1972 and 1975. These soldiers first popularized the use of marijuana, which they consumed frequently in the two African colonies. Until the mid-1980s, however, heroin consumption affected only a very small number of Portuguese, who encountered the drug while traveling abroad. But since then, heroin consumption has increased rapidly, as have the use of synthetic drugs and all forms of multidrug use. According to the morgue in the Portuguese capital, at least one death by overdose is registered each day in greater Lisbon. Authorities estimate that the number of drug addicts, mainly heroin users, has climbed from 30,000 in 1987 to more than 100,000 in 1994. Since Portugal's entry into the European Community in 1986, which acted as a catalyst for economic growth, the country is no longer relatively isolated from the outside world. As the economy averaged 4.5 percent growth per year between 1986 and 1990, drug traffickers took advantage of the opening of Portugal's borders to introduce new products of all kinds. Initially, German, Dutch, and Greek traffickers supplied Portugal's heroin market. But Turkish networks slowly made inroads, using the Istanbul-Zurich-Lisbon route, and are now in direct contact with established Portuguese distributors. Police seized 41 kilograms of heroin in 1992, and 92 kilograms in 1993, of which 50 kilograms originated from the Netherlands and 5 kilograms from Turkey. Wholesalers are often nationals of Guinea Bissau, West Africa. Authorities seized 6.5 kilograms from Guinea Bissau citizens in a working-class neighborhood of Lisbon on April 15, 1994. On April 27, Catio Balde, the brother of Guinea Bissau Minister of the Interior Aboubacar Balde, was sentenced to eight years imprisonment. Gang warfare caused the death of a Guinea-Conakry national on November 9. Cape Verde nationals, who make up by far the largest number of foreigners arrested in 1993 in Portugal (eighty-seven), are also active in small-scale trafficking between Amsterdam and Lisbon. Numerous gypsies specialize in street dealing. Heroin is consumed principally in the poor sections of Lisbon—such as Casal Ventoso, Curraleira, and Cambora—as well as in the Se quarter of Oporto. According to the public prosecutor, 60 percent of property crimes are drug-related. Of 745 armed robberies registered in Portugal's cities in 1993, more than 100 were committed with syringes claimed to be "contaminated" with the AIDS virus.

Heroin is also found in rural areas, such as Tras-os-Montes in the north, which nevertheless harbors a hardworking, deeply religious Catholic community. By the year 2000, membership in the European Union will lead to the disappearance of one million small farms. And since economic growth in Portugal sank to a mere 1 percent in 1993, urban areas no longer offer work. Because job opportunities in France and the rest of Europe too have been considerably reduced, this restructuring of Portugal's rural areas has been accompanied by an explosion in unemployment. Thousands of young people from villages and small towns are already affected by drugs. Yet Portugal is not powerless in the face of this epidemic. It has developed a treatment strategy, called "Project Vida," that balances prevention and enforcement. Project Vida brings together a network of drug abuse aid centers, established in 1987, modeled on the well-known "Taipas Center."

While heroin is destined entirely for the local market, over the past two to three years Portugal has become an important transit country for cocaine and cannabis by-products (see Map 7). As for cocaine, the recent reinforcement of border controls by Spain's Customs Surveillance Service (SVA) has led traffickers to fall back on the Portuguese

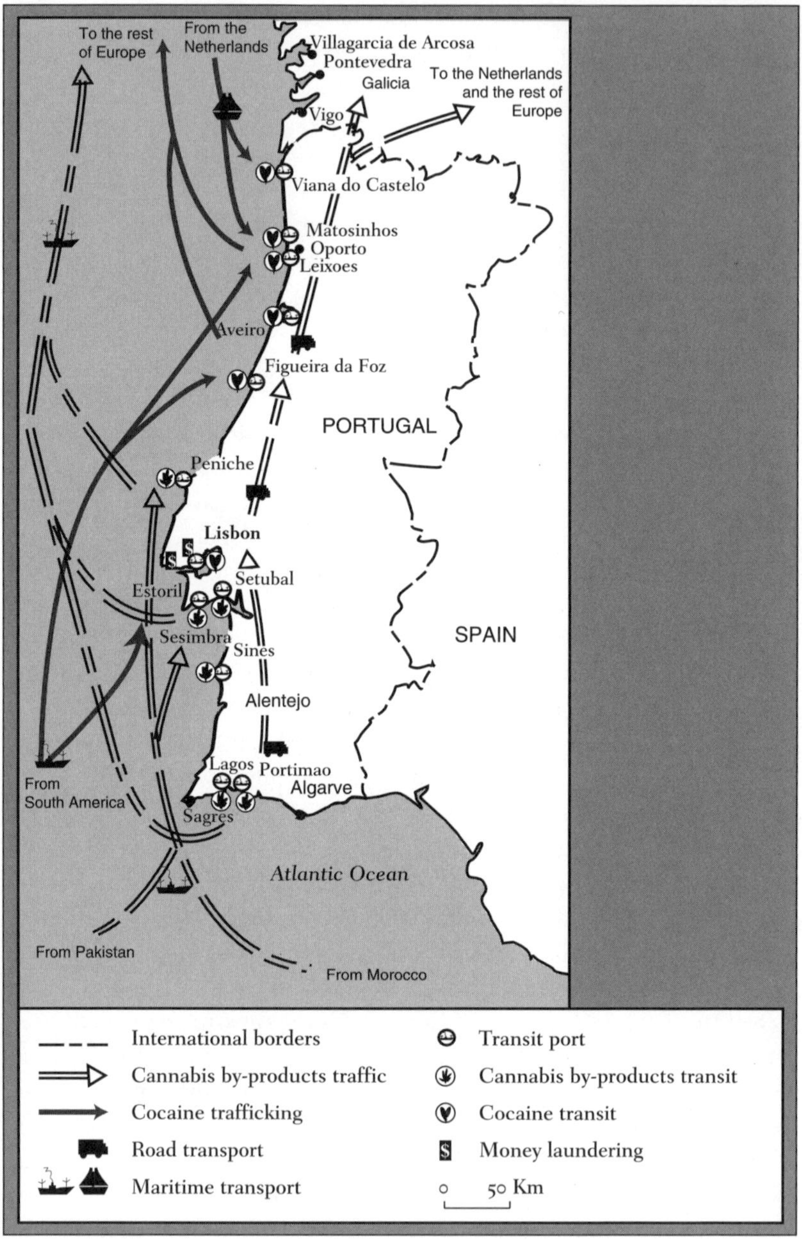

Map 7. Portugal's Transit Trafficking Routes

littoral. On August 1, 1994, law enforcement agents seized 1.4 tons of the drug on a ship registered in Honduras on its way to Spain. Cocaine from Latin America is sent to the ports of Lisbon, Aveiro, Figueiro da Foz, Matosinhos, Viana do Castelo, and especially Leixoes, which acts as the port for Oporto. The drugs are forwarded for the most part along Portugal's northern coast, where navigation conditions are hazardous but surveillance nearly nonexistent. Trafficking is organized by Galician mafia groups, which include businessmen from Vigo, Pontevedra, and Villagarcia de Arcosa, Spain. Large shipments of cocaine, averaging over 1 ton, are sent primarily to the Netherlands but also to other European countries. Between late October and early November 1994, Portuguese officials seized over 60 kilograms of cocaine at Lisbon airport, most of it destined for other European countries. There is also a domestic market for cocaine—mainly among artists and intellectuals—which is not fueled by fallout from transit trafficking but is supplied directly from the Netherlands.

International hashish networks have opened new routes both through Portugal and along its coast. On April 22, French customs officers confiscated 9.5 tons of Moroccan hashish from a tugboat registered in Belize. The ship had called in at Portimao and was bound for the Netherlands. During July alone, some 11 tons of cannabis derivatives were seized in the course of several law enforcement operations in Portugal. The isolated coast and calm waters of the Alentejo and Algarve regions are also widely used by hashish traffickers, who can count on extensive logistical support on land.

A Laundering Galaxy

The government, concerned about its image given that it has been chosen as the seat of the EMCDDA, is preoccupied with the potential for money laundering in Portugal. It prompted Parliament to pass an anti-laundering law in January 1993 and to ratify a European Union guideline on the matter on September 15, 1993. However, the "reprivatization" of almost the entire banking sector, which had been nationalized following the "carnation revolution" of 1974, and the arrival of numerous foreign companies have certainly provided an opportunity for the recycling of funds of dubious origin. In late May the DEA and the Portuguese Criminal Investigation Department organized a seminar on laundering in the Iberian Peninsula in Vilamoura in the Algarve. Police representatives there told the press that laundering already existed in Portugal on a "not negligible scale." Twenty people were indicted on such charges in 1994, but the lack of "experience" of the Portuguese justice system and the loopholes remaining in the law make the outcome of the trials uncertain. Meanwhile real estate, the hotel sector, casinos, the lottery, the bingo games organized by sports clubs, and purchases of objects made of gold and other precious metals are the preferred means of laundering money.

Oddly enough, the Portuguese police made no public mention on this occasion of the offshore banking systems of Madeira (seventeen banks and several hundred companies) or the Azores. Another sensitive spot is Estoril, where the casino is owned by a Macao businessman who heads several establishments in this Portuguese "special territory," reputed to be a laundering hub for members of the Hong Kong triads. It so happens that the Orient Foundation, an institution headed by left-wing personalities whose function is to subsidize cultural, economic, and technical cooperation with Southeast Asian countries, was initially financed by the Macao government. One-third of this government's revenue originates in the eight casinos, which entertain a daily average of 50,000 customers. While major banking operations can no longer be carried out anonymously in Macao, no financial control is imposed on gambling establishments.

5. The Mediterranean Basin

Cyprus and Lebanon play a special role in the eastern Mediterranean. While not really drug producers (although there are several heroin and cocaine labs in Lebanon), they increasingly serve as offshore shelter and home base to international terrorist groups and intelligence services of every stripe—not to mention emerging mafia-type entrepreneurs, arms dealers, and money launderers. Morocco, meanwhile, has consolidated its position as the world's leading supplier of hashish, most of which enters Europe via Spain and France. The European Union, from whom the Moroccan authorities are seeking aid, is not convinced that Morocco is truly determined to attack drug production and trafficking. As for the Italian crime syndicates, despite reeling from recent blows, they have proven their ability both to redeploy their forces (notably in the Balkans) and to make new alliances on the Italian political scene.

Cyprus

The latest report of the Cypriot Ministry of Justice notes that drug consumption is not a problem in Cyprus but that the island has become a trafficking hub. Today the large-scale operations in Cyprus of criminal organizations from the Middle East (Lebanon, for instance) and especially of Russian gangs have been added to the more "traditional" activities of the Turkish-Cypriot mafia in the north of the island and Greek organizations in the south.

The Turkish-Cypriot mafia cashes in on Cyprus's partition into two zones. In the north, which is occupied by Turkey, crime rates have risen by 400 percent in the last ten years. The 300-strong local mafia in this region specializes in supplying heroin for the Turkish families that control a large share of the London market. The institutional "no man's land" of the self-proclaimed Republic of Northern Cyprus is also the refuge of Asil Nadir, a Turkish-Cypriot businessman, for whom the British government has unsuccessfully filed a request for extradition on charges of wrongdoing involving around US$2 billion. The British equivalent of the U.S. Securities and Exchange Commission is still in the dark concerning the origin of Nadir's wealth. The Cypriot police cannot intervene in the north, due to the zone's special status, which permits illicit activities to flourish.

In the south, several Greek networks trafficking in heroin and hashish from the Middle East to western Europe, the United States, and Canada have been destroyed by the authorities. The same networks allegedly also acted as intermediaries for cocaine destined for the Middle East. Russian networks specializing in cocaine are now establishing themselves in Cyprus, as evidenced by the arrest on July 10, 1994, of a twenty-one-year-old Russian national. She had arrived in Cyprus via Moscow, Madrid, and Sao Paulo, Brazil. In Brazil, she purchased 2.5 kilograms of cocaine, which she took with her to Moscow. This emergence of Russian organized crime following the breakup of the Soviet Union is precisely what worries the authorities most. Indeed, over 100,000 Russians visited Cyprus in 1994, and Russian has become the most commonly spoken foreign language on the island. Cyprus Airways and Aeroflot run daily flights between St. Petersburg, Moscow, and Larnaca. The planes are booked up weeks in advance. In the last five years, over 2,000 offshore companies from eastern Europe have opened shop alongside the 8,500 such firms already operating in Cyprus. It is an open secret that a large number of these firms are laundering money from illicit activities, especially the drug trade.

Geopolitical and historical reasons, which have more to do with the Cold War than with Cyprus's position in the international market and its leniency in financial matters, explain the boom in the commercial and financial activities of firms from eastern Europe in general and the CIS in particular. Under Archbishop Makarios in the 1960s, Cyprus shared the leadership of the nonaligned movement with Tito's Yugoslavia. The island thus became the financier of Eastern bloc states and a privileged conduit for the massive arms sales of these countries (Yugoslavia, Czechoslovakia, the USSR, etc.) to the world's hot spots. Cyprus was governed by a makeshift majority, mainly made up of the Communist party (AKEL), which was also the island's biggest investor and which initiated the establishment of joint ventures with Eastern bloc European countries to trade in foodstuffs and build infrastructure (ports, roads, water systems) in the Middle East. The oil crisis of 1973 and the war in Lebanon brought a qualitative change to these commercial relations, adding the trade in arms, oil, and drugs. An added boost to business in Cyprus was provided by the transfer of nearly all of Beirut's offshore companies, fleeing the war, to Nicosia. Relations between people and organizations have thus been forged over three decades and strengthened by the presence of a large Turkish- and Greek-Cypriot diaspora in both the East and the West. When, after the collapse of the USSR, the former Soviet *nomenklatura* launched into business for private profit, it found an extremely favorable situation on the island—the old connections needed only to be reasserted and put to good use.

The Cypriot press reported how one Russian national arrived in the village of Perapeti with a suitcase full of dollars, intent on buying a luxury restaurant and bar. Another carried several million dollars in cash, going from bank to bank and opening accounts. Thus, new businessmen are flooding in. But the other side of the coin is that these "investors" in turn attract racketeers. On August 27, twelve Russians were deported by the Cyprus government on suspicion of extorting payments from Russian "businessmen" working in Cyprus. Arms and a large sum of cash were seized in the operation.

LEBANON Significant quantities of hashish are still being seized—28 metric tons in 1994, on top of 609 kilograms of cannabis oil. Most of these drugs probably come from the stockpiles collected during the last few years. The head of the Lebanese investigative squad, Selim Sleem, declared on September 16, 1994 that a mere 34 hectares (81.6 acres) of cannabis were grown in the Bekaa Valley, Lebanon's principal drug-producing area, in 1994. These crops were destroyed with help from the Syrian military during the harvesting season. However, Sleem added that today Lebanon, which used to be a drug-producing country, was becoming primarily a hub for heroin and cocaine trafficking. Seizures of the latter substances are constantly on the rise (33 kilograms of heroin and 201 kilograms of cocaine in 1994). Lebanese police and Syrian intelligence seized 100 kilograms of cocaine base in the port of Beirut on November 14. The drugs were found hidden in a container of blue jeans arriving from Colombia. Sleem acknowledged that the drugs were to be transformed into cocaine hydrochloride in Lebanon (on January 9, 1992, 150 kilograms of cocaine base from Colombia bound for Lebanon had already been seized by French agents off Le Havre, on the Atlantic coast). Furthermore, the Lebanese authorities told the UNDCP that between 2.5 and 3 tons of morphine base are transformed into heroin in secret laboratories in Lebanon every year.

In late October, the United States requested Syria's aid in neutralizing large-scale narcotics traffickers in the Bekaa Valley, a region under Syrian control. Interpol allegedly has a list of forty-five "godfathers," including members of Parliament and other political figures. On November 24 Lebanese courts obtained the lifting of parliamentary immunity for Yahya Shamas, a Shiite member from the Baalbek-Hermel region who is considered to be close to Damascus. In the middle of a parliamentary debate, Shamas accused Roy Hraoui, the son of the head of state, of being involved in drug trafficking. Shamas also claimed that the head of the Syrian intelligence service, General Ghazi Kanaan, had set him up. These charges suggest that the whole affair was in fact a feud between traffickers. Elsewhere, young Lebanese Shiites originally from the Baalbek region, where poppy and cannabis crops were banned two years ago, have now moved on to working in resale networks in Switzerland, Germany, Russia, and other former Eastern bloc countries. The information was first published in the German press and was later confirmed by several cases, including the arrest in Beirut on May 16 of a twenty-six-year-old Lebanese national carrying 2.8 kilograms of heroin hidden in his luggage on the way to Kiev, Ukraine. The lack of resources in the Baalbek area has pushed nearly 40 percent of the youth there to emigrate. Repatriated drug money allows families who stayed behind to survive. The prohibited poppy and cannabis crops brought six to ten times more revenue than legal crops now generate.

On January 8, 1995, the government proclaimed antilaundering measures. The announcement came at a time when business circles intended to turn the "new" Beirut into a major financial center. The announced measures were the result of a UNDCP initiative. They should be further defined by a commission comprising representatives from the Ministry of Justice, the Ministry of the Interior, Lebanon's central bank, and the Association of Lebanese Banks. Up to now, the law forbids the Treasury and the courts to investigate the bank accounts of Lebanese nationals and foreigners. The United States is pressuring the Lebanese government to lift banking secrecy.

Morocco

Still the world's number-one exporter of hashish and Europe's number-one supplier, Morocco has taken time out from its "war on drugs," declared in the fall of 1992. The European Union, supposedly an ally in the fight, is keeping its distance, since there is little concrete evidence of Rabat's political determination to attack the roots of the problem. Meanwhile, Morocco's major role in drug trafficking—including hard drugs—began to emerge as a topic of political debate in the national media, which means that the official line is no longer being unanimously parroted.

Hashish: Rabat Confirms Its No.1 Ranking

The previous OGD report, based on a 1993 in-depth investigation conducted in the field, ranked Morocco first in the worldwide export of cannabis resin (hashish). Estimating the surface area under cannabis cultivation in Morocco's northern Rif Mountains to be between 65,000 and 75,000 hectares (155,000 to 180,000 acres), the OGD assessed the country's potential annual hashish production to be between 1,500 and 2,400 tons. Moreover, OIPC-Interpol (Organization for International Police Cooperation) statistics place 1993 seizures of Moroccan cannabis throughout the world at 142.5 tons (112 tons in Europe alone—up 23 percent from 1992—and 25 tons in Morocco, as reported by local authorities).

Published late in 1994, the interior ministry's report, titled "Morocco's

General Policy Concerning the War on Narcotics Traffic and Stimulation of the Economic Development of Northern Provinces," unwittingly provides indisputable confirmation of these estimates. First, it reveals that in 1993 over 87 tons of cannabis resin were seized within Morocco (the only seizures officially reported to Interpol are those involving international trafficking or foreign nationals). That means that at least 205 tons of Moroccan hashish were seized throughout the world in 1993. Next, the surface area under cannabis cultivation officially acknowledged by Rabat, 50,000 hectares (120,000 acres), and the figures for average yield per hectare (listed in the paper's appendix) indicate an annual hashish production of 1,250 tons. It should be added that, as of January 1995, partial data for 1994 suggest a general increase in seizures of cannabis resin (mainly of Moroccan origin) throughout Europe. Moreover, according to local information supplied to the OGD, crops are continuing to spread to the northwest, in the Larache region on the Atlantic coast.

Hue and Cry

The publication of the OGD's report sparked vehement protests from Moroccan authorities. In May the National Narcotics Commission (founded in 1977 and chaired by the minister of health) issued a long communiqué to "reestablish the truth and demonstrate the fallacious nature of charges made against Morocco." The OGD report stressed Morocco's emerging role as a hub for hard drugs, notably cocaine, en route for Europe. It noted, moreover, the spread of barter practices, namely, the exchange of Moroccan hashish for hard drugs (notably Turkish heroin) in Spain and the Netherlands. Furthermore, the growing importance of purely Moroccan networks in the Netherlands-based distribution of heroin and cocaine was confirmed in 1994. The rise in drug addiction in large Moroccan cities is directly linked to these phenomena. The commission's reply was nevertheless categorical:

> This allegation prompts the following comments:
>
> ✦ no European country has ever notified the National Central Bureau of a seizure of hard drugs coming from Morocco;
>
> ✦ the fact that these drugs were seized in Europe proves that Europe itself serves as the transit point and hub for hard drugs coming from Latin America and heading toward Morocco. Morocco, moreover, is a growing victim of such traffic.

In a chapter titled "An Unflagging Determination: War on Drugs," the white paper repeats this argument almost word for word. But the introduction reads: "Morocco is confronting attempts to transit, import and consume so-called hard drugs like heroin and other psychotropic substances. The worrying fact is that several countries in eastern and northern Africa are increasingly used by traffickers as transit points for hard drugs coming from South America in particular." And in the fall of 1994, Casablanca hosted an international conference of law enforcement officials, devoted exclusively to the issue of the transit of hard drugs. Furthermore, a major seizure on Moroccan soil served to contradict official pronouncements; on October 11, in cooperation with German police, Moroccan authorities in Casablanca seized a container that had originated in Ecuador and arrived via Hamburg, in which 57 kilograms of cocaine were hidden. The drugs, shipped by a network composed of Colombians, Moroccans, and a Pakistani, were to be reshipped from Tangier to the person in Madrid who placed the order.

The OGD report also questioned Morocco's real determination to conduct a war on drugs, as proclaimed by King Hassan II in the fall of 1992. Noting the inefficiency of the army's system for controlling the country's northern maritime borders (an inefficiency amply demonstrated by the increased seizures in Europe), the report pointed out that enforcement concerned only small dealers. This was confirmed in 1994 by the return to Tangier's political scene of individuals blatantly implicated by the government at the start of its "war on drugs." The commission duly took up this "allegation."

> Concerning the blockade of maritime borders, which was begun in October 1992, requiring the mobilization of over 5,000 men, and costing over $70 million, and which the report claimed has been dropped: men are regularly relieved in order to protect the mobilized troops against the nefarious effects of overfamiliarity with the local population. Moreover, given the efficiency of the deployment, traffickers have adopted new methods and are using routes beyond the perimeter under surveillance.

Apart from the fact that it is paradoxical, to say the least, to vaunt the efficiency of a blockade that is so easy to circumvent, the admission that the troops charged with coastal surveillance are susceptible to temptations (such as corruption?) would appear to constitute an unmistakable "slur on the reputation of the Royal Armed Forces," to quote from the indictment that earned three years imprisonment for union leader Ahmed Belaïchi, found guilty of having denounced the brutality of the coastal blockade.

Finally, the white paper sternly denies that drug money has any influence on Morocco's economy, taking issue with the OGD's report point by point. Most observers assess the sums involved at US$2 billion and consider them the country's prime source of foreign currency. The official line, however, merely admits that "during a meeting with FATF on November 19, 1992, Morocco did not disguise the fact that it believed foreigners were importing funds originating from the narcotics trade. These funds take the form of investments in industrial and commercial firms and real estate, rather than being deposited in bank accounts." The white paper would have it, then, that Moroccan networks supply their customers free of charge. Similarly, the Ministry of the Interior explained that "no causal link can be established between the increase in [contraband] and the laundering of drug money." The annual revenues from contraband goods—basically smuggled from the Spanish enclaves of Ceuta and Melilla—are officially reported to be in the neighborhood of US$2 billion, and have risen sharply in line with the increase in the production and export of hashish. In 1992 the annual report of the U.S. National Narcotics Intelligence Consumers Committee pointed out that contraband importation of manufactured goods into high-tariff countries remains a classic way to launder money and boost profits. It enables drug traffickers to increase their profits by a factor of two or three.

Beyond the stilted official discourse, reactions to the OGD's report suggest that it touched a sore point. The Moroccan opposition daily *L'Opinion* wrote that "the [report's] accusations are extremely serious and demand . . . an immediate reaction from the Moroccan government, because remaining silent would mean acknowledging the accusations in their totality, thereby rendering them credible." Yet the newspaper went on to admit that "obviously, there is some truth in the OGD report, but several accusations would seem to be more a question of exaggeration than anything else." It is worth noting that the term used was "exaggeration," not slander or lies. Perhaps the taboo concerning the drug issue is about to be lifted. Badia Skalli, an elected representative of the opposition USFP party, made the following open declaration to the Tangier weekly *Les Nouvelles du Nord* (January 13, 1995):

> ... according to our sources, it would seem that people apparently above suspicion are engaged in trafficking, like certain members of Parliament. As far as contraband goods go, this is also a familiar scourge from which thousands, indeed millions of people make a living, and not only in the north. Given this situation, which contraband activity should be targeted? To me, it seems obvious that here again we should go for the big wigs, those who take in billions.

Finally, a member of the Moroccan government publicly raised the issue of national crime syndicates for the first time. At a conference in Rabat on January 6, 1995, Minister of Justice Mohammed Idriss Alaoui Machichi indicated that organized crime existed in Morocco and that such criminality threatened the country's economic, political, and social structures.

The European Union's Reservations

On September 21, 1994, Morocco's minister of agriculture and the head of a European Commission delegation signed a financing agreement (amounting to US$3.5 million) for the protection and participatory management of forest ecosystems in the Rif Mountains, as part of a series of pilot programs launched by the EU to develop Morocco's northern provinces. But this symbolic initiative should not disguise the fact that cooperation between Brussels and Rabat is now a dead letter. Moroccan authorities nevertheless persist in asking the EU for its $2 billion contribution (over five years) to Morocco's cannabis crop substitution plan. Rabat in turn claims that it is willing to devote a total of $3 billion to the project. The Europeans are using Morocco's lack of determination in its war on drug trafficking as an excuse for freezing all investment.

The Moroccans, meanwhile, are developing a "give and take" argument:

> No Moroccan finds it tolerable for Europe to ask Morocco to fight clandestine emigration and drug trafficking while a neighboring country like Spain allows its police and customs officers to stand by as merchandise flows illegally toward Morocco. These days, Sebta (Ceuta) and Melilla survive exclusively on contraband and the time has come to put an end to this situation by a principled campaign on an international level.

The author of this statement, Mohammed Abbassy, president of Tangier's Chamber of Commerce and Industry from 1977 to 1983, is a former leader of the majority RNI party. Similarly, Rabat seems to be awaiting the outcome of the debate on decriminalizing—indeed legalizing—cannabis derivatives in Europe before undertaking its own costly programs. The "war on drugs" therefore increasingly appears to be just one issue within Moroccan-EU negotiations of wider political and economic scope.

Spain

Spain's role as a major conduit for drugs into Europe has only expanded in 1994. Colombian, Turkish, and Italian criminal organizations operating in partnership with local gangs continue to be firmly established in Spain, despite periodic setbacks due to police operations. However, judges specializing in drug-related crime complain that they are not well-equipped to fight the increasingly sophisticated drug traffic. The reform of the penal code has not yet been debated, and the provisions of the Antilaundering Law are still in the planning stage. One of the demands of the Association of Judges is that a group of experts be set up to assist courts in drug cases. The law obliges magistrates to divulge the identity of their informers. The result is that no less than twelve of Judge Baltasar Garzón's informers have been murdered since he started specializing in the fight against drugs. It has been noted that numerous defendants in drug cases are businessmen or industrialists who, experiencing financial hardship, get involved in trafficking in order to restore flagging businesses. They can now count on the help of the numerous lawyers working for the narcos.

A Mafia Potpourri

Some of the most significant cases that occurred in Spain during the last two months of 1994 amply demonstrate the diversity of criminal organizations operating on Spanish territory. César Arango, a Colombian who has been described as the representative in Spain of Fabio Ochoa (one of the bosses of the Medellin cartel, currently in jail in Colombia), was arrested in early November. According to the police, Arango is responsible for importing 150 kilograms of cocaine that were seized in July. Arango and his wife own four houses, several shops, one BMW, and two Mercedes. Cash worth up to US$250,000 in various currencies was discovered at their home, along with jewelry and abundant literature on tax havens.

Two record seizures were carried out in December 1994. The first involved the confiscation of close to 10 tons of hashish from a Galician fishing boat on December 8. In the second, which occurred on December 13 in both the Madrid and Asturias provinces, 118 kilograms of heroin were seized from the same network. In the latter case, the traffickers' boss was a Turk, also the owner of a legal business importing seafood. One of the Spaniards arrested was a prison warden.

Operación Dinero was launched simultaneously in the United States, Canada, Italy, and Spain on December 15. Eighty-eight people were arrested (including sixteen in Spain), and 9 tons of cocaine were seized. The boss of the Spanish branch of the gang, Pascuale Claudio Locatelli, was a *capo* of the Neapolitan Camorra with links to the Cali cartel, who was laundering drug money through a chain of supermarkets in Italy, the Ostuni Agriculture and Industry Savings Bank, the ACP bank in Zagreb, and companies in Gibraltar. The criminal organization masterminded, among other things, the transportation of 5 tons of cocaine that were seized in Canada in February 1994; the shipping of 7 tons of hashish, intercepted in England in November on the *Poseidon,* a ship owned by a Frenchman; and the transportation of 800 kilograms of hashish, confiscated in Spain on November 21. In addition, the police seized US$58 million and paintings by Rubens and Picasso.

In late January 1995, a new record was broken by Spanish customs when they seized 2.5 tons of cocaine, destined for Galician godfathers, in the middle of the Atlantic.

The Law Against the Judges

The power wielded by criminal organizations in Spain stands in sharp contrast to the relative impotence of the Spanish judicial system. Baltasar Garzón, who is back in his old job as an examining magistrate, gave the OGD special envoy the following explanation: The jurisdiction existing at the investigative level has yet to be translated into sufficiently precise provisions in the penal code. A perfect illustration is the judgment issued on September 27 by a Madrid court in the wake of Operación Nécora, the most dramatic raid ever to have been carried out against Spanish importers of Colombian cocaine and Moroccan hashish. Coming after three years of preliminary investigation and eight months of hearings, the court's acquittal of seventeen defendants caused an uproar. Those acquitted included two men considered to be among the main godfathers of the Galician cartel: Manuel Charlín Gama (the "patriarch" of the "clan of the Charlines"), who owns a fleet of boats allegedly used by narcos to transport tons of cocaine; and Alfredo Cordero González. The prosecutor had requested a twenty-three-year prison sentence for both men. Manuel Charlín will nonetheless stay in jail, as he was incriminated in another drug case by Judge Garzón, following the accusations made against him by Manuel Baúlo, another repentant Galician godfather who used to smuggle cigarettes before converting to cocaine.

The judge's work was made more difficult on September 12, when Baúlo was murdered by three Colombian hitmen. Celso Barreiro, a businessman, and Carlos Goyanes, a renowned jet-setter (who had already been released in an earlier case) also walked free. Laureano Oubiña, the "Boss of Bosses", and his wife, Esther Lago, for whom the prosecution had requested thirty-one years, were found not guilty of drug trafficking but were sentenced to twelve years and a fine of 1,280 million pesetas (about US$12.8 million) for money laundering and tax evasion. As for the other twenty-eight sentences passed, the prevailing impression is that it was the fall guys who paid the heaviest price.

Javier Zaragoza, the antidrug prosecutor, declared that the sentences were too lenient and appealed to the Supreme Court. According to magistrates interviewed by the OGD special envoy, such leniency cannot be explained by possible corruption or intimidation of the court, which merely interpreted the law in the most traditional and restrictive way. In the cases of Charlín Gama and Cordero González, there was no direct proof, so any sentence would have had to be based on circumstantial evidence. In particular, the court did not take into account the testimony of a repentant trafficker, Ricardo Portabales, and ruled that most of the wire-tapping evidence presented by the examining magistrate, Baltasar Garzón, was inadmissible. The sentences were strongly criticized by the spokespersons for the Association for the Fight Against Drug Trafficking, as well as by members of the Madrid association Mothers Against Drugs. Members of the Vigo (Galicia) Érguete (Stand up!) committee demonstrated violently outside the tribunal and attacked some of the acquitted defendants when they came out of the court building. Another 30,000 people demonstrated in Vigo. Such mobilization of public opinion is pressuring the government to adopt a more clear-cut position on this matter and to listen to the judges' demands. In late January 1995, the Supreme Court still had not come to a decision. However, on January 15, Carlos López Riñao, the man in charge of the National Plan Against Drugs, replying to magistrates' associations, announced that the government would submit the law on control of seized goods to Parliament in February 1995.

Italy

Year one of Italy's Second Republic was supposed to represent a fresh start. But Silvio Berlusconi's government did not even make it through 1994, and Judge Di Pietro, symbol of the Mani Pulite (clean hands) operation, threw in the towel. The mafia and other crime syndicates, despite setbacks suffered since 1992, have adapted to the new international situation and turned instability and war in the Balkans and the Caucasus into a source of profits. According to Gianni De Gennaro, former head of Italy's drug squad (DIA), the arrest of "Boss of Bosses" Toto Riina means that the mafia is now controlled by three of Riina's lieutenants: Giovanni Brusca, Leoluca Bagarella, and Bernardo Provenzano. The three men are in hiding and were not in the dock at the trial that opened in February 1995 for the assassination of Judge Falcone. The prosecution holds that the decision to liquidate Falcone was taken by the entire "Cupula."

According to a report by the Italian trade association Commercio, organized crime in Italy controls 24 percent of the construction industry, 15 percent of supermarkets and hypermarkets, 15 percent of hotels, and 70 percent of the cement market. The same source claims that the Camorra churns out large quantities of forged dollars, which it channels to the Russian mafia in exchange for "synthetic drugs produced by the Russians in enormous quantity, prostitutes (including minors), and weapons."

Although drugs do not constitute the main source of income for Italian crime syndicates, the level of seizures (as of December 9, 1994) suggests that profits are far from negligible: 6.5 tons of cocaine (up 24 percent over 1993) and 1.13 tons of heroin (up 87 percent). Seizures of cannabis derivatives are also up, by 163.32 percent. It is finally becoming apparent that despite the change in government in 1994, the mafia—for decades linked to the Christian Democrats—had already made alternative plans and that today, as in the past, it is able to infiltrate the very heart of the political system.

Old and New Spheres of Action

On May 8, 1994, a police operation code-named "Macedonia" led to the breakup of a vast heroin network in the Balkans, one in which Italians collaborated with Turks, Macedonians, and Albanians. The operation demonstrated that Italian crime organizations were opening up new spheres of action and broadening their alliances. It transpired that the speedboats used to carry clandestine Albanian immigrants across the border were also used for drug and weapons trafficking. One week later, Operation Giano in Bologna put an end to a vast arms trade after two years of investigation. Weapons, purchased in Switzerland and the former Yugoslavia, were shipped from Lombardy and Emilia-Romagna in the north to Calabria and Sicily in the south and then delivered to mafia and 'Ndranghetta bosses. In early October, another dragnet broke up a mafia and Camorra network that operated in Croatia, exchanging heroin and cocaine for weapons smuggled into Italy. This network functioned for two years, and it was only the accidental explosion of a Soviet missile in the hands of a mafioso in Udine that tipped off prosecutors. Most of these contraband activities take place along the Slovenian border and in the Adriatic.

These networks also operate in a far more traditional sphere of action for the mafia: Latin America. In mid-June, a contraband weapons connection between the former Yugoslavia and Colombia was uncovered in Verona. In a relatively new twist, the Colombians acquired weapons in exchange for heroin, which they have begun producing in recent years, shipped to Italy via Spain and Holland. On October 15, the police dismantled a group working out of Milan and Reggio di Calabria that was engaged in trading weapons for cocaine with Bolivian, Peruvian, and Colombian drug dealers.

Perhaps less significant was the March seizure from a truck in Turin of 5.5 tons of cocaine (a European record) unloaded at Genoa. For according to police sources, the operation was monitored by the police from start to finish and entailed more than just surveillance of an ordinary delivery, as suggested by the arrest of former police officers and current customs agents. Operation Dinero, jointly conducted on December 15 in Italy, Spain, and the United States, also mobilized similar resources; but the payoff does not seem to measure up to the effort involved. In contrast, a joint Italian police–FBI operation on September 17 brought to light a vast network headquartered in a New York pizzeria.

Colombian cocaine delivered by the Cali cartel was imported into the United States and Italy, while the network also exported heroin from Italy to the United States. According to Italian authorities, the three main crime syndicates—the Sicilian mafia, the Neapolitan Camorra, and the Calabrian 'Ndranghetta—collaborated in the undertaking. The assistant prosecutor from Reggio di Calabria also stated that the 'Ndranghetta had taken over some of the mafia's drug trafficking networks.

The Mafia and Politics

An incident that occurred on May 26, 1994, in the Reggio di Calabria courthouse sent a warning shock throughout Italian society. Toto Riina, on trial for murder, took advantage of a recess to make televised threats against "antimafia" figures. Referring to Gian Carlo Caselli (district attorney for Palermo), Luciano Violante (former chair of the parliamentary commission on the mafia, former Communist, and member of the left-wing PDS party), and Pino Arlacchi (a legal expert on the Cosa Nostra), Riina exclaimed, "They are evil-minded Communists. The government should watch out what they're up to." These threats were taken all the more seriously, since a week earlier a bomb had destroyed PDS headquarters in the village of Piana degli Albanesi. In general, the mafia has continued to attack the left. The courthouse incident suggests that crime syndicates have not given up trying to intimidate politicians, even when their former allies are now facing trial.

One of the leading Christian Democrats, Antonio Gava, a former minister of the interior, was arrested in Naples on September 20 during a vast anti-Camorra operation. He had been implicated by Pasquale Galasso, a former Camorra bigwig turned state's witness. Gava was placed under house arrest for health reasons and since then has been awaiting notification of his indictment. Furthermore, the parliamentary immunity of Giulio Andreotti, who held thirty-three ministerial appointments and was seven times prime minister, was lifted by the Italian Parliament in June 1994. He was sent before the court by the investigating magistrate of Palermo on charges of "associating with the mafia." Baldassare Di Maggio, a former chauffeur for Toto Riina who later testified against his boss, claims to have witnessed a meeting between Riina and Andreotti on September 20, 1987, at the villa of cousins Antonio and Ignacio Salvo. The Salvos are financiers who functioned as the Sicilian go-betweens for the Christian Democrats, represented by European Parliament member Salvo Lima (assassinated in 1992), and the mafia. Di Maggio added that Riina and Andreotti exchanged the Cosa Nostra's ritual kiss.

Andreotti claims he is being framed. The press, however, has turned up other damning testimony. Pilots have reportedly declared that on several occasions they carried out "secret flights" to Sicily for the former prime minister, flights not announced to civil aviation authorities. Moreover, the prosecutor has uncovered an unexplained gap of five hours in Andreotti's agenda in Palermo on September 20, 1987, during which he reportedly managed to get free of his escort in order to meet the head of the Cupula. Andreotti claims he does not know the Salvo cousins, as unlikely as that may seem. But a new prosecution witness, Salvo Lima's chauffeur, allegedly drove Andreotti to their place several times. In another blow to Andreotti, former Christian Democratic politician Gioacchino Pennino contributed further testimony concerning Andreotti's links to the Cosa Nostra in late January 1995.

But the mafiosi currently behind bars can hardly complain about the new government. One of the Berlusconi administration's first moves was to attempt to disqualify prosecution use of mafiosi-turned-state-witnesses (of whom there were over 1,000 in 1994), the judges' main weapon. On August 19, Environment Minister Altero Matteoli, backed by Minister of Justice Alfredo Bondi, suggested closing the high-security prisons on islands like Asinara, off the coast of Sardinia. Formerly used to hold members of the Red Brigade, Asinara was reopened following the assassinations of Judges Falcone and Borsellino—400 of Italy's most dangerous criminals, including Toto Riina, are now incarcerated there. The plan to transform the island into a holiday camp was blocked only by the protests of judges and opposition officials.

On October 21, Silvio Berlusconi had to appear before a parliamentary antimafia commission to explain his attacks on television news stories on the Cosa Nostra, including his declaration that "fewer than a hundred mafia bosses manage to give Italy a bad name." Berlusconi's comments were interpreted by the opposition as a lack of political determination to combat criminality. Probably to repair this damage, Berlusconi announced that the 7,000 soldiers deployed in Sicily in July 1992 following the Falcone assassination would remain in place for another year (they were scheduled to be withdrawn at the end of 1994). At the opening session of a U.N. conference on crime held in Naples from November 21 to 23, he declared that "the antimafia struggle is the most important item on our agenda."

Liaisons Dangereuses

The Berlusconi firm Fininvest came under investigation as early as January 1993 during the Mani Pulite operation. Berlusconi's brother Paolo was arrested, and one of his close colleagues, Marcello Dell'Utri, was indicted for drawing up false invoices. The Palermo prosecutor's office, meanwhile, has been working on potential Berlusconi links with the mafia since spring 1994.[1] The Justice Department is particularly interested in disturbing coincidences, having noted that "the Rasini bank, which was partner to the young Berlusconi's early real estate operations, was also banker to major mafia godfathers."[2] Berlusconi also belonged to Masonic Lodge P2 and was backed by Lucio Geli's banks. Former godfather Gioacchino La Barbera, one of the most famous mafiosi to turn state witness, explained to judges that Berlusconi was considered "a friend" by Cosa Nostra circles. Fininvest people reportedly contacted La Barbera in 1992 to get his backing for their installation of television broadcast equipment around Palermo. Another mafioso-turned-witness reported how the mafia intervened to prevent the kidnapping of Berlusconi's son.

But the key charges against Berlusconi are made by one of the main state witnesses, Salvatore Cancemi, head of the Porta Nuova family and member of the Cupula. "He asserts that Fininvest paid 200 million lira annually (US$200,000) to protect its interests in Sicily. It was the boss of the Cupula, Toto Riina, who managed the affair."[3] Another affair that has resurfaced is Berlusconi's hiring of Vittorio Mangano as general factotum in 1974. Mangano, a cold-blooded killer and torturer who had worked for the Corleone family, was allegedly recommended by Dell'Utri, head of advertising for the Fininvest group and leader of Berlusconi's Forza Italia political movement. Dell'Utri, moreover,

---

1. Fabrizio Calvi and Leo Sisti, *Les Nouveaux réseaux de la corruption,* Paris: Albin Michel, 1994. Most of the information on Silvio Berlusconi has been drawn from this book, which is based on legal files.
2. Ibid.
3. Ibid.

boasted that he was a friend of one of the most terrible Palermo *capi*, Filippo Marchese. Strangely, it was Mangano, no longer in Berlusconi's employ, who was responsible for collecting Fininvest's annual payment of 200 million lira.

Filippo Alberto Rapisarda, a "shady" financier from Sicily, told judges that Dell'Utri and his twin brother, Alberto, had been recommended to Rapisarda by Gaetano Cina, a representative of the Sicilian mafia clan headed by Mimmo Teresi and Stefano Bontate. Police also possess tapped telephone conversations between Dell'Utri and Mangano concerning what appears to be a delivery of heroin. Berlusconi has also been linked to Flavio Carboni, a crony of Pip Calo, the Cupula's treasurer.

These *liaisons dangereuses* perhaps explain why the mafia clearly backed Forza Italia during the elections on March 27–28, 1994. That, at least, is the conclusion to be drawn from the publication of tapped phone conversations during which Giuseppe Mandalari, a freemason and notorious mafia "consultant"—sentenced to three years in prison—exclaimed the day after the elections: "A total victory, terrific, our friends have won the election!"

The judges' investigations into Berlusconi's group nevertheless suffered a serious setback when the minister of justice withdrew Judge Di Pietro from the case involving bribery of the State Accounting Office by Fininvest, uncovered last November in the context of Mani Pulite investigations. Di Pietro subsequently resigned on December 6, casting a great deal of doubt on the outcome of these investigations.

6. Sub-Saharan Africa

Sub-Saharan Africa's integration into the worldwide system of drug production and trafficking was confirmed and strengthened in 1994. Corroborating information on the development of cannabis crops—whether in Nigeria, Ghana, Guinea, Burundi, or South Africa, to name only a few countries—is being received with increasing frequency. Numerous reports also warn of the appearance of poppy cultivation in Côte d'Ivoire, Nigeria, and Chad. According to the latest report of the Customs Cooperation Council, seizures of African marijuana by customs officials around the world soared from 3.6 tons in 1992 to 40 tons in 1993. French customs officers have noted a surge of trafficking in African pot, seizing 1,973 kilograms of it in 1994 (as against 614 kilograms in 1993). In more than one way, marijuana is playing a part in conflicts such as those of Rwanda or Burundi. Furthermore, Africa as a whole is a hub for the trade in hard drugs, and African networks appear to have expanded their reach, as indicated by the arrests of Africans in possession of significant quantities of heroin in Laos and cocaine in Bolivia. In November 1994, 60 kilograms of Pakistani heroin destined for a Senegalese network were seized in France. Political change in South Africa has accelerated these trends.

Nigeria[1]

In 1994 Nigerian law enforcement officials seized 91.65 kilograms of heroin, 90.76 kilograms of cocaine, close to 20 tons of marijuana, and 94 kilograms of various synthetic drugs. The other drugs seized included 66.5 kilograms of ephedrine and 22 million tablets of Pemoline. However, the seizures were not enough to change Nigeria's image as a narco-regime in the eyes of the international community. Thus, on August 29, 1994, U.S. "drug czar" Lee Brown declared in Lagos that the United States was still not convinced that Nigeria was "doing its utmost to discourage drug trafficking within its territory." Sanctions followed in March 1995, as Nigeria was included on the American blacklist of "uncertified" countries. It is estimated that Nigerians sell 30 to 40 percent of the heroin currently available on American streets.

Traditionally, Nigerian traffickers get their supplies from Thailand and Pakistan. But in 1994, Nigerians were also spotted or arrested in Laos and Cambodia. In Europe, while not totally moving out of the heroin trade, Nigerians are increasingly dealing in cocaine. These days, their supplies come not only from Brazil but also from the countries of the Andes, as indicated by the December 14, 1994, arrest in Bolivia of a Nigerian woman who had purchased 16 kilograms of cocaine and intended to have the drugs transported by an Equatorial Guinean national holding a diplomatic passport. Worldwide seizures of Nigerian marijuana have shot up from less than 2 tons in 1992 to 34.6 tons in 1993. Close to 8 tons of the weed were uncovered in Amsterdam in two containers originating in Lagos.

Heroin Turns into Cassava

At the end of 1993, Brigadier-General Musa Bamaiyi was appointed head of the National Drug Law Enforcement Agency (NDLEA), in a move indicating the army's intention of taking the antidrug fight into its own hands. Musa Bamaiyi, a Christian, had a reputation for incorruptibility. In late May 1994, he fired eighty-nine agents of the NDLEA Kano branch who had been bribed by a trafficker in Lebanese Pemoline. Their

1. Liberia, Sierra Leone, Benin, Mali, Niger, Senegal, Togo, Côte d'Ivoire, Ghana, Equatorial Guinea, Chad, and Zaire were reviewed in the OGD 1994 report, *État des drogues, drogues des États,* op. cit.

leader, Major O. Afishi, was killed by unidentified gunmen while he was being driven under NDLEA escort to a Kano bank where he had deposited his share of the corruption money. Furthermore, the "Akubueze" affair is still sending shock waves of scandal across Nigeria. The NDLEA singled out Joe Brown Akubueze as a major drug baron after his December 1993 arrest following the seizure in Nigeria of just under 250 kilograms of heroin packed in 649 bags of about 350 grams each. Akubueze had traveled to Bangkok to organize the shipping of these drugs. However, journalists working for the weekly magazine *Newswatch* have discovered that the so-called godfather had gone bankrupt when he was running an automobile spare parts business, that he did not own a house or an apartment, and that he could not even afford to send his children to school. Observers therefore are now inclined to think that the real sponsors of the traffic, who allegedly include a woman "jet-setter," have been left alone.

Furthermore, questions have arisen about the fate of the bulk of the seizure, as twelve of the aforementioned bags had vanished by the time the case reached the courts. An OGD correspondent in Nigeria has heard accounts by recently appointed NDLEA officers and diplomats in Lagos stating that a mixture of cassava flour and ground starch had been substituted for at least part of the heroin seized before being incinerated. Once the substitution was carried out, the remaining heroin was taken to the Oju-Ina district, a Lagos ghetto, where it was repackaged and sold. The resulting sudden influx of heroin has caused an increase in the number of users, in particular in the Idumota district, a stronghold for "area boys," as the local street gangs and drug dealers are known. Other major areas for the consumption of heroin—and other drugs—include the exclusive districts of Ikeja (Allen Avenue), Ikoyi, and the nouveaux riches sanctuary, Victoria Island.

In an interview published in the August 29, 1994, issue of *Newswatch,* Brigadier-General Bamaiyi admitted that Nigeria was no longer just a transit country but was rapidly turning into a drug-consuming one as well. He proposed the death penalty as a more efficient way to fight drugs. "It is not too much to kill somebody. After all, within the military . . . we accept casualties," he said. What should, however, be a problem for General Bamaiyi is that the wives and children of numerous serving and retired officers are themselves directly involved in the traffic.

Forged Passports for Real Traffickers

There are numerous indications that corruption within the NDLEA is far from being rooted out. According to Decree No. 33/94, signed into law in early 1995 but applying retroactively from 1990, all Nigerians sentenced for drug trafficking abroad have to be retried when they return home. If found guilty, they are liable to two to five years imprisonment, in blatant violation of the legal principle of double jeopardy. In fact, replies General Bamaiyi, they are tried again "for bringing Nigeria's name to disrepute." In democratic countries, convicts are not deported to their countries of origin after serving their sentence if the courts have reason to believe that they might suffer reprisals there. They are instead placed under house arrest while a third country willing to accept them is found.

Taking advantage of their knowledge of the situation of Nigerian ex-prisoners in foreign countries, certain ex-traffickers working within the NDLEA supply the relevant information, at a price, to networks specializing in forged passports from West African countries. These are sent to the "house arrestees" abroad and allow them to be repatriated to a country neighboring Nigeria, from which they can cross the Nigerian border on foot and vanish into the countryside. A similar method is used by drug barons in order to hire experienced smugglers. Since it is very easy to obtain naturalization in West Africa, passport traffickers have the Nigerian ex-convicts abroad sign documents renouncing their citizenship and then supply them with real papers granting them another African nationality.

Pressure from drug-consuming countries has spurred the Nigerian government into action. Thus, Brigadier-General Bamaiyi announced on December 15, 1994, that immigration officers whose signatures appear on passports held by non-Nigerians arrested on drug-trafficking charges would be liable to the same sentence as the convicted traffickers. Despite Bamaiyi's moralizing drive, *Newswatch* journalists have been able to expose other corruption cases within the NDLEA, notably unjustified travel expenses and extortion practiced on the families of inmates waiting to be tried in the agency's jail.

Guinea-Conakry

In Guinea, the boom in urbanization, the population explosion, the breaking up of the family unit, academic failure, and the social consequences of structural adjustment programs—which have yet to be offset by economic growth—have all had an impact on the development of illicit activity. Since 1984 the public sector has hired hardly any graduates, and 50 percent of civil servants have been made redundant.

An unstable political situation, evidenced by opposition demonstrations questioning the validity of electoral rolls, subsequent repression, and the postponement of the legislative and presidential elections, contributes to the rise of drug addiction and crime. Torture sessions in police stations, which are commonplace and sometimes lead to deaths, have been denounced by Amnesty International. On several occasions the army has opened fire on peaceful demonstrators, killing scores. Finally, the influx of refugees from neighboring Liberia, said to number close to a million in 1994, is another factor contributing to the increase in crime.

Cannabis Crops Across the Territory

Like the datura plant, which grows in Guinea and can be used as a narcotic, cannabis has long been used in local traditional medicine and during rituals such as the worshiping of ancestors. Nowadays, cannabis is smoked and grown everywhere in the country. Cultivation takes place mainly in the following areas:

- the coastal region—around Forécariah, home of the Soussou people, and on the border with Sierra Leone, where the Loma (or Toma) people live on both sides of the border. Coastal Guinea, the main producing area, supplies the capital, Conakry, which is a mere 25 kilometers (15 miles) away. Some 100 kilometers (62 miles) to the north, in the Kindia and Madinnaoula regions, small crops can be found hidden among vegetable gardens.
- the Upper Guinea region—near Siguiri, a district capital, close to the border with Mali, which is also a tobacco-growing area. Cannabis can also be found around Mandiana, not far from Mali and Côte d'Ivoire. The region around Mandiana is one of the areas best suited to Indian hemp cultivation. Once it has been harvested, cannabis can be traded in Kankan, a large commercial center. Eradication campaigns took place in the region in 1982–83. Finally, in the diamond producing regions of Kerouané and Benko, small plots of the weed can be found hidden among food crops.

- Guinea's forest area—around the Kissidougou district on the border with Sierra Leone and slightly farther south, around the Guéckédou district, near the borders with both Sierra Leone and Liberia. This area hosts Liberian refugees who fled from the zones under Charles Taylor's control. Cannabis is now intensively grown in the fields they abandoned back in Liberia, and they have themselves introduced cannabis cultivation in Guinea. The same situation prevails a little farther east in the Macenta district, as well as in N'Zerekoré and Lola, in the Mount Nimba mountains. Farther north, large crops can be found around Beyla, home of the Koniambé people, as well as near Sinko, a *sous-préfecture* (district subcapital), where experimental tobacco growing is carried out.

Apart from marijuana, the police sporadically seize heroin and cocaine, but above all large amounts of psychotropic substances (barbiturates, ephedrine, diazepam). Broadly, the drug trade has two components: Cannabis and diverted medicines are aimed at the young and the poor, while hard drugs are sold to well-off consumers: expatriates, international experts, and Lebanese traders. Police say the latter group is difficult to infiltrate.

Because of the free movement of individuals resulting from Guinea's membership in the Economic Community of West African States (ECOWAS), borders are porous. Thus, Guinea is an ideal place for the transit and consumption of drugs. Cocaine arriving by sea from Liberia and bound for Europe apparently only passes through Guinea, which would explain the near absence of seizures. Although no statistics are available, it appears that stepped-up law enforcement in Senegal and Côte d'Ivoire in 1993 diverted part of Africa's international drug trade toward Guinea.

Cross-Border Trafficking

On either side of the borders with Guinea Bissau, Sierra Leone, Liberia, Côte d'Ivoire, and Mali live populations sharing the same history, customs, and language. Some villages are even split in the middle by the border. Very many vehicles cross these borders, and drug detection is made even more difficult since the drug squad has no branches in the provinces and neither *gendarmes* nor customs officers are adequately trained. In the north, when it is in spate, the traffic on the Niger River toward Mali is also difficult to control. The drug squad has only one rubber dinghy, and it cannot be used when water levels are low. This also applies to the 300-kilometer-long coast: Dug-out canoes, pirate boats, oil tankers, and fishing boats sail along from Guinea-Bissau to Liberia and are subject to no control. There are thirty mooring points at Conakry's autonomous port. The port, where it is almost impossible for law enforcement agents to intervene, is a place of intense trafficking activity. Furthermore, the companies that mine bauxite (Guinea is the second largest world producer) have been granted a privileged customs status, which usually means that they are exempt from any form of control.

After living in autarchy for twenty-five years, the country needs investment if it is to take off economically. The government therefore allows the establishment of new firms without asking questions about the origin of their funds. Corporate end-of-year statements do not always reflect the true level of activities. Some rich merchants are also suspected of involvement in illegal trading with neighboring countries. The building industry could be used for money laundering, especially in cities such as N'Zerekoré and Kankan. According to sources in the judiciary, banks do not cooperate with law enforcement agencies and refuse to make background checks on funds paid by bankers' orders.

THE GAMBIA The military officers who seized power on July 23, 1994, in order to "fight corruption" have made the war against narcotics one of their priorities. The Anti-Narcotics Brigade, accompanied by drug addiction specialists, has undertaken a countrywide tour to teach grassroots communities how to identify certain narcotics and to request that those peddling drugs be turned in to the authorities. This public awareness campaign goes hand in hand with increasingly stiff sentences handed down by the courts for drug trafficking. Cannabis trafficking, which only recently brought three to four months in prison, now leads to between three and six years. Sentences can be for ten years in the case of hard drugs. This effort, however, has yet to slow the arrival in the Gambia of cocaine from Brazil and heroin from Asia via Nigeria, Kenya, Cape Verde, and Senegal.

A new technique used by traffickers is to hide local or imported drug stocks in rural areas and introduce them little by little into urban centers such as Banjul and Serekunda, where several hundred drug users live. Thus, police raids rarely result in large seizures. Official seizure statistics for 1994 list 352 kilograms of cannabis, 3.5 kilograms of cocaine, and 500 grams of heroin. But the amount of heroin passing through the Gambia en route for either Senegal or Europe is certainly far greater. While Gambian networks previously were especially active in Scandinavia, in 1994 they appeared in countries such as France, where settlings of accounts between Gambian traffickers killed two people in December 1994.

The heightened law enforcement has not affected small cannabis growers, who inhabit regions where cannabis stocks can be hidden with relative ease, such as on the islands at the mouth of the Gambia River. On the contrary, these farmers have seen a spectacular rise in prices: One kilogram of marijuana, which fetched between 80 and 100 dalasis (US$8 to $10) prior to the coup d'état, today sells for 400 to 450 dalasis. Farmers are all the more optimistic now, as this year's abundant rains washed the islands' salty earth, rendering it much more fertile. In early December, farmers increased their cannabis nurseries in expectation of the first of two annual cannabis harvests, which are virtually their sole resource.

BURKINA FASO The drug problem in Burkina Faso is becoming more acute, particularly because of the country's location. Landlocked within the heart of West Africa, Burkina borders on six other states, several of which are trafficking hubs: Niger to the east and northeast; Mali to the north and northwest; Côte d'Ivoire to the southwest; and Ghana, Togo, and Benin to the south. In early 1994 the government set up a National Committee for the Fight Against Drugs in application of Decree 93/231/PRESS/PM of July 26, 1993.

Cannabis, known locally as *yamba,* is grown for domestic consumption almost everywhere in the country. But in some parts, such as the central western region—along the Sissili and Nahouris Rivers, to the north of the Ghanaian frontier—there are larger plantations supervised by Ghanaian nationals. In 1993 fields were destroyed in Tiebele, Leo, and Boromo, and the local police seized 105 kilograms of marijuana in this region. A significant part of this production is probably meant for export. Seizures are not directly related to quantities, since the country is also used as a point of transit, especially by Ghanaians who export to Mali, and from there to North Africa.

Burkina is also a place of intense trafficking of psychotropic substances, mainly from Nigeria but also from Ghana and Togo. The drugs are either destined for local consumption or passing through on their way to Côte d'Ivoire, Mali, or Niger. The biggest seizures have been made either at borders or at the airport from passengers traveling on Ethiopian Air Lines from Bombay. Heroin and cocaine, so far in relatively small amounts, use the same routes.

Glue, solvents, synthetic drugs, and marijuana are used by street children, the unemployed, and those working in the informal economy of petty street merchants. But drug abuse is not confined to urban areas. In every rural village, hawkers sell amphetamines as panaceas especially good for increasing strength. Farmers consume high quantities of the substance during the rainy season, a period of intense farming activity, from May to November. It must be pointed out that a large number of farmers do not have draught animals. Because the stimulating effect of amphetamines gradually decreases, farmers tend to use ever-larger amounts, until they eventually suffer serious health troubles. But people do not necessarily make the connection between these ailments and their use of the "medicines." On special occasions such as christenings and weddings, women crush and mix the drugs with drinks and tea. It has been noted that amphetamine consumption is highest in areas under strong Islamic influence, such as Bobo Dioulasso. By contrast, in areas where *dolo* (sorghum beer) is drunk, amphetamines are almost unheard of.

In the east of the country, near the Malian border, gold washers also consume great quantities of these amphetamines, especially because their income is essentially commission-based, their fixed wages being very low. Sometimes, concession owners even crush amphetamines in the workers' food unbeknownst to them in order to increase their performance.

MAURITANIA The country's geographical situation—straddling North Africa and sub-Saharan Africa and bordering Senegal to the south, Mali to the southeast, and Algeria and Morocco to the north—has resulted in its increasing use as an alternative transit route for narcotics. Mauritania also links South America with Spain via the Canary Islands. This link represents an asset for cocaine traffickers, who have recently started using Mauritania as a transit point. The existence of a vast diaspora of Mauritanian businesspeople throughout the world has also fostered the trade in illicit substances. Furthermore, stricter anti-narcotics measures in neighboring countries could push traffickers to look for new routes, especially as the peace process in the western Sahara will probably result in more widely opened routes to the north.

Cannabis crops have been reported to the drug squad in southern Mauritania, in the area irrigated by a dam built on the Senegal River. Cannabis is either grown in small plots or scattered among other crops. There are very few marijuana traffickers in Mauritania. About a dozen are active in Nouakchott, the capital, and a handful in Nouadhibou and the rest of the country. These are mainly people who have connections to the police, customs, and so on. Most of those arrested by law enforcement authorities other than the drug squad have little trouble buying their freedom. Former police officers, and even a *gendarme,* whose activities are well known, have turned to drug trafficking. Reports from Rosso, a town on the border with Senegal, indicate that customs and police officials resell seized marijuana. The U.S. State Department report for 1992 went even further, noting that "high level officials are rumored to be involved in trafficking."[2]

It appears that cocaine traffickers have started using Mauritania as an alternative transit route. Cocaine arrives by ship from Brazil, goes through the port of Nouadhibou, and then continues to Spain and France. Air links are also used. In January 1992, a Mauritanian national who had traveled to Brazil to purchase 4 kilograms of cocaine attracted the attention of the police. The drugs were hidden in a refrigerator and sent as air freight. They were discovered during transit in Paris. Tipped off by their French counterparts, Mauritanian police arrested the trafficker as he came to pick up his merchandise at Nouakchott. Another 500 grams of cocaine were seized in January 1993. Mauritania's proximity to the Canary Islands, a Spanish possession, makes it attractive to Latin American traffickers. Direct links between Mauritania and the Canary Islands are available three times each week. Las Palmas, the capital of the Canary Islands, is a refueling point for fishing boats and could be used by trafficking networks. Shipping routes also link Mauritania with France, in particular via the port of Rouen. With no effective control measures currently in place, the volume of traffic is probably much more significant than seizure statistics indicate.

2. Bureau of International Narcotics Matters.

The heroin seized in Mauritania is *Brown sugar* (No. 3 heroin) from Southwest Asia. Nigerian and Ghanaian couriers have been arrested in transit at Nouakchott airport. Women from the Côte d'Ivoire and Benin, traveling from Abidjan or Cotonou, have also been found in possession of small amounts of drugs hidden in their vaginas. Seizures of heroin amounted to 58 grams in 1992.

Although Mauritania is very poor, its banking system could serve as an effective vehicle for money laundering. Banks receive cash deposits from Mauritanian merchants with activities the world over. In addition, the banks handle the savings of Mauritanian immigrant workers, especially those living in the Persian Gulf. Some cases of unexplained wealth have been observed.

Addressing the situation, the new drug law (Chapter 2, Article 6) requests banks to report suspicious transactions. Prison sentences are to be handed down to any banker knowingly abetting such activities.

CAPE VERDE Although alcoholism and prostitution, especially child prostitution, are far graver problems, production, consumption, and traffic in drugs do exist in Cape Verde.

Indian hemp—known locally as *liamba, maconha, padjinha,* or *pof*—was first consumed before it was actually cultivated. It appeared around 1975–76 with the mass arrival of Cape Verdian immigrants fleeing the civil war in Angola. Nowadays, cannabis is grown in the capital, Praia, in pots placed on balconies or in small gardens. But there are larger cultivation areas within the islands of Santo Antao and Santiago, where the climate is particularly suited to the plant. According to the police, production on the island of Santiago is concentrated in the Santa Catarina district. Some producers claim that this is their only means of survival. Given the information currently available, it is very difficult to estimate how much land is dedicated to cannabis. However, judging from seizures, production could reach 600 to 1,000 kilograms per year on the island of Santiago alone. Cape Verde is also used as a transit point. In 1992 fishermen who had put in for lunch in the desert islet of Raso discovered 3 tons of hashish. The drugs were in transit, probably from Morocco to Europe. It is not known whether the fishermen stole some of their discovery or whether the police did so, but hashish consumption, hitherto unknown in Praia, started following this seizure.

Although the police have no information on networks operating in the region, a few spectacular seizures indicate that the islands of Cape Verde are probably used as a regular point of transit for large-scale cocaine trafficking from Latin America to Europe. In 1989, 45 kilograms were discovered inside an unclaimed suitcase from Brazil. In 1990, a record seizure of 500 kilograms was carried out in Sao Vicente aboard a yacht. Some observers fear that international organized crime may have become interested in the islands' potential as a transit point for the cocaine trade. Indeed, in 1991 an additional ton of cocaine was seized in Vigo, Spain, on a yacht that had called in at the Cape Verde archipelago.

Rwanda-Burundi

Following the June 24, 1994, demonstration by Hutu and Tutsi refugees between the RPF- (Rwandan Patriotic Front) controlled camps of Ndera and Kabuga, where posters were displayed accusing, among others, Jean-Christophe Mitterrand of being a "drug dealer," no confirmation of the rumor going round the capital could be obtained. The demonstrators charged that the son of the then French president was involved in the operation of vast cannabis fields belonging to General Juvénal Habyarimana, the former president of Rwanda, in the large Nyungwe forest in western Rwanda.

No Smoke Without Fire

The Belgian press has insinuated that French troops intervening in the Gikongoro prefecture, which is located within the "humanitarian safe zone," and the foreign legionnaires patrolling the Nyungwe forest are there partly to wipe out any trace of these illicit activities from the area. Thus, the issue here is not so much the economic role played by drugs in the conflict, which is probably minimal, but their use as a propaganda tool.

Production and trafficking are nonetheless indisputable realities. In the past, destruction of cannabis plantations did take place in the Nyungwe forest. Some 150 hectares (370 acres) were destroyed in 1989, for instance. But that was after a denunciation by the Burundian government, supported by international organizations involved in drug control, which furnished the Rwandan government with their precise location. Yet the crop was located in inaccessible clearings, where rows of Indian hemp alternated with rows of sorghum. When intervention could no longer be delayed, General Habyarimana's government just transformed it into a propaganda operation, a great *umuganda* (collective work) complete with military intervention, helicopters, and so on.

François-Xavier Nsanvuwera, a public prosecutor with the Kigali Lower Court between 1990 and 1993 and a member of the opposition to General Habyarimana's government, told the OGD correspondent that the mayor of Kivu and other people from the area who had been arrested and accused of being responsible for the crop—and freed since—were merely scapegoats. Members of the new administration have voiced their intention of reopening the drug trafficking cases that their predecessors buried in oblivion.

As soon as they started intervening in 1990, the French were aware of official involvement in various types of trafficking. Indeed, French Embassy police sent the following letter to President Habyarimana:

> Your penitentiary at Butare is a well-known center of trafficking of narcotics produced in Rwanda, and the director of this institution is a very active link, enjoying great credibility with his French trafficking friends because of the direct and regular contacts he maintains with you ... The drug market in your country is a threat to our country.[3]

During the genocide that claimed the lives of hundreds of thousands of Tutsis, Radio Mille Collines encouraged the members of the Hutu militias (the *interahamwe*) to smoke cannabis before going out to kill.[4]

The proof that cultivation on a significant scale never ceased in Rwanda is that from the late 1980s until the rocket attack of April 6, 1994, which cost the Rwandan and Burundian presidents their lives, over 60 percent of the cannabis seized (from 500 to 1,000 kilograms depending on the year) in Burundi had been smuggled from Rwanda. The provinces and towns of Cibitoke, Kayanza, and Muyinga alone account for over 60 percent of the seizures carried out in the fourteen Burundian provinces. Furthermore, Burundian Hutu rebels from Rwanda who attacked Burundi through the province of Cibitoke are said to have acted under "cannabis intoxication."

In late June 1994, new incursions of Hutu extremists belonging to the Palipehutu party, which is banned in Burundi, caused the death of

3. Cited in Colette Braeckman, *Rwanda, histoire d'un génocide,* Fayard, Paris, 1994, p. 256.
4. Ibid., p. 107.

several soldiers of the Tutsi-dominated Burundian military. The spokesman for the Burundian Ministry of Defense, General Jean-Bosco Daradangwa, declared that on this occasion "significant quantities of weapons and drugs had been seized." The various factions in the conflict take advantage of Burundi's geographical location, which makes it a hub for cannabis trafficking not only from Rwanda but also from Tanzania and Zaire, where 30 percent of confiscated drugs originate. Between Zaire and Burundi, traffickers cross the Ruzizi River on canoes. Fishermen hiding the weed in bags of cassava, corn, or coffee also cross Lake Tanganyika from Zaire and Tanzania.

Big Wigs and "Little Rascals"

Moreover, Burundi has also begun to be used as a heroin-trafficking hub, as suggested by the seizure of 1.4 kilograms in 1989 and 6 kilograms in 1991. In 1992, a first-ever seizure of over 1 kilogram of cocaine was carried out. Among others, high-ranking military officers have been involved, as was reported in the local press. Given the Burundian police's meager means and the unrest prevailing in the country, it can be assumed that these quantities do not reflect the actual scale of the trafficking. According to Interpol, heroin networks use the Karachi/Bombay-Nairobi-Bujumbura-Brussels/Paris-Frankfurt air route.

Within Africa, Kampala-Kigali-Bujumbura could be an alternative air route and Kenya-Tanzania-Burundi a land route. This traffic has local spillover and, according to the director of the Kamengue Neuro-Psychiatric Center in Bujumbura, the capital hosts over 100 heroin users (aged eighteen to twenty-five), usually from well-off families. A gram of heroin costs 5,000 Burundian francs (FBU)—about US$20, compared with 3,000 Belgian francs ($100) in Brussels. Some users allegedly became drug-dependent as they tried to gain entry into the trafficking circles in order to make fast cash. Another drug being used in these circles is flunitrazepam, a hypnotic and anxiolytic drug marketed by the French company Roche under the trademark Rohypnol, which is diverted from its medical purpose.

In urban areas musicians, together with members of the Jamaica-born Rastafarian movement, are marijuana consumers. These users were first supplied by domestic output. Indeed, as in neighboring Rwanda, cannabis will grow in most areas of Burundi. Under the name of *urumogi,* it is used by breeders to treat cattle. The Batwa pygmies use it

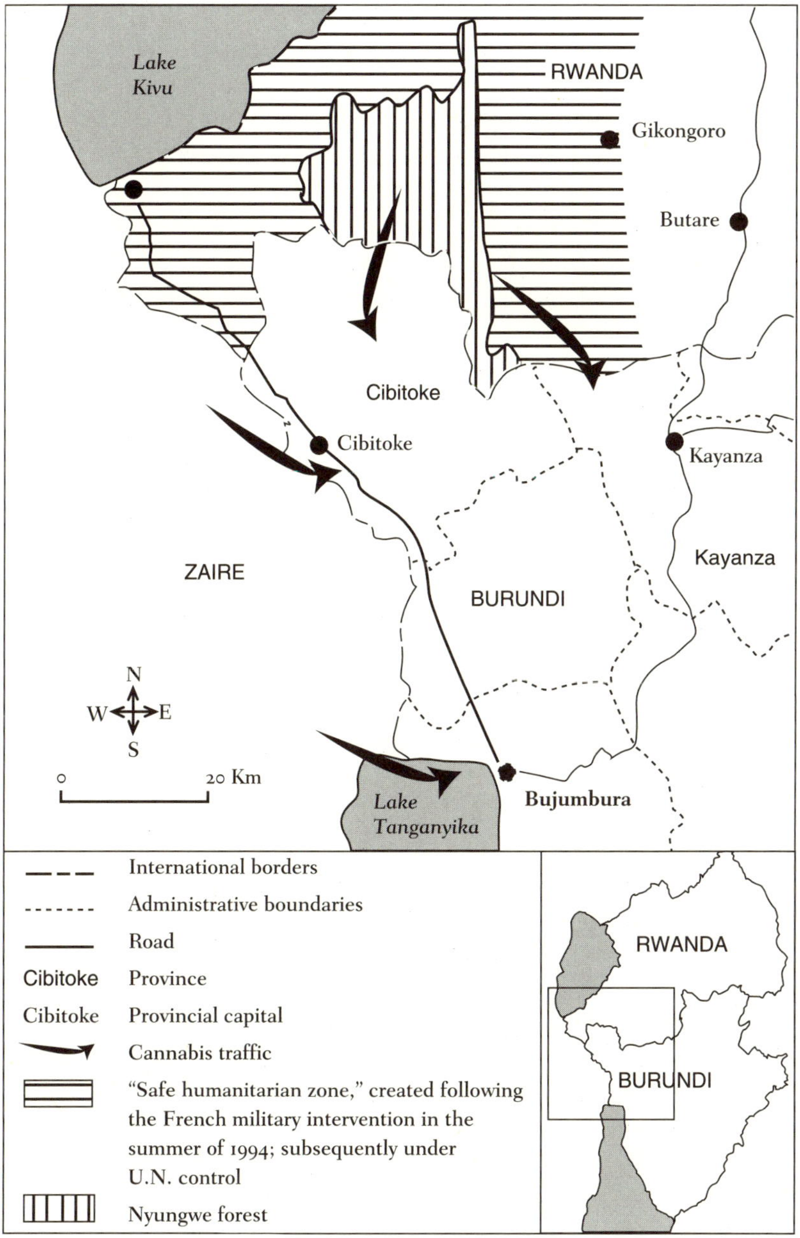

Map 8. Cannabis Trafficking into Burundi

against hunger and cold as well as in certain rituals. It is cultivated throughout the country, on small surfaces hidden among other crops and inside housing compounds. Expatriates have also contributed to the increase in local use, as demonstrated by the fact that cigarette street merchants offer joints to guests at Bujumbura's two hotels, Novotel and Méridien, where foreigners usually stay. The rising demand has made it necessary to import cannabis from neighboring countries, as described above.

The biggest drug users in Burundi, however, are street children. Some 2,000 of them (aged eight to sixteen) have been counted in Bujumbura in recent years. But today, several thousands of new *batimbayi* ("little rascals" in Swahili) have come flooding in following the ethnic violence of October 1993, which killed from 50,000 to 100,000 and sparked the exodus of another 700,000 people. They are often beggars or delinquents who take drugs in order to forget poverty, hunger, the cold of rainy-season nights, police corruption and beatings, and the rapes they suffer from adults. Most inhale gasoline or smoke marijuana, which costs a mere FBU20 (a beggar can make from FBU50 to FBU100 a day). The Burundian nongovernmental organization Humanitarian Help for the Protection and Development of Destitute Children (ODPE), which houses eighty youths in six hostels, cannot cope with such a massive problem by itself. Furthermore, the deteriorating political and ethnic situation, which puts the country on the verge of a catastrophe comparable to that in Rwanda, can only foster drug use by both street children and adults as they try to escape from violence and fear.

South Africa

At a conference on drugs held in Pretoria on November 12, 1994, Nelson Mandela acknowledged that the end of the *apartheid* regime had led to an increase in drug trafficking: "With our borders opening up, our more relaxed immigration laws and all the people arriving from all over the world, we are becoming a haven for drug traffickers." In August, when the rumor spread that drug traffickers were plotting to murder Tokyo Sewale, outspoken drug critic and prime minister of the provincial government of Gauteng (the region around Johannesburg), Nelson Mandela had already voiced concern over the scope of drug trafficking and asserted that the police must turn their attention from political repression to the fight against crime.

A Perverse Effect of Democratization

Since the end of white rule, South Africa has had a brutal encounter with drug problems of the sort found not only in Third World nations but also in rich countries. Endemic unemployment, other urban problems in the townships, and the wave of violence that preceded the national elections are all behind increased criminal activity and the consumption of cheap drugs, notably marijuana and methaqualone. At the same time, the existence of an affluent population has also spawned a market for "hip" products like cocaine and LSD. Furthermore, the lifting of sanctions against South Africa and the opening of air routes between Pretoria and numerous other countries are now being exploited by international traffickers who appreciate the quality of South Africa's infrastructure and are intent on turning it into a transshipment hub linking Asia, Europe, and the United States. A police spokesperson stated in early September that in the month following the elections, 35,000 Nigerians had entered the country and that 90 percent of arrested cocaine traffickers were Nigerian nationals.

Another factor encouraging drug trafficking is the lack of border checks. Major quantities of drugs arrive in South Africa through the kingdom of Swaziland, which they reach by road from Maputo (the capital of Mozambique) or by air from Kenya. Weapons from Mozambique follow the same route—700 items, including a cannon and 500 AK47 rifles, were recently seized near Komatipoort in eastern Transvaal. According to Colonel Neels Venter, head of South Africa's drug squad, some 100 major trafficking networks operate in the country. On August 25, 13 kilograms of cocaine were seized in a Johannesburg hotel and five Nigerian dealers were arrested. In 1993, 80 kilograms of cocaine were discovered and 236 dealers arrested (as against 11.5 kilograms and 108 dealers in 1992). Seizures of LSD have more than doubled in the same period, climbing from 5,000 to 11,000 doses. The quantity of heroin uncovered in the country, however, is still negligible, despite what is probably substantial transshipment traffic.

South Africans also operate beyond their own borders; a cocaine network was dismantled in Brussels and a heroin network was broken up in the United States early in 1994. South Africa is also the continent's primary exporter (and consumer) of marijuana (*dagga*), which police assert is the main cash crop across practically the entire country. Favorable climate and soil conditions enable cannabis to grow wild and to reach a

THC content of 11 percent across practically the whole of South Africa. Over 1,600 tons of grass were seized or destroyed in 1993.

As far as other drugs go, the most widely consumed substance since the early 1980s has been methaqualone, a depressant known locally as Mandrax and used as a stimulant either combined with alcohol or crushed with marijuana (a mixture called "white pipe"). In 1993, 3,550,000 doses were seized and 3,338 dealers were arrested. Some 80 percent of the Mandrax made in India and Pakistan is destined for the South African market, after passing through other eastern or southern African countries. Two thousand tablets from Mozambique were recently seized in Swaziland. Part of the imported Mandrax is now reexported to Great Britain. Furthermore, police note with alarm the establishment of drug-related Thai prostitution networks and Chinese criminal organizations from Taiwan and Hong Kong. Despite all this, alcohol abuse remains the number-one problem among both the black and white populations. South Africa contains over a million alcoholics, 5.8 percent of the population over age fifteen.

ZAMBIA Police seizures of large quantities of marijuana, which is consumed traditionally here, fool no one. The real stakes are in heroin and cocaine trafficking. Indeed, Zambia is a transit country for Southwest Asian heroin and Latin American cocaine. But both substances are also destined for rich South Africans and, increasingly, young upper-class Zambians. South Africans also use Mandrax (methaqualone, Quaaludes), which is blended with marijuana and smoked. The trade has become so common that Mandrax tablets are used as currency in Zambia. Six packages the size of a 300-page paperback book are enough to purchase a Toyota Corolla automobile. A dozen packages will buy a Mercedes. The laundering of the proceeds from these illicit activities has been made easier by a government program of privatization of state-owned enterprises. Not only is corruption rife within the police and customs, it is present at the highest echelons of the state.

Thus, Wina Nakatindi, the minister of social affairs, and her husband, Sikota, vice president of Parliament, resigned on January 9, 1994, following public accusations linking the two to drug trafficking. The couple were detained for four months in 1985, under the Kenneth Kaunda regime, in connection with a drug-trafficking investigation. Their resignations came less than one week after that of the foreign affairs minister, Vernon Mwaanga, also accused of involvement in drug-related activities. Nonetheless, they retained their parliamentary seats as members of the ruling party, the Movement for Multiparty Democracy. This series of resignations came after Zambia's principal creditors complained to Zambian representatives at a Club of Paris meeting about suspected involvement of "certain" national leaders in drug trafficking.

On July 4 Zambian President Frederick Chiluba dismissed his justice minister, Ludwig Sondashi, for "improprieties in conducting the affairs of his ministry." On July 6, during a press conference, Sondashi declared that he had proof President Chiluba had enriched himself with drug money, by way of finance companies set up by the health minister, Michael Sata. Chiluba immediately filed slander charges against his former justice minister. The repeated scandals underline the role played by drug trafficking in Zambia.

7. *Southwest Asia*

Southwest Asia is the world's leading producer of opiates. In 1994 the extent of this production was accurately assessed for the first time. Domestic markets, notably in Pakistan and India, absorb a major part of that production. And although exports in the direction of the United States continue to slide, the region remains by far the leading supplier of opiates to western Europe and, in all likelihood, the CIS. The Golden Crescent also exports considerable quantities of hashish. In the past year it has become apparent that Pakistani heroin distribution networks (both wholesale and retail), formerly based mainly in Great Britain, are beginning to operate throughout northern Europe, notably in the Netherlands and France. Some of these networks, abetted by Pakistan's military intelligence service, are used to finance Islamic fundamentalist groups in Indian Kashmir. This state of affairs, however, in no way inhibits European countries and the United States from competing for Pakistani weapons contracts.

Afghanistan[1]

According to the annual reports of the U.S. State Department, Afghanistan's annual opium outputs for the years 1987 to 1993 fluctuated between 585 and 685 tons. For several years, U.N. representatives and members of the OGD, both of whom carried out field investigations during the harvest season, have considered that American figures grossly underestimate the real scale of opium production in Afghanistan. Already in January 1992, an article published by the *Geopolitical Drug Dispatch* estimated the 1991 output at 2,000 tons and announced that the following harvest "could reach 3,000 to 4,000 tons." But it was not until the UNDCP carried out a thorough survey on the ground in spring 1994, reviewing all "suspect" provinces, that concrete evidence emerged.

The World's Top Opium Producer

Although the UNDCP did not publish the survey's final report, the OGD obtained access to its contents through Western diplomatic sources in Islamabad, Pakistan. The current poppy crop in Afghanistan is sown on 80,000 hectares (192,000 acres) of land, and will produce a harvest of between 3,200 and 3,300 tons of opium. This puts Afghanistan ahead of Burma, which produced between 2,600 and 2,800 tons of opium in 1993–94. The two principal poppy-producing regions in Afghanistan are Nangahar in the east and Helmand in the west, each expected to provide 1,500 tons this year. Uruzgan contributes 150 tons, Badakhshan only 50 tons, and other provinces—such as Nimruz and Zabul—a few tons. Poppies are generally planted in the most fertile soil. One hectare produces on average 40 kilograms of "wet" opium, or about 30 kilograms of "dry" opium. In the Helmand region, where crops are irrigated, returns are respectively 60 kilograms and 45 kilograms per hectare. Traders pay farmers the equivalent of US$40 for 1 kilogram of "wet" opium, $60 for "dry" opium. Revenues from the country's opium production amount to $220 million annually, to which must be added the profits from the heroin manufactured locally.

The void resulting from the absence of a viable state for fifteen years goes a long way to explaining why Afghanistan has become the world's top opium producer. But things got even worse after the collapse of

1. Iran was reviewed in OGD 1994 report, *État des drogues, drogues des États,* op. cit.

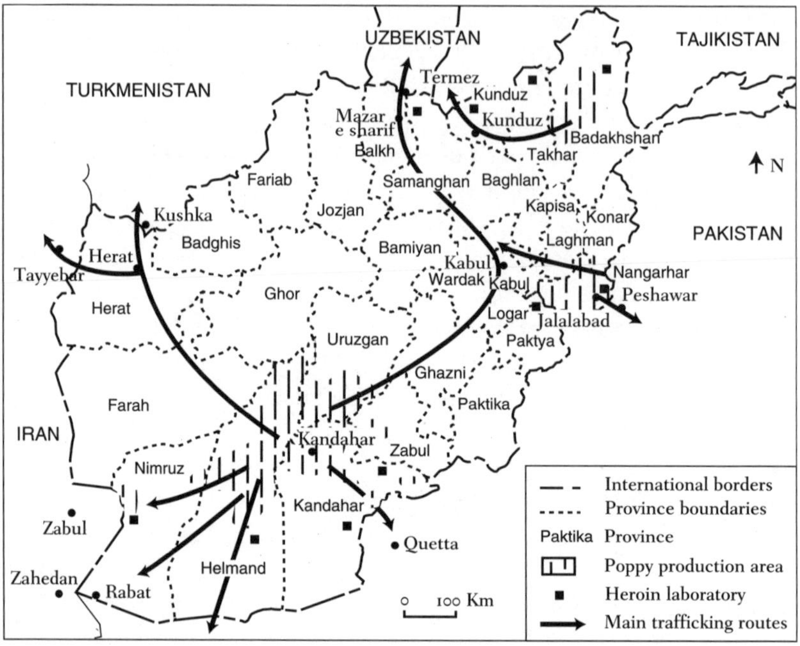

Map 9. Afghanistan: Opium Production and Trafficking Routes

the Russian-supported communist regime and the subsequent chaos resulting from the internecine fighting among the various *mujahedeen* factions. Poppy revenues are a key element in the peasant economy of a country devastated by years of warfare, to which 1.5 million refugees have returned over the last three years. Yet poppies are equally beneficial to former *mujahedeen* guerrilla commanders, who impose a tax of from 10 to 20 percent on sales. This is especially true in Helmand province, where areas of increasing opium production are for the most part controlled by Commander Rasul Akhunzada of the Harakat-e Inqilab party. Akhunzada has even planted poppies on his own land. The commanders' treasure chest is overflowing all the more now that an ever-increasing portion of the opium crop is being transformed into heroin inside Afghanistan rather than being sent to laboratories in the tribal zones of neighboring Pakistan as before. The draconian antinarcotics measures implemented in Iran have encouraged the relocation of morphine base and heroin laboratories from eastern zones near the Pakistani border to areas farther north, along the permeable border with Tajikistan, Uzbekistan, and Turkmenistan. From there the drugs are shipped to the West via these and other republics of the CIS.

Haji Qader, the governor of eastern Afghanistan's Nangahar, Laghman, and Kunar provinces, has undertaken a poppy eradication campaign since late 1994. With the help of dozens of tractors, he is reported to have tilled 100,000 *jeribs* (48,000 acres) sown last autumn, in particular in the Khojiani and Surkh Road districts of Nangahar. Qader asserts that 70 percent of poppy crops in Nangahar will be destroyed by spring 1995. Certain local commanders, some of whose power lies in control of the poppies, are opposed to the eradication of poppies on their territory.

Publication by the OGD of the results of the UNDCP survey initially provoked a strong reaction from Haji Qader and the *shura* (assembly of traditional authorities) of Nangahar. As reported in the Pakistani press, the UNDCP was requested to cease its activities in the region. But hard feelings were short-lived. The UNDCP's commitment to implementing alternative crop programs seems to have convinced the governor of Nangahar to launch his campaign against opium. The permanent reduction of poppy crops during the coming years will depend on the ability of the UNDCP and, more generally, of the international community to respond to the needs of affected farmers, whose revenue will be diminished beginning in spring 1995.

According to information obtained in Washington, D.C., by the OGD, the U.S. DEA believes that the UNDCP's estimates are not far off the mark. They are, however, resolutely opposed by the CIA, which uses satellite images to back its view. State Department statistics for 1994, which will be officially published in the spring, reportedly estimate Afghan opium production at 950 tons, compared with 685 tons in 1993. The only scenario that could make this very low estimate become a reality in 1995 would be, first of all, if the *Taliban* continued with their string of victories in Afghanistan and gained lasting control of large swathes of Afghan territory. Next, these Islamic religious students would have to put into practice their proclaimed desire to put an end to narcotics production. However, while reports from the field mention the repression of petty trafficking and consumption by the *Taliban,* they are also alleged to have acknowledged that for the moment, poppy growing remains crucial for the survival of local peasants.

Pakistan

An increasing amount of Afghan opium is transformed into heroin in Afghanistan itself. Part of it is exported via Iran or via the former Soviet republics of Central Asia, but a large number of heroin laboratories continue to operate in Pakistan's tribal areas. Exporting 30 to 40 tons annually, the country remains the world's largest heroin exporter after Burma. Another 70 to 80 tons of heroin are destined for the local market, some 1.5 million users. Hashish production has never been estimated but is certainly very large. In the last quarter of 1994, uprisings in the tribal zones used the excuse of religious fundamentalism but were really about preserving hashish and heroin as a source of revenue. Elsewhere, the involvement of certain sectors of the military in drug trafficking was made public due to internal political strife. On December 10, 1994, Prime Minister Benazir Bhutto, whose electoral campaign was partly funded by heroin barons, decided to submit very tough antidrug measures to a parliamentary vote. The proposed measures include the death penalty for traffickers and a requirement that banks report suspect transactions. In late January a vast military operation resulted in the destruction of twenty-six laboratories in the tribal zones and the seizure of 400 kilograms of heroin and 165 tons of hashish. This sudden zeal emanated from the fact that U.S. President Bill Clinton had to decide in February whether Pakistan would be "certified" as doing its utmost in the fight against drugs. The maneuver paid off on January 10, 1995, when bilateral talks on regional security between Pakistan and the United States were renewed. The Americans had suspended the talks in 1990 because Pakistan was suspected to possess, or be actively seeking to obtain, nuclear weapons. Renewing the talks might make it easier for Islamabad to obtain the delivery of thirty-two American F-16 fighter planes for which Pakistan had already paid US$680 million, but the delivery of which had been frozen.

Drugs and Weapons

Pakistan's Anti-Narcotics Task Force (ANTF), created in June 1994, seized 700 kilograms of heroin on August 28 in Peshawar, the capital of Pakistan's Northwest Frontier province. On August 17, 68 tons of hashish had been confiscated in two separate seizures in Pakistan's southwestern province of Baluchistan. Observers do not believe that these sudden successes were the result of luck alone. Pakistan needed to prove the effectiveness of the ANTF, which is under the control of the military. In addition, the Pakistani government itself announced that the European Union has made it known that economic aid to Pakistan is dependent on Islamabad's antinarcotics efforts.

Pakistan's most spectacular drug hauls, such as the 3.2 tons of heroin seized in October 1991, have always occurred at a time of delicate international negotiations, usually with the United States. It has even been asked whether the various seizures involve the same drugs, stocked for exhibition at such opportune moments. This time, Great Britain and France are competing to sell three or four submarines to Pakistan. France, which has already provided Pakistan's current submarine fleet of two Agostas and four Daphnés, finally won the order, worth close to US$1 billion. The signing of the contract was announced on September 21, 1994, by the French minister of defense, François Léotard. The deal also included the Mesma propulsion system and some SM-39 Exocet missiles, two devices that will give the Pakistani navy a significant advantage over other naval forces in Southwest Asia. In addition, France offered three Bréguet-Atlantique-1 maritime patrol aircraft, which could be used as spare parts to repair three similar aircraft supplied to Pakistan in 1976.

Explosive Revelations

In this context, it was in Pakistan's interest to minimize its role as the principal supplier of heroin to Europe, and to France in particular. Its military had been, and still is, suspected by Western intelligence agencies of using hidden accounts funded with profits from the heroin trade to pay for a portion of its arms purchases, as well as its secret nuclear research program (including the acquisition of enriched uranium and plutonium bought on the black market of the former Soviet Union). The trafficking began as Pakistan's army intelligence, Inter-Services Intelligence (ISI), became intimately involved in the war in Afghanistan in the 1980s. It continues today within the framework of aid to Muslim rebels in Kashmir and Tajikistan. Military officers implicated in the trafficking have family links to heroin kingpins in Pakistan's Punjab province and the autonomous tribal zones of the Northwest Frontier province.

In 1994 a political leader publicly confirmed for the first time the links between the secret service and drug trafficking. In an interview published by the *Washington Post,* former prime minister Nawaz Sharif

(1990–92) claimed that the then army chief of staff, General Aslam Beg, and the head of ISI, General Asad Durrani, had proposed to him in early 1991 a project in which heroin would be sold on a large scale as a means of financing undercover activities. Nawaz Sharif said he opposed the plan. Aslam Beg, now in retirement, and Asad Durrani, now Pakistan's ambassador to Germany, have denied Sharif's accusation. Subsequently, Sharif claimed that he never granted an interview to the Pakistani correspondent of the *Washington Post,* Kamran Khan. Khan is a highly respected journalist who was nearly murdered in 1991 by drug traffickers. He maintains that he interviewed Sharif at his home in Lahore in May 1994.

Sharif's statement, which came after an outcry he had provoked earlier by declaring that Pakistan possessed nuclear weapons, was probably aimed at destabilizing the military, the ultimate objective being to question the soldiers' current support for Benazir Bhutto. The former prime minister's declaration, while perhaps only partly accurate and subsequently denied, still amounts to blackmailing the military. However, it must first be noted that ISI's use of drug money to finance covert operations began during the war in Afghanistan, more than a decade earlier; second, it is very unlikely that the military bothered to ask permission from a civilian prime minister before engaging in this kind of operation.

In its April 30, 1994, issue Britain's *The Economist* exposed the Mehran Bank as a money-laundering center for funds used by the opposition to Benazir Bhutto during the 1990 election campaign, as well as by Islamic fundamentalists fighting in Kashmir and by certain generals, including Aslam Beg, for their private use. For good measure, Pakistani President Sardar Faruq Leghari himself admitted that the drug mafia had succeeded in penetrating politics at the highest level. Though he refused to identify drug barons with seats in Pakistan's Senate and Parliament, Leghari was referring in particular to the return to active politics of the Khattak and Saifullah families.

Tribalism, Fundamentalism, and Heroin Trafficking

Pakistani paramilitary forces patrolling the border with Afghanistan fought heavy battles with Pashtun tribesmen in early November in Bajaur Tribal Agency, 85 kilometers (52 miles) north of Peshawar. The Pashtuns were besieging a military camp and had taken eight soldiers hostage. The pretext for the kidnappings, as for those that occurred a few days earlier at Mingora in the Swat Valley, was to demand the application of Islamic law. Another demand, the true motivation for the rebellion led by Sufi Mohammad, was the cancellation of the decision by authorities to attach the Bajaur region to Peshawar administratively. Up to now, Bajaur was administered from Malakand, where justice is administered by the tribes. This "special" statute of tribal agencies means that police and judicial authority are exercised through assemblies (*jirga*) of local "grey beards," or elders. These tribal agencies have become a refuge for thousands of outlaws, as well as for some 200 permanent heroin laboratories. That represents large sums of money and helps explain the problem. Pashtun tribesmen are well armed, and possess Stinger missiles acquired from the Afghan *mujahedeen*. The fighting has left dozens dead and wounded.

Nepal

Nepal's location on the map, between Southeast and Southwest Asia, goes a long way to explaining the drug situation there. The air links with Southeast Asia and the 1,700-kilometer-long porous border with India have turned Nepal into a trafficking hub for heroin on its way to the Western world. Another threat was added recently—the activities of Afghan and Kashmiri organizations. Nepal also produces and exports marijuana and hashish of universally acclaimed quality, and is becoming a money-laundering center of increasing significance. Growing unemployment, the worsening of living conditions in general, and the spread of corruption among politicians are the main factors encouraging popular involvement in drug-related activities.

A Crossroads for Drug Routes

In mid-December, Nepalese police exchanged heavy gunfire with members of a sixty-man caravan engaged in loading thirty-six sacks, each containing about 50 kilograms of cannabis derivatives. The traffickers were operating on one of the many "secret" landing strips existing in the area, in a forest near Birgunj, in southern Nepal. Porters here are paid US$6.50 to deliver the drugs, at the end of a grueling four-day march, to Swanbarsha, India. The only "mule" to be arrested declared that 150 people from his village, Dhading, in central Nepal, worked on a regular basis for an Indian trafficker called Mulmi Sahib. The 1,200 kilograms of marijuana and the 1,000 kilograms of hashish seized from January to October 1994 are but a drop in the ocean of cannabis flooding India.

Some regions in northern India, notably Baranbaki, are centers of opium and morphine production. Laboratories are located in the towns of Raxaul and Kakarbhitta, on the border with Nepal. On a daily basis "mules" smuggle opiates into Nepal. Some of the drugs fuel local consumption, but most are reexported. Heroin and hashish seizures were carried out in September from the false bottoms of tea crates exported by an American air freight company. Drugs are also increasingly being sent by mail, especially during the tourist season.

Compared with such large-scale trafficking, the 20 kilograms of heroin, 5 kilograms of opium, and 3,000 bottles of opium-based syrup seized in 1994 are of little significance, as is confirmed by the case of the Sherpas, an ethnic group that traditionally provides porters and guides for Himalayan expeditions. During 1994, at least eight Nepalese Sherpas were arrested on arrival in the United States. The Sherpas were carrying in total more than 8 kilograms of heroin, all hidden in false-bottomed suitcases, according to U.S. Customs. An OGD investigation in Nepal resulted in confirmation from Nepalese antinarcotics agents that arrests of Nepalese nationals abroad are on the rise. Some fifty were detained in 1993, while this number was reached in only the first six months of 1994. The majority were arrested in Hong Kong for hashish or heroin trafficking, though others were picked up in Thailand, Singapore, Japan, Australia, Iran, Germany, and the United States. According to police, certain Sherpas, who are in constant contact with foreigners, may have been recruited by their climbing clients. Most of the time, the Sherpas do not carry drugs when they leave Nepal. They go and pick them up in Bangkok or Hong Kong before flying to their final destination. While they earn only a few hundred dollars each season as porters, they can make several thousand dollars on a single trip as a "mule."

However, Nepalese police officials told the OGD correspondent that the eight individuals arrested recently in the United States were probably either Tibetan refugees or Indians who wanted to pass themselves off as Tibetans in order to settle in Nepal and obtain passports. To support this claim, they told the OGD that certain members of the Tibetan community in Nepal have become rich for no apparent reason. No one bothers asking them the origin of this sudden wealth, which is not necessarily the result of drug trafficking. Members of Indian minorities in Assam, Nagaland, Manipur, and Mizoram have also been arrested in possession of heroin, which came from Burma or from the Baranbaki region of India.

After opening up drug routes through the Hindu Kush, numerous Afghans and Kashmiris are now settling in Nepal and claiming to be Indian nationals. Only Kashmiris, who are often political refugees, can rightly claim to be Indians. Indian politicians, whose opinions were widely publicized in the media, have often accused Kashmiris of being prone to participate in the anti-Indian activities of the ISI, Pakistani's army intelligence service. These allegations were rejected by Islamabad.

Laundering Potential

Despite the presence in Kathmandu of the only legally operated casino between Macao and Beirut, Nepal has thus far not been signaled as a money-laundering center. However, the Nepalese Department of Revenue Investigation (DRI) is examining numerous cases. In the last quarter of 1994, fifteen cases of illegal transactions were brought to court by the DRI. Lokman Singh Karki, the director of the DRI until late 1994, was strongly criticized when he ordered the arrest of Mohan Gopal Khetan, a well-known industrialist representing many multinational corporations in Nepal. Mohan Gopal Khetan deposited the money from his commissions in a Hong Kong bank, without telling the Nepalese Treasury. He used this money either for "investment" in other countries or to obtain bank guarantees in Nepal. This is a classic money-laundering scheme. Gopal was freed on US$2.4 million bail, and his case has yet to be tried. Furthermore, at least eight major international banks with headquarters in Hong Kong, Thailand, Pakistan (Habib Bank), India, and Western countries have opened branches in Kathmandu. This is an astonishing number, given that Nepal's financial market is quite small.

Another laundering trick is to buy gold. Indeed, under the neoliberal policies currently being phased in, any person who spends more than one month abroad is authorized to buy up to 10 kilograms of gold and 150 kilograms of silver, with the state receiving a 5 percent tax. The measure has resulted in a rise in precious metals imports. Gold is then reexported to India, where it is sold for hard currency, which is smuggled back into Nepal. According to the DRI, these funds are often proceeds from the drug trade. Launderers also buy electronic goods in Hong

Kong, Singapore, Dubai, and Thailand and import them into Nepal with fake certificates of purchase.

As in India or Pakistan, the *hundi* system, which consists in exchanging hard currency for local currency across thousands of miles by a single phone call, is also massively used in Nepal. The Nepalese police have so far arrested seven businessmen who were illegally dealing in currency and have seized US$100,000. However, the police freed the offenders after pocketing half of the money. On January 5, 1995, $3,600 in cash and $28,600 in traveler's checks were discovered in the toilets of a Royal Air Nepal plane departing for Hong Kong. On the same flight, a Danish national was arrested in possession of $100,000 and DM1,400 in cash as well as $25,000 and £15,700 in traveler's checks. The money was concealed in the man's bandages.

India

India's geographic location makes it an important transit zone for Pakistani drugs and Burmese heroin. Pakistani trafficking is facilitated by current unrest in the Indian provinces of Punjab and Kashmir, secretly supported by Pakistan's ISI. There is no proof that ISI masterminded the attacks that bloodied India in 1993, but it is certain that the organization has infiltrated the local Muslim mafia. In the case of heroin arriving from Burma, monitoring has been made difficult by local conflicts that persisted throughout 1994 in the seven northeastern states. Finally, the southern state of Tamil Nadu has become another hub, probably related to the activities of Tamil rebels in neighboring Sri Lanka. Heroin seizures in 1994 amounted to 906 kilograms, roughly the same quantity as the previous year.

But India is also a major drug-producing country. First there is marijuana, 150 tons of which were seized in 1994. Next, legal opium production continues to be partly diverted (2,072 kilograms were seized and 1,016 people were arrested), and secret labs produce significant quantities of synthetic drugs, notably methaqualone (32 tons of which were seized during the year). Finally, India exports precursor chemicals to Pakistan; and there are also increasing signs of money-laundering activity.

A Web of Conflicts

In terms of drugs of Pakistani origin, the biggest episode of 1994 involved not heroin but hashish, 6,532 tons of which were seized during the year. In June the discovery of three tons of hashish in the Israeli port of Ashdod led to the breakup of a Madras network that police say has exported dozens of tons of hashish and 4 tons of methaqualone since 1992. The merchandise belonged to Arif Patel, an Indian living in Great Britain, who worked with a Madras businessman, himself in cahoots with the Muslim mafia based in Bombay. Meanwhile, Pakistan's minister of the interior, Naisrullah Khan Babar, declared on March 20, 1994—subsequent to his squad's seizures of nearly 100 kilograms of highly concentrated acetic anhydride—that the Indian authorities were themselves covering up illicit trade in precursor chemicals used to transform opium into morphine base and heroin.

The northeastern states are another source of problems for the Indian government, for that is where Burmese heroin both passes through and is consumed, partly because a bilateral agreement allows members of local tribes to move freely across the border to a distance of 40 kilometers. Border trafficking is also encouraged by conflicts that have flared up in the region, in which the Tibetan-Burmese mountain tribes oppose federal forces or fight among themselves. Immigration from the Bengal plain toward this region rich in oil, wood, and tea has sparked anti-Indian sentiment. Collusion between corrupt politicians and rebel smugglers has increased, as has illegal trade in heroin, teak, and gems (jade) crossing the Burmese border.

In the Imphal Valley in the state of Manipur, the Meithei tribe's Popular Liberation Army (PLA) operating out of Bangladesh also relies on the region's vast marijuana crops for funding. The same goes for the Bangkok-based National Socialist Council of Nagaland, the wealthiest and most militarily efficient of all rebel movements. In July 1994, Naga separatists killed twenty-two members of the rival Kuki tribe, by way of reprisal for the murder of four Nagas by Kukis the previous week. The real stakes behind such clashes, however, concern control of National Route 39, down which Burmese heroin travels.

On return from a meeting held in Rangoon at the end of 1994, authorities from India's Narcotics Control Board (NCB) declared that Khun Sa has become the main purveyor of heroin in the Indian states of Manipur, Nagaland, and Mizoram—despite the fact that Khun Sa's zone of influence, Shan State, is far from the Indian border. These allegations, uncritically transmitted by the Indian press, should therefore be seen as an extension of the local campaign by the Burmese dictators to lay sole blame on "the opium king of Shan State" for an illicit trade in which they are heavily involved themselves, particularly along the Indian border that they control militarily. The Indian delegates to Burma are not fools but are keen to display goodwill toward Burma in order to counteract Chinese influence. They therefore offered to supply their Burmese counterparts with two trained dogs to strengthen border controls.

The third drug front is located along the coast of the state of Tamil Nadu. According to Joginder Singh, head of the Indian drug squad, this coast has become the scene of intensive heroin and marijuana smuggling. The situation has allegedly been exacerbated by pressure put on the Bombay mafia since March 1993; police enforcement in the west has driven activity to the east coast. Some 110 kilograms of heroin were seized in the area in 1993 (including 66 kilograms during a single seizure in May). The drugs would probably have been sent to Sri Lanka by one of the 70,000 Sri Lankan refugees living in India and then forwarded on to Europe or the United States. Airports in Madras and Tiruchirapalli are also employed.

Local Production and Money Laundering

Five hundred tons of opium are produced each year on 13,000 hectares (31,000 acres) by 130,000 farmers, primarily in the states of Rajasthan and Madhya Pradesh, destined for the national and international pharmaceutical industry. It is estimated that 25 percent of this opium is diverted toward heroin factories, with the complicity of civil servants. To restrict this "leakage," crops have been limited to one hectare per farmer, and monitoring is henceforth to be conducted by tax office employees. Computerization of data reportedly prevented the diversion of 60 to 100 tons of opium in 1994. In order to stamp out such practices completely, NCB officials would like the government to put an end to the export of opium products. They feel that the impact of this activity on the spread of opium and heroin addiction far outweighs the US$20 million that the exports bring the government. But as pointed out by R. K. Chandrar, manager of one of the processing labs, "if legal crops are outlawed, farmers will grow poppies anyway because it represents an important source of income for them."

Furthermore, finance ministry officials declared in spring 1994 that investigations were being carried out into Bombay stock market activities that allegedly covered money laundering from drug and gold smuggling. The supposed presence of Colombian narco-capital has not, however, been proven. Some observers feel that parallel business, taken as a whole, represents some 60 percent of India's legal economy.

8. *Southeast Asia and the Pacific Rim*

The Golden Triangle (covering parts of Burma, Thailand, and Laos) is second only to the Golden Crescent in worldwide production of opium and heroin (between 2,700 and 2,800 tons of opium in 1994). Poppy crops are also grown in Vietnam, Cambodia, and China (in Yunnan province, where the opium harvest reportedly approached 200 tons). But it is Burma that remains the world's number-one producer of heroin, with some 200 tons annually. The military dictatorship governing Burma continues to skim off a significant part of drug profits. Exports not only supply the markets of wealthy countries (United States, Australia, Europe) but also heavily affect the region itself, notably in southern China. This situation has not prevented Chinese authorities from reinforcing their links with Burma, a geostrategically attractive ally that provides China with an outlet to the Indian Ocean. In Thailand, another transit hub for Burmese heroin, accusations leveled by the United States against a number of entrepreneurial politicians have begun to shed a little light on the weight that drugs carry in Thai affairs.

Thailand[1]

While Thailand produced only about 20 tons of opium in 1994, it remained, along with China, the main transit point for Burmese heroin. The heroin trade is carried by local Thai traders or traders of Chinese origin, with the complicity of powerful politicians and military officers, who recycle their profits in legal economic activities. The links between drugs and the Thai establishment are rarely discussed by Western governments, since Thailand is still perceived as a bulwark against Chinese expansionism. Western countries see China's foreign policy as a threat to their interests in the region, fearing in particular that Burma may grant its Chinese protector the use of naval bases on the Indian Ocean.

Narco-Legislators in the Hot Seat

However, in March 1994, the United States did deny a visa to Monkol Chongsuthamanee, a member of Parliament for the town of Chiang Rai representing the opposition Chart Pattana (National Development) party, even though the visa had been requested by the Thai Ministry of Foreign Affairs for an official visit. The reasons given by the U.S. Department of State were the same as those invoked two years earlier to deny a visa to Narong Wongman, of whom Monkol is a "close aide."

Politician and businessman Narong, from Prae in northern Thailand, long ago established himself in trafficking heroin from Laos and Burma. He is responsible for dozens of assassinations of suspected informers and business rivals. During his heyday in the late 1980s, Narong's refineries (located mostly in the Udomxai region of northwestern Laos) were producing over 100 kilograms of heroin annually. The business, run by his sons, also included heroin from Burma as well as marijuana from Laos. In 1991, he donated 500 million baht (US$20 million), mostly laundered drug money, to the newly formed Samakkhi Tham party (STP), an alliance between businessmen and the powerful clan of military officers from year 5 of the Chulachomklao military academy. The STP appointed Narong its chairman and counted among its ranks such "influential" figures as Sonthaya Khunpluem, the son of "Kamnan Poh," godfather of the port of Chonduri, which is an important hub for all types of illegal trade. The STP easily won the March 1992 elections but lost control of

1. Cambodia, Vietnam, and Japan were reviewed in the OGD 1994 report, *État des drogues, drogues des États,* op. cit.

the state following the uprising against General Suchinda Kraprayoon, who had replaced Narong as a result of U.S. accusations. In the aftermath of the turmoil, the STP was dissolved. Narong now heads a smaller and less influential party. Another Thai politician who was reportedly deemed to be "undesirable" in the United States in March 1994 was Thanit Traitvuth, a member of Parliament from the eastern province of Trat and a well-known local drug baron. Thanit has extensive business interests inside Cambodia, which apart from drugs also include gems and timber.

On May 10, the affair took a new turn. A declaration made the week before by the U.S. Embassy in Bangkok was confirmed by a San Francisco assistant U.S. attorney: Parliamentary member Thanong Siripreechapong had been indicted by a federal grand jury in San Francisco in November 1991 for involvement in drug trafficking on U.S. territory. His house in Beverly Hills and a Mercedes automobile had been seized. The decision had until then been kept secret. He resigned from Parliament on May 21. Thanong had been charged with importing 45 tons of marijuana into the United States between 1977 and 1987, allegedly for profits of US$10 million. The assistant U.S. attorney announced that the United States will probably request the politician's extradition from Thailand.

The news caused an uproar in Thailand, where Thanong is a major figure. He owns a hotel chain called Little Duck, which certain journalists allege was financed with drug money. In 1987 the chain sponsored a beauty queen who later became Miss Universe. Thanong was a member of the opposition Chart Thai party, a large grouping that has refused to join the governing coalition. The Thai foreign minister, Prasong Soonsiri, declared on May 18, 1994, that seventeen politicians, including members of Parliament, were suspected by U.S. authorities of involvement in the drug trade.

The allegations were first confirmed in July, when the U.S. Embassy announced that it had denied a visa to Vatana Asavahme, former deputy minister of the interior and leader of the Chart Thai party. Vatana, a representative for Samut Prakar, near Bangkok, has significant business interests in Chiang Rai, amounting to scores of millions of dollars according to local sources. During the past ten years, he has acquired large tracts of land along the Mekong River close to the town of Chiang Saen, where the borders of Burma, Thailand, and Laos meet. A shopping center and a four-star hotel are being built for him, and he has also ordered speedboats that will link Chiang Saen to the Chinese town of Jinghong. This investment could have been funded by drug money. Moreover, several people who sold him land were murdered. The killer was identified as Kamman Leuk, the local representative of godfather Ban Tak Mao Pleun, who is established in Chiang Rai and enjoys contacts "at the highest level." Vatana and Kamman Leuk are linked to Veerapool, an associate of Narong Wongman. Veerapool joined Narong and Monkol to found the STP. The involvement of members of Parliament in the drug trade is not surprising; the real question is, why did the United States wait until 1994 to raise this issue?

The Contradictions of U.S. Policy

Thanong's activities, like those of many others, have been known for nearly twenty years. But with the end of the Cold War drug barons have replaced Communists in the U.S. lexicon of foreign evils and threats, and even America's friends and old allies such as Thailand can no longer take advantage of their position as "frontline states" in the struggle against communism to avoid being implicated in drug trafficking. Above all, the U.S. administration has begun to integrate the war on drugs in this region with pressure applied during more globally oriented negotiations, whether geopolitical or economic.

This strategy lays bare the internal contradictions of the U.S. administration. Those State Department officials wishing to push a harder line are far from having the support of all the diplomats at the U.S. Embassy in Bangkok. Some, in particular DEA agents, are trying to minimize the scandals in order "not to embarrass a friendly country." It is interesting to note that only opposition members of Parliament were put in the hot seat, despite the fact that certain groups in power, in particular serving or retired military officers, could just as well be implicated. But they are charged only when they are arrested abroad. Thus, a Hong Kong court ruled on October 4, 1994, that General Thanat Phaktiphat, an attaché to the Thai chiefs of staff, could be extradited to the United States. He was arrested in December 1993 on charges of having smuggled large quantities of heroin into Hong Kong. It must also be noted that the biggest seizures made by the Thai police result most of the time from information from their counterparts abroad. Thus, 1994's largest heroin seizure, carried out on December 6, in which 124.7 kilograms were confiscated from a fishing boat off Phetchaburi, was made possible by the collaboration of the DEA and the Dutch antidrug police.

Burma

When the Burmese military overran the headquarters of the Karen army at Manerplaw on January 25, 1995, the last stronghold against the Burmese narco-dictatorship of the State Law and Order Restoration Council (SLORC) disappeared. The refugees living in the "capital" of the "free" Karen state included elected officials of the Democratic Alliance of Burma who have been hunted by the junta since their victory in the 1990 election, as well as leaders of the student movement who spearheaded the democratic uprising of 1988. The accord reached in 1993 between the Kachin minority and the SLORC makes Khun Sa, the well-known opium warlord who proclaimed the independence of his Shan State in 1994, the only remaining leader still openly at war with Rangoon.

The Burmese military launched offensives against Khun Sa's Mon Tai Army (MTA) in late 1993 and in 1994 (see Map 10). The dry season, which normally lasts until May, is usually the period chosen for military operations. Time will tell whether the SLORC's campaign was really aimed at eliminating the "Opium King," or whether it was only a smokescreen destined to appease international public opinion. Indeed, Rangoon's propaganda blames Khun Sa for nearly all of Burma's heroin exports, even though he could hardly be entirely responsible. Furthermore, the campaign, which has the blessing of Burma's trading partners, serves to mask the well-established involvement of the Burmese military junta in the lucrative drug trade.

Turmoil in Shan State

Fighting between troops loyal to Khun Sa's MTA and the Burmese military flared up in November 1994 in northeastern Burma's Shan State, casting doubt on the SLORC's military credibility while simultaneously reinforcing that of the "Opium King's" nationalist forces. Khun Sa's latest offensive came at a crucial phase in the negotiations between Rangoon and the Karen and Mon ethnic nationalist movements. A gas pipeline traverses the Karen and Mon regions, linking Thailand to the gas field in the Gulf of Martaban, soon to be exploited by the French oil

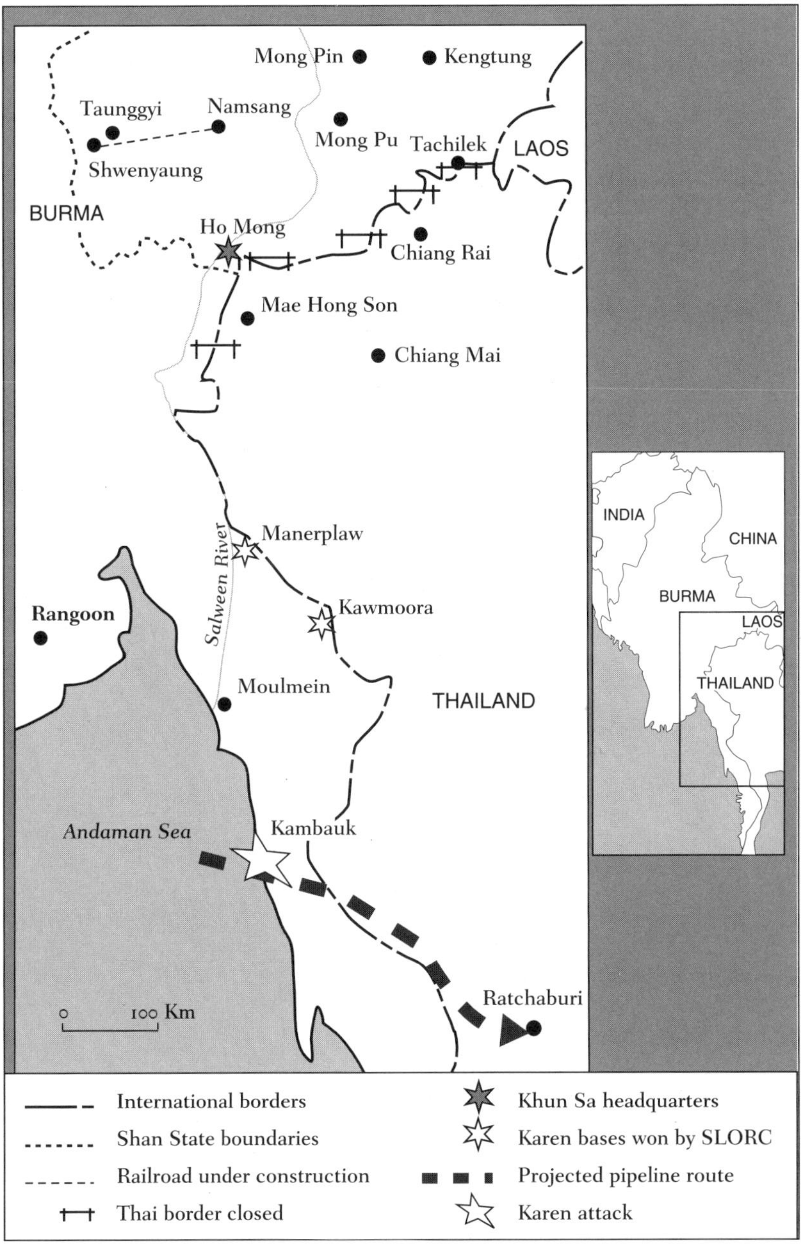

Map 10. Burma: Geopolitical Stakes

company Total. The MTA claimed responsibility for the capture in mid-May of six of the seven outposts at a Burmese army garrison at Mong Kwawt, a town in eastern Shan State that the army had seized early in the campaign. Fighting continued on May 22, 1994, near the Burmese border town of Tachilek, and on the new highway linking Tachilek with Kengtung on the Chinese border. The MTA's success in the offensive, which allegedly resulted in the deaths of several hundred Burmese army soldiers, has been neither confirmed nor denied by Rangoon.

Khun Sa has also launched a public relations campaign from his "capital" of Ho Mong. In April, Peter Bourne, a former U.S. presidential adviser in the Carter administration, visited him. Bourne told the *Bangkok Post* that he had come on a personal visit to speak with Khun Sa and determine his willingness to eradicate opium poppy cultivation in a hypothetically independent Shan State. Bourne said he was impressed with the Shan movement's political agenda, which makes Khun Sa much more than the head of a drug-trafficking organization. Khun Sa's image as a nationalist leader was earlier reinforced by the rallying to his cause of Sai Lek, the leader of the Shan State Progress party (SSPP), whose troops had merged with the MTA in 1992. Sai Lek's death after a long illness in Ho Mong on January 6, 1995, has weakened Khun Sa's nationalist claims. However, it should not affect the merger of the SSPP and MTA forces.

The inability of the Burmese army, made up of over 300,000 well-armed and battle-hardened men, to overcome a rebel force of only 20,000 has raised several questions. The MTA's surface-to-air missiles, acquired in Cambodia, Laos, and in the international marketplace, are not enough to explain why the Burmese military has not used its air force. Ho Mong is a proper town, with barracks, warehouses, a hospital, a hotel, and other buildings. It presents a conspicuous target for the Burmese air force, which has never before been stopped by humanitarian considerations or by a desire to spare the civilian population. Are the SLORC leaders in Rangoon so unsure of their control that they hesitate to mobilize elite units, garrisoned in Burmese cities, against Khun Sa? Or does Khun Sa continue to pay royalties on his trafficking activities to certain members of the junta, despite his overt challenge to Rangoon authorities?

Closing the Thai Border

The border separating Burma from the Thai provinces of Mae Hong

Song, Chiang Mai, and Chiang Rai was closed in July 1994 on orders from Bangkok. The Thai government was thereby seeking to cut supplies to Khun Sa's troops. The 6,000 permanent residents of the town of Ho Mong, the headquarters of the MTA and the capital of the self-proclaimed, independent Shan State, depend entirely on Thai markets for their supplies. This has been the case ever since the Burmese military started occupying the west bank of the Salween River. From early October, at the start of the dry season, the Burmese military began to apply stronger pressure.

According to Thai newspapers, some Khun Sa supporters have left the area, fleeing hunger. Thai authorities, under stronger U.S. pressure since the "narco-legislators" scandal, arrested the envoy Khun Sa had sent to negotiate a border reopening. The Thai press rushed once more to conclude that Khun Sa was being dealt a fatal blow. But smugglers are known to import rice and other foods into Ho Mong, where prices have tripled. To offset the impact of the closure of the roads he built, Khun Sa could fall back on some 4,000 mules and their drivers. Aware that supply routes are his most vulnerable point, the Shan State's main warlord long ago stockpiled large quantities of weapons, ammunition, and food. As fighters have priority over food, it is civilians who are most affected by the current situation. Furthermore, it is not certain whether the Thai generals in command at the borders (especially those of the secret service who have had links with Khun Sa for a long time) are enforcing an efficient blockade. Information that reached the OGD in January 1995 indicated that Thai control of the borders had considerably loosened and that Western tourists are still crossing into Burma as they have always done.

Khun Sa himself may have an interest in making the picture look bleaker than it is, in order to divert attention from the opening of new supply routes. Indeed, it is known that his influence has recently expanded into new Shan areas, particularly east of the town of Taunggyi, which was under the control of the Pa-O minority national army until it signed a cease-fire agreement with the Burmese government in early 1991. MTA forces have also allegedly occupied the hills south of Namkham-Muse near the border with Yunnan, facing the Chinese town of Ruili. Although Khun Sa, with help from Taiwanese engineers, is maintaining a very tight network of fortifications around Ho Mong, rumors circulated by mid-October that he intended to transfer his headquarters in eastern Shan State, by the Mekong River, on the border with Laos. The Burmese-Thai plan of action against Khun Sa has disrupted his activities other than drugs (teak, precious stones) and has diminished the volume of the heroin passing through his authority. Evidently, the future of the MTA depends directly upon its financial reserves and its ability to redeploy itself. But above all, it depends on the Burmese military. And it has no real interest in getting rid of the man whom international opinion blames for all drug-related activities in Burma, because the military dictatorship is thereby cleared of responsibility, even though it is probably the main beneficiary of the drug trade. In the United States, a debate over whether human rights violations constitute sufficient grounds to withhold help for the Burmese antidrug campaign is raging in the administration and Congress. By contrast, the fact that SLORC members are organizing the trafficking is completely overlooked.

China, despite the problems caused by the transit of the heroin manufactured in northeastern Burma, a region controlled by SLORC allies, is nonetheless quite pleased with the SLORC. Thus Khin Nyunt, the head of the Burmese military secret service, went to Beijing for a three-day official visit in late December 1994. Fighting heroin trafficking was on the agenda, and the international press recalled that Rangoon had just ordered military hardware worth US$400 million—helicopters, armored vehicles, assault rifles, and fast patrol boats—which was supposed to be used against Khun Sa in the spring offensive. Considering the amount of foreign currency Burma has in reserve, part of the order will probably be paid for in heroin money, the SLORC's main source of hard currency.

Laos

The main concern of international antinarcotics agencies in Laos is domestic opium production and heroin manufacturing. However, the country is increasingly being used as a transit point for heroin manufactured in the neighboring Golden Triangle.

Traditional Use and Exports

Poppies are grown by 60,000 families in 2,200 of the 6,900 villages of the ten provinces of northern Laos. Crops cover just under 20,000 hectares (48,000 acres). Yields may vary widely, from 0.5 kilograms to 33.5 kilograms per hectare. According to Laotian authorities, opium production hovered between 125 and 130 tons in 1992 (230 tons, according to U.S. counternarcotics services). Part of the harvest, 61 tons in the northern provinces and 2 tons in the rest of the country, is smoked by 42,000 consumers inside Laos. A further 15 to 18 tons are used for medical purposes (against intestinal diseases, coughs, mental illness, arthritis) or during ceremonies (funerals, births, christenings, etc.). Traditional opium use thus absorbs some 80 tons annually. Of the remaining 50 tons or so, some (the exact amount remains to be determined) is exported to Thailand—where prices are higher than in Vietnam and China—while the rest is transformed into heroin in Laos itself.

The recent adoption of market economics has not benefited numerous rural areas in the least, especially in the north. But it has created new needs. In such conditions, it may be feared that poppy fields, the farmers' only cash crop, will expand, especially as heroin laboratories have been detected in the northwest, in the provinces of Oudomsay in 1988, and in Bokeo in 1990. It is rumored that the laboratories are still functioning in both provinces as well as in Louang Namtha. Laotian antidrug agencies claim that these "are difficult to access and the mobility of the laboratories impedes precise location." The United States Bureau of International Narcotics Matters report for 1993 is more explicit: "The U.S. government continued to receive reports of military and official corruption and collusion in narcotics production and trafficking." In previous years, the State Department had accused the Mountainous Area Development Corps (MADC), under the command of the Third Army Division, the official mission of which was the development of the Hmong minority, of controlling heroin laboratories and protecting the transit of Burmese heroin.

In early December 1994, four Laotians working for the UNDCP on a development project in Palaveck in the Vientiane province were killed in an ambush. Although both the UNDCP and the Laotian government are trying to suppress the incident, observers say the workers were killed by the guerrilla movement of the Hmong minority, which is still active in the region.

Heroin Transit

The authorities fear that intravenous heroin use, which is rife across the border in Burma, China, and Thailand, could contaminate Laos and spread AIDS. The heroin consumption in urban areas set off by the Vietnam War disappeared in the late 1970s, but some cases have recently been reported among craftsmen in certain northern villages.

The threat is all the more real since heroin manufactured in neighboring countries also passes through Laos. Thus, in 1994 African networks attempted to use Vientiane airport to that end. On August 19, Laotian customs officials seized 8 kilograms of heroin from a traveler with a Benin passport and the next day found 31.8 kilograms in the luggage of another African carrying Liberian papers. According to sources interviewed by the OGD correspondent, those smugglers were probably Nigerians. Thinking that it would be easier to get through customs in Laos and that they would not be searched again when in transit through Thailand, they had arranged flights from Vientiane to their destination in West Africa via Bangkok. It took a request by U.S. narcotics agents, puzzled by the presence of Africans at the Vientiane boarding gate, for the Laotian customs officers to search them. Attempts to smuggle heroin manufactured in Burma or Thailand have been made before, but this was the first time such large quantities were seized from Africans. In late January 1995, 15 kilograms of heroin were seized in Hanoi from two Laotian nationals. This record seizure came shortly after a network smuggling heroin between the Savannakhet province of Laos and Vietnam was dismantled.

China

Chinese officials are the first to admit that anarchy reigns in the many areas of the country teeming with bandits, drug traffickers, and warlords. According to the authorities, 5 tons of drugs were seized in 1994 (an increase of 130 percent over the previous year), 4 tons of these were heroin. Nearly 2,000 smuggled weapons were also seized. Most of these seizures occurred on the borders of Golden Triangle countries. According to a report published on May 3 by the official *China Daily*, "The contrasts between the swift growth of consumption and the precarious revenues in certain sectors have induced farmers to abandon their sense of duty and to use criminal methods to appease their appetite for wealth." As for the *People's Daily*, on November 18 it quoted Deng Xiaoping as having asserted, the previous year, that the government had to fight crime with one hand and pursue reforms with the other. During the U.N. conference on organized crime held in Naples, China's minister of justice, Yang Xio, presented statistics revealing the existence of 150,000 crime syndicates, plus another 600,000 affiliated gangs of lesser importance.

The Limits of Enforcement Policy

To counter this situation, the government has launched vast enforcement campaigns. During August 1994 it targeted illegal weapons factories throughout the country. In October, a large-scale operation against prostitution and drug trafficking was launched in Guangdong province to the south. According to the official Xinhua press agency, that operation alone led to the execution of forty-four criminals on October 25 (fourteen of them were implicated in prostitution networks, the other thirty in drug trafficking). Some 82,000 people were arrested (including 407 civil servants), and 4,500 criminal gangs were dismantled.

But Chinese authorities are aware that civil servants and military officials are themselves involved in trafficking. The problem was raised during a very important meeting held in Beijing on August 4, 1993, at the instigation of the Central Committee of the Communist party and the General Council of the Supreme Court. The agenda was titled "National Workshop for Combating Contraband Activities." The main topics of discussion were the involvement of state enterprises in contraband activities alongside army and police officers who "abuse their power by participating in these activities." There are some indications that the government has decided to stamp out corruption. Thus, the seventeen people executed in Kunming (capital of Yunnan) in October included police officers and an individual linked to China's Burmese allies, Yang Muxian. Yang, a Burmese national of Chinese stock living in Kokang, was arrested in May for having smuggled hundreds of kilograms of heroin into Yunnan. Until 1989 his elder brother Yang Mulen commanded a unit of the Burmese Communist party, which is recognized as a local militia by the Rangoon government, a Chinese ally. Thus Burmese government protection no longer guarantees impunity in China. However, only heroin trafficking has been targeted so far; investments made by Burmese drug barons are still welcome in an underdeveloped region sorely in need of capital.

Furthermore, the fact that drug enforcement efforts in Yunnan have been assigned to the People's Armed Police (PAP), the largest domestic security force, founded in 1980, shows that Beijing has no confidence in local authorities. It is the PAP that led the offensive against the armed gangs in Pingguyan, near the Vietnamese border.[2] It would seem that the PAP does not even warn local authorities prior to launching its operations. However, the fact that Tao Siju, minister for public safety, who was then also political commissar for the PAP, declared in 1992 that the Hong Kong triads were "patriotic organizations" whose "investments were welcome" raises questions about the true scope of the fight against corruption.[3]

The PAP has the power to police illegal activities within the armed forces. Thus, a colonel and some 100 men from the battalion he commanded were recently arrested for heroin trafficking on a vast scale between Burma and China. This involvement of Chinese army officers in drug trafficking only confirms a recent Interpol report from Bangkok asserting that a Chinese military camp was producing *shabu* (methamphetamine) under the command of a general who shipped it to the Philippines in batches of 200 kilograms. Thanks notably to accurate information contained in the Interpol report, the Philippines' Economic Intelligence and Investigation Bureau (EIIB) was able to intercept two Chinese ships, the *Harbor Star* and the *MV-Trade,* off the island of Bataan to the north of the archipelago; the ships contained 22,000 cartons of cigarettes and 150 kilograms of *shabu*. The thirty-three Chinese nationals aboard, including military officers like Tiu Heng Peng, were arrested. Weapons and uniforms were also seized. The Chinese Embassy in Manila first declared that it "thought the Chinese ships were on an antismuggling mission," expressed its "regret" over the incident, and asked that its nationals be extradited. Filipino Minister of Justice Franklin Drillon rejected the request, on the grounds that the ships were not equipped, nor their crews trained, for such missions.

"Traditional" Money-Laundering Techniques

The policy of economic openness has encouraged the Chinese diaspora to repatriate its capital back to China, especially the "special economic zones" of Guangdong and Fujian. According to a July 1994 DEA report, Chinese traffickers repatriate heroin profits by using a system of transferring funds based on word of honor. Called *hui k'uan* (deposit money) in Mandarin and *phoe kwan* (house of message) by the Chiu Chow—

2. *La Drogue, nouveau désordre mondial,* op. cit., pp. 62–63.
3. *État des drogues, drogues des États,* op. cit., p. 160.

and similar to the *hundi* and *hawalah* systems used on the Indian subcontinent—it is an outgrowth of the activities of traders who supplied the diaspora of Chinese coolies with rice in the late nineteenth and early twentieth centuries. In China it was first of all used to remedy the disorganized state of the postal service and legal bank transfers. In short, the system involves giving a sum in hard currency to someone abroad, who then gives an order to a contact in China to pay the equivalent in local currency to a designated recipient. The system can work in both directions. Thus, in October 1993, Chinese authorities seized US$1.38 million belonging to a supermarket in Fujian province, originally generated by heroin trafficking in the United States. Such practices can take place only in societies where very strong bonds of blood and alliances between clans exist. But since such practices leave no written trace, all antilaundering measures are ineffective. These transfers thus occur on a large scale, from Taiwan toward Thailand and China.

HONG KONG More heroin was seized by Hong Kong authorities in the first three months of 1994 than in the whole of 1993; and more ICE (3,4-methylenedioxyamphetamine, a psychotropic drug that first appeared in South Korea and Japan in the 1970s) than in the past two years. The upward trend continued during the second half of the year. In mid-December, the police seized a record 100 kilograms of ICE on a truck from China. Intensified economic activity makes it increasingly difficult to monitor the borders. For example, 10,000 trucks go through the Ma Chau border post every day. During the first half of 1994, the number of arrests for drug trafficking was 35.8 percent higher than for the same period in 1993. Already in 1993, the number of arrests on trafficking charges had risen by 44 percent over the previous year. As far as heroin is concerned, the statistics reflect the surge in Burma's opium output from the 1993–94 harvest. They also indicate the development of triads' activities, particularly in southern China, through which increasing quantities of Golden Triangle drugs pass. A small share of this heroin is for local consumption, which is on the rise; but most of it is for export, especially to the United States, as well as to Australia and New Zealand.

Hong Kong police broke up a makeshift ICE laboratory in March 1994, seizing 22 kilograms. This laboratory, the first to be discovered in Hong Kong in seventeen years, was controlled by the 14K triad, the largest in the territory after Sun Yee On. The early stages of the manufacturing process had been carried out in Guangzhu, in southern China. A gang from that same region had then sent the partially finished product to Hong Kong for refinement. The ICE was intended to be marketed in the Philippines. The medium-term objective of the Hong Kong triads is allegedly to supply Japan as well, and even Hawaii, notwithstanding the fact that the latter has been an ICE trafficking hub for quite some time.

Also in March, Yu Yem-Kin, a prosperous businessman, was sentenced to sixteen years in jail. He too had set up a plant in southern China for manufacturing ICE. His partner, Lee Chauping, alias "the ICE queen" (currently at large), operated from a Hong Kong textile and plastics factory. The police think that the organization manufactured 4 metric tons of ICE, retailing at a price of HK$500 per gram. Another trafficker, from whom 14.54 kilograms of ICE was seized, was sentenced to fourteen years in prison on March 30.

The triads' renewed operations in the drug business are all the more worrying for the authorities as these criminals are increasingly investing in legitimate business interests, and as their leaders are beginning to be accepted in high society. At present, many of them receive an excellent education, resulting in increasing white-collar crime. In addition, more women are becoming prominent triad members. In an attempt to curb laundering and despite the reluctance of the Hong Kong Association of Banks, the government is trying to enforce the measures enacted by the FATF, of which it is a member. The 170 banks registered in Hong Kong resisted a ban on the anonymity of those making "suspect" financial transactions. The antilaundering measures adopted in 1989 did permit the seizure of US$340 million, but no convictions for laundering have thus far been obtained.

TAIWAN The murder of Chang Chin-tu on January 10, 1995, followed by the confession of the killers that their group had been hired by heroin kingpin Huang Shang-feng, is one example among many others of the galloping crime rate in Taiwan. The island is today home to 1,236 gangs with some 10,500 members. They are supported by the presence of international criminal organizations in Taiwan, in particular local branches of the Hong Kong triads. The gangs, protected by members of the police force, have infiltrated Taiwan's political scene. In mid-October 1994, Hsu Ping-feng, deputy leader of the main opposition party, the Democratic Progressive party (DPP), was arrested and charged with importing heroin from Hong Kong. Arrested with him were one of the most popular television hosts and "a local VIP."

The relationship between crime, drug trafficking, and politics in Taiwan has its roots in contemporary history. In the 1920s, the rise of Chiang Kai-shek owed much to the Green Gang, the leading criminal organization in Shanghai, of which he was secretly a member, and which specialized in drugs and prostitution. Its leader, Yuesheng Du, alias Mister Du, had sided with the Nationalists, and his organization actively participated in the elimination of labor unionists and Communists on behalf of Chiang Kai-shek. While Kuomintang troops withdrew into Burma between 1950 and 1961, they continued their trafficking in opium and heroin on a large scale, with the blessing of the CIA. In Taiwan the government then protected members of the Hong Kong triads, such as the godfather White Powder Ma, who took refuge in Taiwan in 1977. Despite international pressure, Ma and his brother, living in luxurious residences, were able to continue to direct the heroin traffic with impunity throughout the region. In the same vein, the Taiwanese government has always refused to extradite corrupt Hong Kong police officers who have come to Taiwan.

It appears that the present democratization of the political regime in Taiwan is now bringing with it a democratization of crime. This situation has been facilitated by the geographic position of Taiwan, which forms a crossroads for Asian trade routes in the Pacific. Traffickers of Southwest Asian heroin have transformed the island into a hub for their exports. The record heroin seizures of 1993 (1.11 tons) will likely be exceeded in 1994. Approximately half of the heroin seized has crossed mainland China, the remainder coming from Thailand, Hong Kong, Vietnam, Singapore, or South Korea. Certain specialists, such as Willard H. Myers of the Center for the Study of Asian Organized Crime in Philadelphia, believe that the Taiwanese government itself is implicated in the organization of smuggling and drug trafficking. In order to do this, Taiwan takes advantage of the economic and military aid it provides a number of countries in Latin America (Guatemala, Belize, the Dominican Republic, Bolivia, Jamaica, and Paraguay) to establish beachheads and to acquire easier access to markets in the United States. It has been proved that networks belonging to the Taiwanese community living in Bolivia export cocaine to Hong Kong and the rest of Southeast Asia.

Taiwan is also a large producer of amphetamines, both on its own territory and on the mainland. On December 22, 1994, the record seizure of 1 ton of finished product and 500 kilograms of partly refined product took place in a laboratory in Taichung County, Taiwan. This narcotics trafficking has two consequences. The first is a large volume of money-laundering activities. For example, on October 1, five stockbrokers were arrested, charged with laundering funds from the sale of heroin in the United States. A Taipei judge was also detained for complicity. The second consequence is a sharp increase in local drug consumption. The number of drug abusers and dealers today is estimated at 200,000. Some 40 percent of criminal offenses are drug-related. This situation has provoked tougher legislation: Capital punishment is now possible for refining and trafficking hard drugs.

SINGAPORE On January 6, 1995, Angela Mou Pui Peng, a Portuguese national born in Macao, was hanged after having been arrested in 1991 in possession of 5.6 kilograms of heroin. The execution of this twenty-five-year-old unmarried Christian mother was scheduled for December 23, 1994, but postponed to allow Peng to spend Christmas with her nine-year-old son. Together with neighboring Malaysia, Singapore imposes the harshest possible sentences on drug traffickers. Peng was the ninety-fifth person to be executed for violating Singapore's 1975 antinarcotics laws, which impose the death penalty on any person found in possession of at least 15 grams of heroin or 500 grams of cannabis. In September, one man found in possession of 1 kilogram of cannabis and another with 2.5 kilograms were both executed.

The execution on September 23, 1994, of Johannes Van Damme, a Dutch engineer, drew international attention to the disproportionate character of the punishment. During a visit to Paris on October 17, Goh Chok Tong, Singapore's prime minister, declared to the daily *Le Figaro* that Westerners "gave too much importance to human rights." Despite the harshness of Singapore's legislation, the number of abusers admitted to rehabilitation clinics rose from 5,700 in 1990 to 7,700 in 1994, according to a report published by the authorities in early October 1994. Observers think that the real number of abusers is much higher and growing fast.

Singapore's severe policies in its fight against trafficking are in sharp contrast to its leniency in laundering matters. It is known that a significant share of the heroin money collected by the Burmese military junta, which is used particularly to purchase weapons, is laundered through Singapore banks. Furthermore, in September 1994 Singapore strongman Lee Kuan Yew, in declaring a series of measures to attract capital to his country, already a money-laundering hub, announced, "We have all the attributes to become the Chicago and Zurich of Southeast Asia." The aim is to lure specialists and financial activities from Hong Kong, the world's second most important financial center, when the British colony reverts to Chinese rule in 1997. Although legislation against money laundering was adopted in October 1993, no charges have yet been filed under it.

THE PHILIPPINES Since July 1994, drugs have been front-page news in the Philippines. For the first time, a popular scandal widely covered in the press has gone beyond the usual corruption of low-level civil servants. This one is more serious because politicians and important government leaders are directly implicated. The scandal broke in the press on July 4, when eleven Indian traffickers were arrested in a Manila suburb. Police discovered in their dwelling a laboratory for the production of methaqualone (a central nervous system depressant with hypnotic and euphoric effects), known as Mandrax in the Philippines and Quaalude in the United States. Police seized 6.9 tons of the drug from the place. Indicted on July 29, the eleven Indians faced the death penalty. However, on August 12, they were allowed to leave the Philippines for Bombay.

Each of the ministries concerned (justice, immigration, police, security) blames the other for the "mixup." Senator Ernesto Herrera Maceda, president of the Anti-Drug Commission, vigorously publicized the affair and criticized the Narcotics Command, the police service, which, according to Herrera, had in its possession proof that the eleven Indians were part of an international trafficking network. The confiscated methaqualone arrived from India and Pakistan in powder form. It was to be packaged in the Philippines before being sent on, for the most part to southern and east Africa. The scandal of the Indian traffickers resulted in the resignations of the director of the immigration service, Zafiro Respicio, and two of his deputies. Respicio was suspected of having received a bribe of 20 million pesos (US$755,000) in return for letting the eleven traffickers go free. Also accused of corruption in connection with the affair were Epimaco Velasco, head of the National Bureau of Investigation (NBI), the Philippines' intelligence service; Ramón Esguerra, the number-two man at the NBI; Reynaldo Lugtu, deputy minister of justice; Silvestre Bello III, former minister of justice and spokesman for President Fidel Ramos's Lakas-NUCD party before Bello resigned; and one public prosecutor.

Ramos, who is trying to improve the image of the Philippines in order to attract much-needed European investment, as shown by his recent official visit to France, reacted energetically to the scandal. He demanded that all persons implicated in the affair be put on trial. Whatever the end result of this public announcement of a crackdown, the fact that politicians and civil servants at the highest level are suspect seems to indicate that trafficking networks in the Philippines enjoy influential support and large sums of money to cover their activities.

AUSTRALIA Australia manufactures amphetamines for local consumption as well as for export to New Zealand. Marijuana, another very popular drug, is either produced locally or imported from the Philippines or Papua-New Guinea. A recent deterioration in the economic situation of farmers in Papua-New Guinea (56 percent of the working population)—notably due to the fall in coffee and cacao prices—has forced peasants living at high altitudes to cultivate a form of cannabis that yields an excellent grade of marijuana, known in Australia as PNG-Gold. A flotilla of small boats then transports it across the Torres Strait separating Papua-New Guinea from Australia. Cocaine arriving from South America (the largest seizure, involving 90 kilograms, took place in 1992 in Sydney), is either destined for the local market or reexported to Hong Kong or Japan. Australian police claim to have evidence that Colombian cartels are interested in that new market.

Although the island-state of Tasmania is a major grower of poppies and producer of morphine (the local Glaxo/Johnson & Johnson outfit supplies one-third of worldwide opiate requirements), only small quantities of opium are diverted locally.

In contrast, it looks as though the Australian market became a major target for heroin dealers from the Golden Triangle in 1994. Nearly 100 kilograms of heroin were seized between January and July. Then in August police made a record haul of 135.5 kilograms in the port of Darwin on the north coast. Some of the 171 packages containing the drug were found on a Thai fishing vessel, the rest having been dropped in crocodile-infested waters. On December 21, the courts convicted members of a gang of importing 51.5 kilograms from Malaysia. On January 14, 1995, 55 kilograms were discovered at the airport. Of the three people arrested, one owned a restaurant in Hong Kong.

The authorities feel that the Hong Kong triads, particularly the 14K triad, are behind 85 percent of Australian heroin traffic. Local distribution, however, is handled by gangs of Asian youths recruited within the local Vietnamese and Chinese communities. The increase in criminal activity was highlighted by the September 5 assassination of John Newman, a Labour member of Parliament from New South Wales, who had declared war on the Asian gangs in "Little Asia," the Cabramatta district to the east of Sydney. One theory is that he was a victim of killers from the 5T organization—some 150 to 200 members strong—which specializes in housebreaking, racketeering, and heroin dealing. Approximately fifteen other Asian gangs operate in Cabramatta alone, where 75 percent of the population is Vietnamese; Newman was trying to persuade the Asian community to break the law of silence, of which it is the prime victim. The assassination provoked strong feelings all across Australia, a country that until now had felt free from the violence associated with crime syndicates and drug traffickers.

9. *South America*

South America still retains its monopoly on cocaine production, which rose last year in the two main producer countries, Peru and Colombia (which is attempting to become self-sufficient in raw material). The OGD estimates that 1994 production was between 1,000 and 1,500 tons. Those figures are greater than the 1993 estimates of 770 to 805 tons published by U.S. authorities. But the Americans also pegged worldwide cocaine seizures at 226 tons—111 tons of which were seized in the United States alone—and it seems highly unlikely that fully 33 percent of total production was intercepted.

Poppy crops are increasingly taking root not only in Colombia but also in Peru, where they have apparently passed the experimental stage (unlike Ecuador, Venezuela, and Argentina). In terms of trafficking, two new phenomena are worth noting: On the one hand, greater numbers of small- and mid-sized groups are springing up all across the continent alongside powerful organizations like the Cali cartel; on the other hand, networks of local traffickers are being consolidated as the Colombians redeploy themselves in Brazil, Chile, Bolivia, and Venezuela. Furthermore, the traffickers' infiltration of economic, political, law enforcement, and military institutions continues apace in many South American countries.

Bolivia[1]

With 35,000 hectares (84,000 acres) of illegal coca crops in the Chapare region, and a further 10,000 hectares (24,000 acres) of legal crops in the Yungas area, in 1994 Bolivia ranked third in the world as a producer of the raw material for cocaine, behind Peru and Colombia. In addition to the seizure of 4,700 kilograms of cocaine sulphate, as well as 1,168 kilograms of base paste, the year 1994 was marked by three critical events: Accusations of narco-corruption were directed at the former president of the republic and his party; the coca growers marched in protest across the country; and the government made its Option Zero proposal concerning coca cultivation.

The MIR's Narco-Connection

On March 27, 1994, Jaime Paz Zamora, former head of state of Bolivia and current vice president of the Socialist International, admitted during a press conference that "mistakes were made in the war on drugs." He nevertheless denied having protected the drug trade. His confession was in fact the upshot of an investigation by the Special War-on-Drugs Force (FELCN) carried out on behalf of the Bolivian Congress. Since December 1990, the existence has been known of a photograph showing President Paz Zamora, leader of the Movement of the Revolutionary Left (MIR), in the company of Isaac "Oso" Chavarría, a former member of the armed forces who became one of the country's leading cocaine traffickers, with links to the Medellin cartel. At their sides were Interior Minister Guillermo Capobianco and Carmelo "Meco" Domínguez, Chavarría's right-hand man. Paz Zamora had always stated that he did not know the gentlemen in question, from whom he had merely rented an airplane.

However, the FELCN's investigation has established that Chavarría had been a card-carrying MIR member since 1986 and that on April 15 of that year he threw a big birthday party for Paz Zamora, facts confirmed by other photographs. The men stayed in touch. "Meco" Domínguez reportedly donated US$100,000 to MIR and made aircraft available to the party for its electoral campaign. The government official responsible for dealing with drug traffickers was none other than Capobianco, who

1. Chile and Venezuela, as well as Central America and the Caribbean, were reviewed in *État des drogues, drogues des États,* op. cit.

resigned on March 13, 1990, following a media campaign led by the *Miami Herald,* although he never answered the allegations leveled at him. The FELCN report now reveals that he had ordered government officials to release drug traffickers and return confiscated aircraft to them. In February 1991, Chavarría encouraged Paz Zamora to appoint Colonel Faustino Rico Toro—a notorious drug trafficker, notably during General García Meza's drug dictatorship early in the 1980s—as FELCN commander. With the future in mind, Chavarría carefully saved all material documenting his relationship with the MIR. Thus it emerged that on February 29, 1994, Oscar Eid Franco, number two in the MIR hierarchy, used a false name to pay a US$25,000 bill owed to the Calacoto health clinic where Chavarría was being treated. One of Paz Zamora's sisters, Rosaria, even took flowers to the convalescent drug baron. In order to be elected president of the republic, Paz Zamora had made an alliance with the party of General Hugo Banzer who, during his years as a dictator (1971–78) was notorious for his links to drug trafficking. In 1987, videotapes showed the continuing friendly relations between close friends of Banzer and Roberto Suárez, the "Cocaine King" at the time.

The legal proceedings against Paz Zamora and the MIR leadership, initially under the control of judicial authorities, have been transformed into a political trial within congressional jurisdiction. On December 16, the Chamber of Deputies decided to send several MIR members to court, after months of hesitation and haggling among the parties. Oscar Eid Franco was thus arrested on December 26 by FELCN agents. Seven MIR figures, including two sisters of former President Jaime Paz Zamora, were called to appear at court hearings. As for Rico Toro, his extradition to the United States was granted by the Bolivian Supreme Court on February 1, 1995, after the magistrates were subjected to strong pressure by the U.S. Embassy.

Cocaleros *and Option Zero*

On August 29, several thousands of *cocaleros* (coca farmers) were to march 600 kilometers from Chapare to La Paz to protest against the repressive policies from which they suffer. Bolivian law stipulates that coca farming is permitted on a temporary basis so long as alternative crops have not been introduced into the area. On July 10, 1994, the Bolivian government signed an agreement with the United States in which La Paz committed itself to eradicating 3,200 hectares (7,680 acres) of coca fields by the end of the year. In exchange, Washington was to provide US$20 million in credit to help steady Bolivia's balance of payments. On July 13 some 800 members of the Rural Mobile Police Units (UMOPAR), an antinarcotics force commanded by the U.S. DEA, launched a vast operation along with FELCN agents, supported by an American AWACS E-3 aircraft. Dubbed "New Dawn," the operation targeted "Colombian cartels" in the Chapare region. Observers believe that whereas most large-scale traffickers escaped capture through paying bribes to the authorities, the brunt of the law enforcement action fell on poor local farmers. One of them died under torture. Numerous union activists were arrested, including the principal leader in the region, Evo Morales. The leaders of nongovernmental organizations attempting to assist the farmers were also detained. All were accused, without proof, of planning a "narco-guerrilla" war. The Church and human rights organizations in Bolivia denounced the UMOPAR and FELCN brutalities. Farmers said that the development projects financed by the United Nations and the United States had failed. They said that funds were insufficient, and that the participation of representative union organizations was never sought, either in the planning or implementation stages.

Three thousand protesting coca farmers, most of them from the Chapare region but later joined by some growers from Yungas, arrived in La Paz on September 12 after having walked 386 kilometers (241 miles) in two weeks. The protest was supported by large sectors of public opinion. After unsuccessfully trying to disperse the *cocaleros* by force, the government of President Gonzalo Sánchez de Lozada first gave the impression of ceding to their demands. In particular, the government admitted that the alternative crop development project had been a failure. And like his predecessor, Jaime Paz Zamora, Sánchez promised to launch an international campaign to legalize the use of coca leaves. The stated objective is not only to cater to the traditional coca consumption of Bolivian farmers but also to create a legal market for industrialized by-products and to export them in the form of herbal tea bags (*mate*), toothpaste, and so on. The conclusions, published in November 1994, of a study jointly carried out by Bolivian and French scientists of the Bolivian Institute of High Altitude Biology (IBBA), set up in 1991, showed that regular coca "chewers" have more endurance and are better adapted to living conditions high up in the mountains. This supports arguments against the total eradication of coca.

The government's acceptance of the *cocaleros'* demands was undercut by a measure announced by the Bolivian minister for sustainable development, José Guillermo Justiniano, during a Paris Club meeting held from November 2–4, 1994. The proposal, named Option Zero, aimed to eradicate all of Chapare's coca bushes and turn the region into a national park and a center for the industrial and service sectors, "relocating" 45,000 families in frontier areas in the process. It is estimated that 300,000 people (4 percent of the Bolivian population) depend directly on the production and transformation of coca leaves for a living. According to a study by USAID-Bolivia (the local branch of the United States Agency for International Development), traffickers earned US$425 million through cocaine exports in 1993, of which $119 million (or 20 percent of legal exports) were allegedly recycled in the country. The opposition and some of the parties within the government think that the Option Zero policy is unrealistic, especially as it is highly doubtful whether the United States and the international community in general are ready to make the financial effort necessary to replace the coca economy.

Peru

In reply to the 1994 OGD report,[2] the Peruvian minister of foreign affairs, Efrain Goldenberg, declared on May 29, 1994 that "Peru is no longer in danger of becoming a narco-state." Notwithstanding, on May 24, the day before several newspapers were to report the judgment passed on the country by the OGD, one general and eleven officers were arrested on charges of involvement in cocaine trafficking in the Amazon. On May 25, the daily *La República* wrote in its leading article that despite the adoption of an antilaundering law on April 6, 1993, "this law was never applied and nobody was ever jailed for laundering drug money, even though a flood of narco-dollars into the economy should permit their detection."

The "Colombianization" of Peru

Recent investigations by the police, researchers, and journalists tend to suggest that drugs in Peru play a far more important role than was hitherto believed. It seems that the country is undergoing a veritable process

2. See *État des drogues, drogues des États,* op. cit.

of "Colombianization." First of all, there are the criminal organizations that Peruvians call "firms." These are not only the representatives of their Colombian counterparts but highly structured autonomous power centers as well. There are about forty such firms in Peru, covering 20 percent of the territory with a population of 1.2 million. Since the end of 1993 there has been a redeployment of coca production and trafficking areas from the Huallaga Valley (especially the Central and Lower Huallaga) toward other Amazon regions along the cordillera (Apurimac, Madre de Dios, Puno), where crops first boomed in the mid-1980s. In the whole of Peru, coca crops probably cover over 200,000 hectares (480,000 acres). In the thirteen major valleys of the Peruvian Amazon, more than 200 "secret" landing strips permit the export of 500 to 600 tons of cocaine base annually. The main places from which the firms allegedly operate are Bellavista, Yurimaguas, Sivia, Palmapampa, Iquitos, the Tambopata Valley (between Puno and Madre de Dios), the northern area (from Tumbes to Chimbote), and of course Lima (the Cieneguilla neighborhood).

Furthermore, some of the firms tend to become independent of the Colombians, manufacturing their own cocaine hydrochloride and setting up marketing networks in consumer countries. One of the first Peruvian cartels to have been identified was that of the five Cachique Rivera brothers from the town of Tingo María. Their organization is active in Amazon localities such as Palmapampa, Pichis Palcazu, Pucallpa, Aguayta, and Zorillos and in major coastal cities such as Trujillo, Lima, and Ica. The Cachique brothers are warned in advance every time the DEA and the Peruvian police launch an operation against them.

Other organizations followed the same path. Police seized 3.343 tons of cocaine hydrochloride on January 11, 1995, in Piura, in northern Peru. The drugs belonged to the firm dubbed by the press Los Norteños (the Northerners), headed by the López Paredes brothers. The brothers had parted ways with the Medellin cartel following Pablo Escobar's death. Instead of supplying cocaine base to Colombian partners, the López Paredes brothers set up their own hydrochloride export network. To do so, they forged links with the Mexican cartel led by the Quintero Payán family of Guadalajara and with other international organized crime groups such as the Japanese *yakuza*. Japanese police in fact assisted in the Peruvian operation against Los Norteños.

The Peruvian firms are more nationalistic and recycle more of their money in their own country than do organizations linked to the Colombians. Estimates of the money generated by the drug trade in Peru vary widely. Average figures hover between US$700 million and $1 billion, or 20 to 30 percent of legal Peruvian exports. The flow of drug money thus has a definite impact on the country's economic situation.

The interest on Peru's external debt—Peru owes a total of US$20 billion—amounted to $60 million per month in 1994. Despite this difficulty and a deficit of the balance of payments, Peru's reserves of foreign currency reached an all-time high of $5 billion in December 1994. There are two explanations for such a favorable situation. The first is that President Fujimori gained the confidence of multilateral lenders (the International Monetary Fund declared Peru to be eligible for loans in March 1993) and that capital is coming back to the country. The second is the presence of narco-dollars. Every week, some private banks send small planes to the Amazon towns to bring back narco-dollars. Hence, part of the foreign currency purchased by the central bank is drug money. The economics minister declared in November 1994 that the government had received $800 million from the parallel economy in 1994. Most pundits agree that narco-dollars have contributed to the success of the stabilization and privatization program of the Fujimori government. The significance of drug trafficking for the Peruvian economy thus carries serious political implications.

Soldiers Against the Army

A series of recent events provided confirmation of the information published by the OGD as early as April 1994,[3] describing in particular how the military had temporarily "regrouped" fifteen trafficking organizations so that taxes paid to the guerrillas of the Shining Path now fall into the soldiers' pockets. At the end of December 1994, more than 100 soldiers, most of them officers, were indicted on charges of, or convicted of, complicity with drug traffickers. A number of high-ranking officers, whom President Alberto Fujimori (then running for a second term) forced to retire following their demands for "the moralization of the military institution," think that those officers chiefly responsible for the army's involvement in drugs have been left unmolested.

3. See *État des drogues, drogues des États,* op. cit., p. 186.

Most corruption cases have been taking place in the central Huallaga region since 1992. Following the declarations of a trafficker called "Vaticano," the accusations of Captains Alan López Tang, Ricardo Falconí, and Major Evaristo Castillo, Captain Gilmar Valdivieso Rejas provided one of the most detailed testimonies to an investigating committee of the Peruvian Parliament on October 31. Valdivieso's testimony confirmed that the former commander in chief of the area of guerrilla activity in Huallaga, Eduardo Bellido Mora—now a military attaché in Israel—provided cover for "operations" such as the assassination in Balsayacu of a group of traffickers by a military patrol in order to grab a load of cocaine base. The commander of the army, General Nicolás de Bari Hermoza Ríos, refused to allow General Bellido to appear before the courts, or even to testify to the judge investigating the charges of drug trafficking against his predecessor on the Huallaga front, General Jaime Araicos. This led a *Caretas* magazine columnist to write that "what is happening in Huallaga has assumed such proportions that it would be incredible if the High Command were not aware of it. If the High Command lets corruption bloom, it must have had good reasons to do so." On January 19, 1995, General Araicos was found guilty of drug trafficking by a civilian judge in Lima. The same judge had once more requested the testimony of General Bellido.

Captain Valdivieso, an officer in the Special Commando Company of Anti-Subversive Battalion No. 26 at Tocache, told how on April 5, 1993, he captured a Shining Path collaborator, "Chatín," in possession of 200 kilograms of cocaine base. "Chatín" was also responsible for the chainsaw murder of an army captain. He was nevertheless released by Captain Manuel Olguín Luna, head of the Bambamarca military base, against payment of US$80,000. The drugs were also returned to "Chatín" for $100,000, along with some AKM rifles, a generator, and two solar panels. Yet the case was hushed up thanks to the intervention of Captain Olguín's sister, secretary to the army's inspector general, General Máximo Bracamonte. The commander of Battalion No. 26, Lieutenant-Colonel Miguel Nájar Acosta, has himself facilitated—for $40,000—the release of a Shining Path leader, Elder John Soto Chávez, nicknamed "Wilson," who was responsible for about forty murders of police officers and civilians. Commander Nájar also collected $2,000 for every 100-kilogram load of cocaine base passing along the rivers and roads close to the military bases of the central Huallaga region—Punto Pizana, Sion, Punta Arenas, and Uchiza. Every Colombian plane picking up drugs had to pay $10,000.

In 1992, Lieutenant-Colonel Luis Aparicio Manrique had the engineers of the Upper Huallaga Special Project (PEAH) in Cañuto build a clandestine landing strip 800 meters long and 50 meters wide. The strip, used exclusively by narcos, was located just one mile away from the military base. Captain Flores Huamani, alias "Viking," assigned to the Bellavista base, was organizing his own drug shipments to Colombia. Military sources close to the joint chiefs of staff confirmed these accusations to the conservative daily *El Comercio*. According to these sources, in June 1994 the military command was forced to forbid the use of helicopters during "secret operations" because they were used to fly cocaine by, among others, Commander Arias Córdova, alias "Chuck Norris."

Cocaine Funds the Military

Because of all this, most Peruvian army officers actively seek an assignment in Huallaga. Because this costs $2,000, an amount beyond the reach of most officers, candidates gang up in groups of ten, each contributing $200. A draw is made, the lucky winner pledges to pay each of his companions at least $1,000 in the future, and the officers who are not directly involved in the trade thereby become accomplices. The army inspectors and officers on the ground who oppose or denounce such practices are systematically assigned to other areas by the High Command. As for Captain Valdivieso, who has gone underground, he is being sued by the army for "insult to his superiors, disobedience, abuse of authority, and false testimony." Three of the main witnesses who could have supported his accusations have been murdered. The retired commander in chief of a military region revealed to the OGD special envoy that an army commando has received orders to eliminate Valdivieso. Major Evaristo Castillo, also under death threats, has taken refuge in Spain, and Captain Falconí is also abroad.

It took the virus of narco-corruption about ten years to infect the whole of the army. A former commander in chief in Huallaga says that the first clues to collusion with the narcos came one year before the army officially intervened against the Shining Path on August 16, 1984. One of the causes of the progressive deterioration was that the officers' allowance was not enough to feed their troops. They first allowed the narcos to pay for the men's food, feeling little remorse since, until 1991, the army was not in charge of the antidrug fight—that was the police's job—and concentrated on the struggle against the guerrillas.

The situation got worse with the rise to power of Alberto Fujimori in 1990 and deteriorated further after his April 1992 coup. Fujimori, whose main institutional support is the armed forces, has exercised a prerogative his predecessors left to the military: the promotion of officers. In reality, Fujimori leaves it up to the man who is the de facto head of the army's secret service (SIN), former CIA officer Vladimiro Montesinos. Montesinos's résumé was published by journalist Gustavo Gorriti in the monthly *CovertAction* in the United States and Caretas in Peru. Following his expulsion from the military in 1977, Montesinos studied law and became the Colombian and Peruvian drug traffickers' favorite lawyer. Not content with defending them in court, he helped narcos escape or "arranged" the disappearance of their files. In particular, he managed to exculpate a group of high-ranking police officers protecting godfather Reynaldo Rodríguez López, who was arrested in 1985. Little wonder, then, that in 1989 it was no big deal for him to "arrange" the vanishing of the files regarding the suspect real estate operations of a then presidential hopeful—Alberto Fujimori. Certain observers, like the writers of the Christian Democrat review *Oiga,* think that the constitutional coup of April 1992, in which Montesinos had a critically important role, was undertaken with the ulterior motive of erasing all traces of army involvement in drug trafficking and human rights violations. Between April 5 and 10, army commandos removed about one-third of the files concerning current cases that were stored in the Palace of Justice and the Office of the Attorney of the Nation. Vladimiro Montesinos was also involved in two recent massacres of civilians carried out by military commandos.

Political Stakes

There is every reason to believe that Fujimori has ensured staunch military backing by letting officers cash in on the profits of the trade in cocaine base, of which Peru is the world's biggest producer. Certainly, the armed forces were prepared to do anything to ensure that Fujimori would be reelected in April 1995. This situation has led the *Caretas* columnist to portray Peru in terms similar to the notion of a "narco-state" advanced in last year's OGD annual report: "A country's situation gets more complicated when the drug trade manages to corrupt a major sector of the armed forces while they hold a decisive part of political power." It is likely, for instance, that the army will avoid exterminating the remaining Shining Path militants operating in Huallaga in order to justify its continued presence in what it sees as a real-life Eldorado.

Indeed, the guerrilla's units were hard hit on two occasions. First came the call for "pacification" made from jail by Abimael Guzmán, the traditional leader of the Shining Path, which resulted in the surrender of some 4,500 Shining Path "sympathizers." Next came a series of attacks launched against the guerrillas between April and August 1994. It seems that some guerrillas are nonetheless still active and that they have redeployed in other areas of the Amazon, where they are probably trying to reestablish the links with the traffickers severed by the military in the former Shining Path preserve of the Huallaga Valley. Seized documents and the confessions of former guerrillas shed light on the role drugs played in funding the Shining Path. On the one hand, the tax on the drug trade was truly established only in 1986–87, after the Maoist guerrillas' return to a region from which they had been partially expelled by the military and the Tupac Amaru Revolutionary Movement (MRTA) in 1984–85. On the other hand, the revenue from the tax was not as great as has sometimes been claimed, amounting at best to between US$8 million and $10 million per year. This money was essentially used to pay for facilities within Peru—houses, cars, infrastructure, lawyers' fees, and so on. However, the Shining Path sometimes took weapons as payment from the Colombian traffickers. Although it has been considerably weakened, the Shining Path still retains a capacity for harm—an ambush against a military convoy in Pucallpa on December 15, 1994, left twenty soldiers dead and fifteen wounded.

The dismantling of Los Norteños ended in an unexpected way. First, it was learned on January 18, 1995, that the diary of one of the arrested traffickers, José Luis Mandiola, contained the telephone numbers of numerous important figures. Among them was General Manuel Ortiz Lucero, Mandiola's cousin and the former commander of the domestic front, with special responsibility for counternarcotics and countersubversion. Deputy Minister of the Interior Edgar Solis Cano, a member of the joint chiefs of staff also in charge of counternarcotics, met with the traffickers on several occasions. And to top it all, General Enrique Torrico, chief of the fifth military region (that of Iquitos in the Amazon), is the godfather of the son of Los Norteños boss Manuel López Paredes.

The conflict with Ecuador came as a timely diversion from a scandal that could have destabilized President Fujimori, then seeking reelection.

Colombia

The "absence" of Pablo Escobar from the drug-trafficking scene in 1994 did more than arouse the legitimate hope of an end to a state of bloody internal war; it also liberated the political class, and Colombian society at large, from inhibitions regarding drug money, which is now only the fruit of a reputedly nonviolent, and therefore "acceptable," drug traffic. Today, every clue points to a deeper infiltration by the narcos, those from Cali in particular, into every level of Colombian politics and economics. At the same time, areas under coca cultivation grew by close to 50 percent between 1992 and 1994. The culprits are the narcos, obviously, yet also the Revolutionary Armed Forces of Colombia (FARC) guerrilla movement, which found defending growers against eradication campaigns particularly rewarding in terms of popular support.

From Narco-Economics to Narco-Politics

In Colombia the interests of domestic traffickers, who for fifteen years have been accumulating enormous amounts of money, and those of the local bourgeoisie and its representatives within the state have become increasingly intermeshed. Since the death of Pablo Escobar and the subsequent "peaceful" atmosphere prevailing on the antidrug front, more drug money—several billion dollars in 1994—has been repatriated into Colombia from abroad. Despite a drop in exports and a dramatic rise in imports, Colombia's gross domestic product is growing to the tune of 5 percent annually. Traffickers not only own 3 million hectares (7.2 million acres) of the best land but also entire sectors of economic activity, such as the construction, tourism, telecommunications, and pharmaceutical industries. In November 1994 a Miami court indicted Raúl Grajales, the owner of a major canned fruit company based in Cali. Little by little, the entire Colombian economy is coming directly or indirectly under the influence of narco-dollars, which are no doubt the principal explanation for the growth recorded in the last few years.

In a recent report,[4] the DEA analyzed the impact of the liberal poli-

4. See *Colombian Economic Reform: The Impact of Drug Money Laundering Within the Colombian Economy* (DEA-94072), September 1994.

cies implemented since 1990 (called the "opening" policy in Colombia) on the recycling of drug money. The report emphasized several key factors that favor laundering: the privatization of major banks; the fact that the foreign currency market is managed by private institutions; the modernization of the banking and telecommunications systems, allowing Colombia to be directly connected to the international financial system; the privatization of ports, hitherto under state control; and the creation of duty-free zones of economic activity throughout the country. Notwithstanding, instead of learning from its analysis by questioning the ultraliberal policies imposed on Colombia by the Bretton Woods institutions (within which the United States wields much power) the DEA concluded that only strict implementation of the antilaundering legislation will keep Colombia from being "the first country to become dependent on the drug trafficking industry."

The narcos' economic weight is felt first and foremost at the local level. In Pereira, Tulua, La Dorada, and many other Colombian towns and provinces, the October 30, 1994, mayoral and gubernatorial elections sparked intimidation and corruption maneuvers by trafficking organizations, for whom local and regional authorities are inevitable targets. Meanwhile, the Colombian Parliament has witnessed several attempts to pass what the press has dubbed "the narco-project"—a legislative package that would have prevented the seizure of property belonging to drug traffickers when this property was registered in the name of a third person. It would also have put an end to the use of "faceless judges" in drug-related trials and investigations. Despite its earlier approval by a special commission by 13 votes to 9, the plan was finally dropped by the Colombian Congress on November 30, 1994. According to some legislators, the "narco-project" has been only temporarily put aside, and not because of its substance but because of disagreement on its exact wording. It could reemerge in the future.

The Narco-Tapes Affair

Forty-eight hours after the victory of the Samper-La Calle Liberal ticket in the presidential election, the Colombian media broadcast extracts from recordings of telephone conversations between the Rodríguez Orejuela brothers, the Cali cartel bosses, and journalist Alberto Giraldo, the traffickers' reputed middleman in political and economic circles. The tapes were transmitted to then President César Gaviria by Andrés Pastrana, the Conservative candidate who finally lost the election. The content of the tapes, which was authenticated by the Colombian authorities themselves, clearly demonstrates that the Rodríguez brothers had maintained repeated contacts through Giraldo with the various presidential candidates or their campaign managers in order to contribute money to their campaigns. The crucial fact—which no one involved has ever denied—is that campaign managers had meetings (at least twice as far as Samper is concerned) with the narcos' spokesperson—and that nobody seems to mind. This sort of meeting is thus considered "natural." General Maza Márquez, the former chief of the Departamento Administrativo de Seguridad (DAS), a Colombian intelligence service, who withdrew in the second round of the presidential election in favor of Samper, ingenuously provided a key to the attitude of "upright men" vis-à-vis the Rodríguez Orejuela brothers in a statement to the weekly *Semana,* which asked about his name cropping up in the recordings: "I received several calls inviting me to talks with Dr. Samper. I agreed to go to the address I was given. There, I found Dr. Samper, Dr. De La Calle, and Dr. Botero... I learned later that it was the house of journalist Giraldo, and for me it was natural because he was a journalist." Now, can a former head of intelligence be unaware of what everyone knows in Colombia—that Giraldo is the public relations officer and middleman for the Rodríguez Orejuelas?

Before any inquiry into the links between the narcos and the campaign managers, the attorney general's office had made it clear that the tapes, authenticated though they they might be, could not be presented as valid evidence under Colombian law. As for Giraldo, after disappearing for a while, he popped up in Bogota to organize nothing less than an exclusive interview with the Rodríguez brothers for *Time* magazine. In the final analysis, Colombia is a country where the heads of criminal organizations are perfectly well known (their telephones are bugged, discussions can be held with them at any time—even concerning money—through lawyers or journalists like Giraldo) but where they carry on living in total impunity.

In such an atmosphere, all U.S. initiatives aimed at convincing the Colombian authorities of the necessity to redirect their "joint forces" against the Cali cartel were doomed to failure—all the more so since they were belated and clumsy. Apart from the alleged role of U.S. agencies in publicizing the narco-tapes, the latest evidence of U.S. diplomatic failure in Colombia came on September 29, 1994. Joseph Toft, the former director of the DEA in Colombia during the six years of bloody war against Pablo Escobar and the Medellin cartel, stated on the day he left his post that indisputable evidence that the Cali cartel had financed Ernesto Samper's electoral campaign. Toft concluded his interview on Colombian television with a detailed indictment of the Colombian regime, which he called a "narco-democracy." Such "revelations" coming from one private individual, but too feebly denied by his former immediate superiors not to betray some form of encouragement, left the impression of a last-ditch effort. The consequences of this "kamikaze" attack were as counterproductive as possible. Toft's words raised a general outcry in the Colombian establishment against a "foreign plot" aimed at tearing the country's prestige to shreds; the DEA presence in Colombia was questioned, lawsuits were threatened, and so on. Washington is now striving to restore the pieces of a diplomacy currently reduced to economic blackmail. Meanwhile, the Samper administration can afford the luxury of laying the blame for the drug trade on the United States, a drug-consuming country led by a president, as Samper is fond of reminding everybody, who himself smoked marijuana, and where the recently reelected mayor of the federal capital, Marion Barry, was caught smoking crack.

Finally, any change in the judicial authorities' attitude toward policies that favor the narcos is immediately followed by a warning. Thus, the personal involvement of the new attorney general Alfonso Valdivieso in blocking the narco-project in Parliament, together with his statements in favor of giving a new lease of life to extradition—a procedure now forbidden by the Colombian constitution—earned him two death threats in a row.

Diversified Outputs

The U.S. market has experienced a rise in heroin consumption and stabilization in the use of cocaine hydrochloride (the fall in the number of consumers has been offset by an increase in the quantities consumed) and crack. The Colombian cartels seem to have anticipated this development; after experimenting with poppy growing for at least ten years, the narcos launched large-scale poppy cultivation in 1990–91 (see Map 11). Poppy crops, which are substantially under the control of members of the Pereira cartel—an affiliate of the Cali cartel—are located mainly

Map 11. Colombia: Coca, Poppies, and Cannabis

in southern and central Colombia, although they have recently expanded into the northeast (in the Cesar and La Guajira regions). The average yield of the estimated 20,000 hectares under poppy cultivation is relatively low: 6 to 8 kilograms of opium per hectare. Estimated annual opium production hovers between 120 and 160 tons, or 12 to 16 tons of heroin. Ten heroin laboratories were detected in Colombia in 1994. Furthermore, DEA spokesperson Ila Brown indicated that 232 Colombian heroin smugglers were arrested in the United States in 1993. Each had swallowed about 800 grams of the drug distributed in several plastic bags (136 kilograms in total, or 13.6 percent of heroin seizures in the United States). For a successful delivery in the United States, a smuggler gets US$3,000. However, the data currently available suggest that because of the poor quality of Colombian heroin, it cannot compete with the No. 4 brand of the drug from the Golden Triangle, which still dominates the U.S. market (68 percent of seizures). The Colombians also cater to the market's new trends: heroin used as a complement to crack and above all, as a consequence of the AIDS epidemic, a strong demand for noninjectable heroin (instead snorted or smoked) of admittedly higher purity but sold at a price equivalent to that of the (far less pure) injectable drug. The Colombians use their long-established cocaine-marketing networks to offer mixed drug batches—1 kilogram of heroin for 20 kilograms of cocaine.

Cocaine economics are currently characterized by a paradox. The U.S. market is saturated, while the trend in Colombia is toward maintaining or increasing production levels. This explains why networks in the United States dealing in crack—the substance most in demand—and hydrochloride are implementing a very aggressive marketing strategy. This consists of extending consumption to rural areas; drastically cutting prices (a dose of crack sells for $2 in New York City); and offering new products, such as *geek joints* (a mixture of cocaine and marijuana sold in Atlanta). Furthermore, it was confirmed in 1994 that Colombian cocaine was making a breakthrough in Asia and eastern Europe, especially in Russia.

This explains why the surface area under coca cultivation in Colombia itself jumped in less than two years from 25,000 hectares (60,000 acres) to the 47,887 hectares (115,000 acres) that were officially detected from January to October 1994. According to certain sources in the ministry of agriculture, cultivation may even reach 86,000 hectares (206,000 acres). This phenomenon supports the hypothesis that the narcos' strategy is one of production diversification, not substitution of coca for poppies. The opening up of new markets also explains why coca production remains level in Peru. The spread of coca crops in Colombia probably betrays the narcos' intention to repatriate the production of cocaine-base paste to their homeland. It could also mean—and these explanations are not mutually exclusive—that certain organizations have cashed in on the "normalization" process at work in Colombia since the death of Escobar and the end of large-scale law enforcement operations. Since the risks are similar, traffickers may have decided to increase their autonomy and shorten the production process while reducing their logistics costs. One example is to bypass the "protection" of Peruvian military officials, who often prove to be too greedy, or Peruvian "firms" that have run out of control.

The Guerrillas Against Eradication

A second explanation for the rise and diversification of drug production in Colombia could be the strategy of the FARC guerrillas. Although they have given up hope of one day taking over the Colombian state, the guerrillas are no longer content with extracting a 15 to 20 percent tax on the base paste produced in the areas under their control. Since it has become the owner of thousands of hectares of land, the FARC has decided to grow coca or poppies and to sell the output to the narcos. South of the Guaviare River, the FARC has set up refining laboratories near the coca fields. At the end of 1994, 1 kilogram of cocaine-base paste brought around US$1,000, while 1 kilogram of hydrochloride (obtained from 1.3 kilograms of cocaine-base paste) sold for $2,000. The FARC's policy accepts the increased participation of growers in the cocaine-manufacturing process. Ten years ago, growers switched from the mere growing of coca bushes to the the more elaborate production of cocaine-base paste. These days, they have started manufacturing cocaine hydrochloride (*perico*), which they sell to the narcos. This development marks a greater diversification of risk. Farmers manage to divert small quantities of chemical reagents destined for local industries for their own use. As a result, in the Puerto Alvira region, chemical products are diverted from a Coca-Cola factory by some of its employees. Traffickers no longer need to worry about finding large quantities of chemical reagents, which recent international legislation has made it difficult to obtain. Nor are they burdened with the responsibility of operating refining laboratories.

The events that took place from mid-November 1994 until the end of the year in the Amazon regions of Guaviare and Putumayo, where the government undertook a gliphosate-spraying campaign on coca crops, shed light on both the strategies of the various players and the importance of what is at stake. In Guaviare, at least 25,000 hectares (60,000 acres) are planted with coca, yielding about 150 tons of base paste every year. The aerial spraying set off an intense protest movement among the population, highlighted by strikes and protest marches supported by the FARC. On November 12, Colonel Leonardo Gallego, the head of the police antidrug unit, fell into a guerrilla ambush and had to battle for three days before he could escape the area. An accord was eventually worked out, with government authorities agreeing not to use the gliphosate on coca crops covering less than 3 hectares (7 acres). Observers believe that it will not be hard for the narcos, who have purchased large tracts of land and often grow over 40 hectares (96 acres) in coca, to circumvent the agreement, for example by dividing large landholdings among the owner's employees. The same goes for the FARC, which will have no problem sharing its holdings among third parties.

Three weeks after the agreement was reached in Guaviare, a similar protest took place in Putumayo, another coca-growing region, where growers occupied five oil production plants. In response to the criticisms arising out of the Guaviare accord, the government reacted strongly and entrusted negotiations to the commander of the army. The agreement putting an end to the growers' movement was reached on January 12, 1995. Under it, all crops are to be eradicated (manually for those under 2 hectares) in exchange for a comprehensive development program for the region, which is one of those most lacking in infrastructure in Colombia.

Brazil

By far the most notable development in the Brazilian fight against drugs was the military intervention in the slums of Rio at the end of 1994, which diverted attention away from several problems. Brazil is a large-scale producer of marijuana for domestic consumption. The country also plays a key role in the passage of Bolivian and Colombian cocaine destined for the United States and Europe (7.5 tons were seized in just one operation in 1994). In addition, Brazil is the main supplier of precursor chemicals to the Andean countries, in its capacity either as a producer or a point of transit. Finally, it has become a refuge for the godfathers of international criminal organizations specializing in the drug trade. As for Operation Rio, in which fighting drugs was probably not the sole objective, it might have serious political consequences.

War in the Favelas

One of the problems that the new president, Henrique Cardoso, has been endeavoring to solve since he came to power on January 1, 1995, surfaced dramatically two months earlier. In early November 1994, the army began going through Rio's main *favelas* with a fine-toothed comb. The intervention occurred after several months of negotiations with the state governor, aimed at preventing the situation from deteriorating and forcing him to take steps that would put Rio State under direct federal control—a measure even more constraining than the military operation. The notoriously corrupt police had become an added factor conducive to disorder. The justification given for the military action in the slums was the war raging between the main local gangs of drug traffickers, including *Comando Vermelho* (red commando). The gangs' use of modern weapons from military barracks, coupled with the fact that they hoisted a Brazilian flag and forced shops to close as a show of grief when a trafficker died, illustrated the city's ungovernability. The narcos often warned the media of certain operations in advance and got plenty of interviews.

But crime was not the only motive for the intervention. For instance, statistics published in early 1995 show that the number of violent deaths is even higher in Sao Paulo. Rio de Janeiro's governor, Leonel Brizola, who also ran in the October 1994 presidential election, was accused—apparently not without reason—of favoring narcotics trafficking in exchange for receiving dirty money for his electoral campaign. Only after he left his post to concentrate on his campaign could negotiations between the federal government, the state government, the army, and the police begin. The new governor, Nilo Batista (a former police minister), though even more involved with the narcos than his predecessor, had to accept the army's intervention. Most officers thought that this type of operation should remain the preserve of the police, but those who finally won the day insisted that the narcos' use of military weapons and of the Brazilian flag threatened national sovereignty—as did, in a more general way, the loss of control over a portion of the national territory. Finally, a compromise was arrived at: The intervention would be swift, limited, and would not involve the occupation of the *favelas.*

In terms of results, the Brazilian army has little to show for its intervention, which was still going on in early 1995. In counternarcotics terms, the effect was certainly dismal. The number of arrests and seizures of narcotics and weapons, affecting merely minor local traffickers, was disappointing. One of the most significant arrests was that of Carlos Alberto da Costa Moreira, found in possession of 10 kilograms of cocaine destined for Luxembourg. The narco recruited personnel of the air carrier Varig in order to send drugs to Italian mafia families. In the most spectacular seizure, carried out in the Parada de Lucas slum during the weekend of January 7–8, 1,000 marines confiscated 91.5 kilograms of cocaine, 292 kilograms of marijuana, and 200 grams of hashish. These amount to real stockpiles, which had been collected ready for the carnival, and represent five times the total of drugs seized in all prior operations.

What else was to be expected of an operation so widely publicized in advance? Numerous barons had taken refuge in neighboring countries, particularly Peru, and sometimes even as far away as Europe and the United States. By contrast, once the soldiers entered the *favelas* with the excuse of fighting traffickers, they established themselves there, and they now coordinate police operations. Although they were supposed to withdraw by the end of 1994, they seem in no hurry to leave. Their continued presence presented an early challenge to the government, which was forced to prolong the intervention until early January 1995. It must also be noted that while numerous intellectuals opposed the military operations and the brutality to which they sometimes gave rise, the majority of Rio's inhabitants still support the intervention. Moreover, the military announced in early January 1995 that it was also going to investigate death squads, which are known to be made up of serving and retired policemen. It is estimated that the death squads have killed 12,000 people, including many street children, throughout Brazil during the last five years. The military decision followed countless anonymous phone calls about extermination groups active in the Baixada Fluminense, a vast neighborhood in northern Rio. The army's willingness to appear as the spearhead of the fight against crime can only undermine the new government by capturing a share of its legitimacy.

The war on drugs in the *favelas* also serves to obscure the fact that slums are not the only places for drug trafficking and consumption. Massive quantities of cocaine hydrochloride are consumed in places of recreation and in well-off circles. Millions of Brazilians smoke marijuana, whose use has long been commonplace. In late November 1994, an official from the Chamber of Deputies was found to be involved in an LSD network. LSD is imported from the Netherlands and has been sold for two years in fashion shops for teenagers in Brasilia, the federal capital. LSD is also used during parties in the Lago Sur residential area.

The Challenge of Organized Crime

Another challenge awaits the president: Brazil's role in the international drug trade. During the Conference on Organized Crime sponsored by the UNDCP in Naples in November 1994, where representatives from 140 countries gathered, Brazil was accused of being a hub for international trafficking in cocaine and precursor chemicals. The Italian Ministry of Justice revealed that the four Italian criminal organizations, the Cosa Nostra, the Camorra, the 'Ndranghetta, and the Sacra Corona Unita had abandoned their former fiefdoms in Peru, Venezuela, Argentina, Colombia, Bolivia, and Uruguay in order to set up shop in Brazil. The Brazilian drug squad then acknowledged that twenty-three international networks were operating within its borders—North Americans, Italians, Israelis, Nigerians, Japanese (*yakuza*), Chinese (triads), and so on. But all these international traffickers are relying on Brazilian organizations, some of which have acquired enough power to deserve the name "cartels." For instance, according to a study by the police, there is a cartel in Mato Grosso, a state bordering on Bolivia and Paraguay, which was set up by former smugglers in legal goods who switched to drugs as a more lucrative undertaking. The Mato Grosso cartel's boss, Fahd Jamil Jorge, is among Brazil's richest and most powerful traffickers. His cocaine supplies come mainly from Pedro Juan Caballero, a Paraguayan town from which the drugs are exported to the international market. Cocaine is often paid for with cars that have been stolen in Rio de Janeiro and Sao Paulo. Brazil is also the main producer of chemical reagents (ether, acetone, hydrochloric acid) destined for the cocaine-refining facilities of Bolivia, Colombia, and Peru. Despite operations carried out in 1993 and 1994 by the Brazilian police, with support from the DEA, against domestic and foreign firms that divert part of their stocks of chemicals to traffickers, there has been no notable improvement in the situation.

A new development in 1994 was the designation of Sao Paulo by various international antidrug institutions as Brazil's most significant center for the drug trade and related laundering activities. While local authorities recognized that major international criminal organizations, notably from Colombia, were already established in the city, the DEA estimated that currently US$5 billion are laundered in Brazil annually, mainly in Sao Paulo.

On January 14, 1995, the Brazilian government announced that the United States, which had been supporting Brazil's antidrug fight for ten years and had contributed a total of $11.7 million during that period, had decided in late 1994 to terminate its antidrug aid to Brazil. According to the U.S. Department of State, the decision was made because "the United States is disappointed by the lack of 'political will' of the Brazilian government to act against drug trafficking and corruption."

Paraguay

Thirty-six years of institutionalized corruption under the dictatorship of General Alfredo Stroessner turned Paraguay into a hub for all kinds of illegal trade. The government of President Juan Carlos Wasmosy, which was elected on May 9, 1993, is powerless in this regard, particularly as the military, which still wields much power in Paraguay, is itself involved in drug trafficking. The penetration of Brazilian organized crime into Paraguay has gone deeper since Operation Rio. Although cannabis is grown in Paraguay—Paraguayan pot is greatly appreciated in Brazil—the country is above all a hub for cocaine trafficking. The cocaine trade can rely on the networks and routes set up for the trade in stolen cars and contraband cigarettes and electronic goods. Coming from Bolivia on small planes, the cocaine travels by road to ports in Brazil and Argentina. In 1994, a spectacular case confirmed the deep involvement of Paraguayan institutions, especially the police and armed forces, in the drug trade.

A Two-Tiered Murder

General Ramón Rosa Rodríguez, the director of Paraguay's National Anti-Drug Service (SENAD) was murdered in the center of Asunción on Monday, October 10, 1994. Although the authorities have not seen fit to clarify the circumstances of the assassination, testimony provided by a series of witnesses enabled the press to work out what happened. In the morning, General Rosa Rodríguez's car was machine-gunned by two unknown men in another vehicle. Superficially wounded, he alerted SENAD's headquarters, and his assistant, Captain Juan Ruiz Díaz, was sent to the scene. Captain Ruiz helped his superior to the car that was to drive him to the hospital. During the drive, the two men "exchanged gunfire," and Rosa Rodríguez arrived dead at the hospital.

The SENAD director was investigating a case that began with the arrest of a civilian pilot, Carlos Amado Recalde, who was apprehended in September after his plane, carrying 343 kilograms of cocaine, had landed in the village of Parque Cué, in the Paraguayan Chaco. The pilot has always maintained that his sponsors were the former president of Paraguay, General Andrés Rodríguez, and the former SENAD director, General Marcial Samaniego. In their defense, both men replied that the cocaine was in fact destined for a "sell and bust" operation being conducted jointly with the DEA. Following the murder of General Rosa, member of Parliament Francisco José Rodríguez asked the U.S. Embassy for clarification. Although it had thus far refused to provide any, the embassy issued a communiqué stating that the DEA does not engage in any operation on Paraguayan territory and that "the DEA has no police powers, its role is limited to providing technical assistance to its Paraguayan counterparts." The first results to emerge from the inquiry into Rosa's death revealed that the van used in the morning attack belonged to SENAD and that the "alleged" perpetrator of the fatal shooting, Captain Ruiz Díaz, led the military police unit that seized the cocaine at Parque Cué. Observers are now wondering whether the head of SENAD was shot because of his investigation into the involvement of the former president, General Andrés Rodríguez, and the leading role the military plays in drug trafficking or whether, involved himself, he was the victim of a settling of accounts within the antinarcotics services, which are known to be thoroughly infiltrated by traffickers.

During his trial, Captain Juan Ruiz Díaz maintained that his superior was killed by a man who had thrown himself inside the car. He also contended that the murder of Rosa was organized by military personnel, politicians, and smugglers whom Rosa was investigating and who were known within the brigade by the code name "Ten for Two." Allegedly included in this group was the "Turks cartel." Turks is the name given to

Paraguayan nationals of Syrian and Lebanese descent. One of the cartel members is Carlos Barreto, governor of Paraguay's Upper Parana department. The cartel was allegedly under the protection of General Roosevelt Benítez, chief of staff of the armed forces, and Oscar Rodrigo and Santiago Zaracho, commanders of the First and Second Army Corps, respectively. Juan Ruiz Díaz has also accused the "navy cartel," headed by Vice Admiral Eduardo González Petit, of involvement in the assassination. González is head of Paraguay's entire armed forces. Captain Ruiz also mentioned another mini-cartel, operating on the border separating Paraguay and Brazil. This group is headed by a businessman linked to former dictator Stroessner, Fadh Yamil, and is believed to control dozens of aircraft landing strips.

10. *North America*

Mexico continues to be the main transit country used by the Latin American cartels to smuggle cocaine into the United States. One novel trend is that land and sea routes are taking over from air routes as the preferred smuggling method. The events that took place in Mexico in 1994 help to explain, at least in part, why cocaine seizures have dropped from 46 metric tons in 1993 to a mere 11 tons in 1994, although the DEA estimates that the flow of cocaine into the United States is not drying up. In early February 1995, 2.4 tons of ephedrine from India were seized in Mexico City. Growing Mexican involvement in dealing on U.S. streets has also been observed. However, the Mexican dealers do not specialize in only one drug. Indeed, each year Mexico produces about 5 tons of heroin (of which 300 kilograms were seized in 1994) and 6,000 tons of marijuana (365 tons seized). U.S. drug policy south of the Rio Grande is ineffectual. Every effort by the United States to pressure Mexican officials to act against traffickers is countered by the powerful interest groups linked to the narcos.

The United States[1]

Ever since the Republicans won a majority in both houses of Congress in the November 1994 elections, the White House has been scrambling to redefine and repackage administration policies in anticipation of battles to come. For President Clinton's antidrug strategists, the new political landscape undoubtedly means a return to hawkish policies reminiscent of Reagan's and Bush's "war on drugs." And almost certainly, drug czar Lee Brown, director of the Office of National Drug Control Policy (ONDCP), will now have to preside over the dismantling of his modest plan to redirect some funds from interdiction and enforcement programs and into treatment and prevention programs.

Conservative Onslaught

Recent changes in the chairs of congressional committees are an indication of the likely direction of future U.S. drug policy. Control of the powerful Senate Judiciary Committee, for example, went to Orrin Hatch, an ultraconservative senator from Utah and a fierce critic of the Clinton administration's drug strategy. In a hearing held before the committee last October, he railed at the drug czar's "reckless abdication" of interdiction and enforcement policies, and declared that "under President Clinton's leadership, we are losing ground" in the war on drugs.

Among the House committees likely to influence the future of U.S. drug control is the House Foreign Affairs Committee, which reviews all foreign aid programs and U.S. operations overseas. Congressman Benjamin A. Gilman of New York, formerly the ranking minority member of the House Select Committee on Narcotics, has an extensive background in drug control and is another outspoken critic of Clinton's policies. When the White House released its first strategy in February 1994, a disgusted Gilman lashed out against the administration's efforts to reduce interdiction in favor of increased treatment and prevention programs, claiming that the move was an "invitation to the drug cartels to expand their drug shipments to the United States." After being installed as the committee chair in November 1994, Gilman made clear his interest in revisiting the drug issue, promising during a press conference that his committee would pay "particular attention to combating international narcotics trafficking."

1. Canada was reviewed in the OGD 1994 report, *État des drogues, drogues des États*, op. cit.

The most immediate effect of the Republican victory may be felt domestically, however. Last fall, the Clinton administration managed to pass a crime bill only after a nasty bipartisan struggle that left many conservative lawmakers disgruntled. The Republicans find fault with two areas of the new law: first, the vastly increased authority of Brown's ONDCP; and second, the money the bill allocates for drug prevention programs.

Strengthening the ONDCP

Congress created the ONDCP in 1988 over the objections of a Republican administration. In 1994 Clinton surprised ONDCP critics by expanding the office's responsibilities to include oversight of all federal agency drug policy budgets and staffs. Brown now has the authority to provide budget recommendations to other agencies in support of strategies developed by his office, and to request agencies to reassign their personnel temporarily to other departments in need of additional staff. The implications of the drug czar's expanded mandate is that more traditional counternarcotics agencies, such as the DEA or U.S. Customs Service, are now obliged to confer closely with the ONDCP when formulating their policies—a process that grates on many Republicans.

Conservative lawmakers also take issue with the efforts Brown's office has made to date throughout the country to enhance treatment and prevention programs, which are a linchpin of the Clinton antidrug strategy. Even under a Democratic Congress, Brown had trouble finding support; when the administration requested $355 million for additional substance abuse treatment programs in 1993, Congress approved a paltry $57 million. Most Republicans view such initiatives as merely appeasing addicts. In the famous "Contract with America" drafted by House Speaker Newt Gingrich (R-Ga.), a section on crime calls for an "anti-crime package including... effective death penalty provisions and cuts in social spending from this summer's [1994's] Crime Bill to fund prison construction and additional law enforcement to keep people safe in their neighborhoods and kids safe in their schools." The "social spending" includes $29 million for drug courts, which give nonviolent, drug-addicted criminals the option of enrolling in treatment programs or going to jail. The amount is tiny during the first year of funding, but by the year 2000 it will total almost $1 billion, as the bill is currently written. The question now is simply how long it will take new congressional leaders to rewrite the bill.

Change and Continuity

Just as Congress is preparing to toughen federal antinarcotics laws, the ONDCP is beginning to get serious about talking to citizens about drugs at a local level. For the first time since its creation, in 1994 the ONDCP convened a series of conferences across the United States to discuss the drug problem with state and local officials, educators, county administrators, police chiefs, and public interest organizations. The meetings were designed to elicit suggestions for the administration's future drug strategies.

The drug czar's office has been required by law to speak to local groups since it was established in 1988. But this provision was completely neglected during the Reagan and Bush administrations. Now that the White House has decided to elicit solutions from grassroots communities around the country, Congress may face strong resistance to further attempts to federalize policies. Indeed, one of the complaints most frequently heard during congressional and gubernatorial campaigns in the fall of 1994 was that Washington intervened too heavily in local political and economic affairs.

Although Brown has tried to emphasize demand reduction, the Crime Bill passed into law in August 1994 continues to use repression as the preferred means of dealing with crime (as well as increasing the powers of the federal government in this matter). Many of the measures it includes are even tougher than those in force under the previous Republican administrations. Thus, certain mandatory sentences, which give judges no leeway as to their application, were increased and new ones were established. Experts consider mandatory sentences, which have been applied massively since the 1980s, especially in cases involving drugs, responsible for the 140 percent increase in the U.S. prison population since 1980. Today, with 1.3 million people behind bars, nearly 70 percent of them serving time for drug-related offenses (almost three times as many as fifteen years ago), the United States has the highest number of prison inmates of any country in the world. Those paying the heaviest price are minorities, especially blacks. In 1992, according to the latest available statistics, the incarceration rate for black males was 2,678 per 100,000; the corresponding figure for white males was 372 per 100,000. Mostly due to the "war on drugs," there are currently more blacks subjected to some form of judicial control than there are black university students.

It is still unclear how the Republican regime on Capitol Hill will respond to Lee Brown's drug control policies overseas. Under Brown, the ONDCP has aggressively courted cooperation on counternarcotics activities from most of the major source countries. Although cocaine trafficking remains a priority, Clinton's Presidential Decision Directive 14 on narcotics, released in November 1993, charged his agencies with developing a heroin strategy. Indeed, official reports indicate that heroin consumption rose substantially throughout the United States between 1992 and 1993.

An Ambiguous International Policy

Brown addressed the heroin issue in 1993 with trips to Southeast and Southwest Asia for bilateral talks on drug abuse and drug trafficking. His strategy of "constructive engagement" with drug-producing nations took a strange turn, however, when he announced at a press conference in April 1994—after a whirlwind tour of Hong Kong, Singapore, Thailand, Malaysia, Laos, and Japan—that government officials in all the countries he visited had urged him to involve Burma in regional efforts to curtail the narcotics trade. "The message was quite clear," the director told reporters. "If we're going to deal with the problem of opium in Southeast Asia, Burma has to be dealt with as well."

Brown's statements surprised and dismayed U.S. human rights organizations, which have long pressed the Clinton administration to reject expanded relations with the SLORC, a narco-dictatorship with an appalling record of human rights atrocities.

But the drug czar seems determined to remove completely the connection between human rights and his counternarcotics initiative. Brown is even pressuring for increased assistance to Peru, which since 1992 has been barred by Congress from receiving U.S. aid other than antidrug or humanitarian funds due to its dismal human rights record. "We need to do more in Peru and Congress just has to help us," Brown said last fall. "Peru must receive more of our attention and more of our resources. We must find a way to separate our counternarcotics interests in Peru from other foreign policy interests, and pursue counternarcotics on a separate track." In practice, however, the exact opposite has occurred. For if the United States feigns to ignore the fact that Burma and Peru are trafficker-states, it is merely in order to watch over its strategic interests in both countries. Burma has become a spearhead for Chinese expansionism, in particular toward the Indian Ocean; and Peru is a nation where the Shining Path Maoist guerrilla group has yet to be totally wiped out.

While the United States presses for multilateral cooperation on the heroin front, the administration's cocaine strategy is in disarray. A bitter turf battle exploded in May 1994 between the Pentagon and the State Department over Andean operations, after the Pentagon decided unilaterally to shut down its military radar network in Ecuador, Colombia, and Peru. Since 1989, the U.S. Southern Command has used four sophisticated radars to track suspected drug-trafficking planes and relay the intelligence to military counterparts in the Andean countries. When Colombia formally adopted a policy last spring of shooting down aircraft that ignored a command to land, the Pentagon turned off the radars, fearing lawsuits from families of traffickers killed by forces using American-supplied information.

The decision provoked an uproar in both the United States and Latin America. Andean leaders complained of American hypocrisy, while U.S. embassies in the region and State Department officials in Washington openly expressed their anger toward the Pentagon. After several weeks of debate, the administration ordered a resumption of intelligence sharing, but it was not until October that the interagency spat was finally put to rest. In an unusual move, Brown convened a meeting of the top U.S. antidrug officials and the American ambassadors to Colombia, Peru, Ecuador, and Venezuela for two days of closed discussions. After the conference, he acknowledged the lack of a coordinated drug strategy between officials in Washington and those overseas, promising to "personally monitor" the problem in the future.

Finally, as Brown struggles to keep his supply-side cocaine strategy together, he faces tough questioning from members of Congress on his decision to request a "controlled shift" (that is, a very small cut) in interdiction funds for the transit zones. ONDCP designed the reduction last year in order to justify putting new money into prevention programs. The drug czar was also responding to mounting evidence, however, that expensive Pentagon detection and monitoring efforts in Central America and the Caribbean were not working.

In Clinton's first year in office, a Democrat-controlled Senate Judiciary Committee released a report stating plainly that the United States "must accept the reality that the enormous resources poured into the

Pentagon's antidrug budget have produced few results." And in the summer of 1994, the General Accounting Office—using data gathered before the ONDCP's cuts went into effect—declared that "the supply of drugs entering the United States via Central America remains virtually uninterrupted." Despite millions of dollars, the use of sophisticated military aircraft, and a vast radar network, the report said, some 70 tons of cocaine passed through Guatemala alone in the preceding year. Most Republicans are not swayed by the evidence. One congressional staff member told the OGD that "regardless of whether detection and monitoring has been cost-effective, the Republicans love it, and there is a definite possibility that they will try to increase the budget again." If that happens, Lee Brown's drug policy is back to square one, with more funds becoming available for enforcement and supply-side policies and a dwindling budget for the treatment and prevention of drug addiction. Few believe that Brown will be able to garner substantial increases in the programs that he favors the most; when it comes to the demand side of the drug control equation, the Republican Congress is just not in the giving vein. This resistance is rather surprising, given the latest statistics showing that, after declining for thirteen years, the consumption of all drugs is on the way up again.

Mexico

From the armed uprising in Chiapas of New Year's Day 1994 to the humiliating rescue of the Mexico City Stock Exchange by the United States Treasury in January 1995, in twelve months Mexico experienced a chain of events unprecedented since the Institutional Revolutionary Party (PRI) began its exclusive rule over the Mexican state in 1929. Throughout this black year, the power acquired by the drug trade in the country seemed to epitomize, if not accelerate, the general crisis of the Mexican political system.

On March 23, 1994, less than three months after the Zapatist National Liberation Army (EZLN) rose up in arms in the Lacandonia jungle of southern Mexico, Luis Donaldo Colosio, the PRI's official presidential candidate, was murdered at an electoral meeting in Tijuana, a border town and drug-trafficking hub between Mexico and the United States, as well as the fiefdom of the gang of the Arellano Félix brothers. Six months later, on September 28, the PRI number-two man, Secretary General

José Francisco Ruiz Massieu, was in turn shot in a Mexico City street. Between the two events, Ernesto Zedillo, President Salinas de Gortari's nominee to replace Colosio as the PRI candidate, was elected to the presidency by a wide majority. Both political murders, affecting major figures of the ruling party, made the presidential succession—a process normally left entirely in the hands of the outgoing incumbent—a far more complicated matter than usual. And in both cases, through rumors and denials, the question of the drug cartels' involvement was raised.

A very peculiar event, at least one that was completely unprecedented in Mexico, was the issuing, just four days after the murder of Francisco Ruiz Massieu, of a press release signed by "Latin America's most powerful drug cartel." There was no other indication of exactly which cartel it was. The communiqué implicitly claimed responsibility for the Colosio and Ruiz Massieu assassinations and threatened to murder more people if the authorities did not end their "campaign against us." Although intriguing, the message was not taken very seriously. It nevertheless ended with a clear threat: "only then will we be able to live in peace in this country, while you sleep easy and carry on stealing as you please." However deeply any given narco-organization was involved in both political assassinations, the essence of this message is its implication that for two decades a more or less tacit agreement—as opposed to a negotiated "pact"—regulated the "connivance" between the state, its local barons, and the major traffickers. This arrangement, already shaky, is now in danger of collapsing altogether. And the bloodiness of recent events indicates just how high the stakes are.

To understand this dual process of escalation, it is necessary to go back to the murder of Cardinal Posadas in Guadalajara in May 1993. Whether it was a "hitch" or a premeditated act, the murder, still unsolved, set off a chain reaction. After the Guadalajara airport shoot-out, the top priority for the Salinas government just a few months ahead of the signature of the Free Trade Treaty, known in the United States as the North American Free Trade Agreement (NAFTA), was to play down the scandal and reassure Washington. Taking the risk of breaking the fragile balance of power defining the respective territories of the various cartels, the government just had to arrest some major trafficker in a dramatic display of strength. The axe fell on "Chapo" Guzmán, the boss of the Sinaloa cartel and the alleged joint perpetrator of the Guadalajara murder. Guzmán's capture in Guatemala, probably as a result of his being let down by a former ally, or "protector," within the state apparatus, could have been interpreted as the first dent in an informal agreement of non-aggression.

Then came the reorganization of the federal counternarcotics forces, a development that upset the old balance to a considerable extent. In principle, the job of the newly created National Institute for the Anti-Drug Fight (INCD), an ad hoc technical coordinating body that the press a little hastily nicknamed "the Mexican DEA," was to plan, implement, supervise, and assess programs against drug trafficking and drug addiction. But during the first months of its existence the INCD was especially noted for its obsession with secrecy, very closely monitoring journalists' access to its own data. However, the most important change implied by the establishment of the INCD was that the *chicos malos* (bad boys), that is, the police officers most closely involved in operations, were stripped of their investigative authority. The INCD was thereby deprived of the *chicos malos'* experience, contacts, and dealings with the underworld, all of which had enabled the police to understand its workings and to carry out, at appropriate times, some major seizures, regulating the market and limiting the possibilities of a war between the cartels. One of the essential communication channels between the central government and organized crime, through the police and certain sectors of the army, was thus blurred or even cut off. The consequences were felt almost immediately. While the antidrug fight faded into the background, as the police and army were busy investigating and designing strategies to confront the sudden arrival on the scene of the Chiapas guerrillas, the *chicos malos* vanished into thin air, as ready as ever to supplement their income with the best offer but this time free from government control.

The powerful cartels of Amado Carrillo Fuentes in Chihuahua state, Juan García Abrego in Tamaulipas state, or the Arellano Félix brothers in Tijuana, remained beyond reach. Feuds between the narcos, which also involved local and federal police officers, multiplied. Smaller, apparently autonomous cartels appeared, mainly in central and northern Mexico. These smaller cartels, numbering about twenty according to the DEA and with mostly ill-identified leaders, experienced rapid growth. Repression was applied to these groups in a highly selective, "à la carte" manner that seemed to coincide with the short-term interests of certain civil servants prior to the August 1994 election.

The involvement of persons linked to the drug trade—rather limited in the Colosio case but more obvious in that of Ruiz Massieu—must be placed in the context of a no-holds-barred renegotiation of the balance of power and growing personalization of the prevailing arrangements between the narcos and their political allies. It should be recalled that from the outset, Colosio's campaign was placed against the backdrop of the Chiapas rebellion, a consequence of which was to open a rift within the PRI. One side advocates talks with the guerrillas. Generally, it stands for a more socially oriented PRI, eager to avoid a potentially explosive worsening of the relations between a corrupt political system thriving on privileges and bribes and the majority of the population, which remains excluded from the benefits promised by Mexico's graduation, through NAFTA, to the status of a First World country. The other camp, formed by the PRI's "dinosaurs," is hostile to a redistribution of wealth and advocates the use of force to deal with the Chiapas rebels. The rift within the ruling party suddenly turned the question of President Salinas's succession and the makeup of the new cabinet and its general policy orientation into burning issues, widening even further the gap between the PRI's internal clans and interest groups. Colosio's murder simply brought down the remaining bridges between the camps.

Indisputably, by systematically rejecting the notion of a political murder conspiracy, the official inquiry into the Colosio assassination lacks credibility and has complicated matters even more. The only independent investigation to have been carried out was probably going to prove, on the basis of several trustworthy witnesses, that Colosio was killed by two bullets shot from different angles by weapons of different caliber. But the investigation came to a halt following the theft of the investigation's files from the Tijuana police headquarters and, on the following day, the murder of José Federico Benítez, the policeman in charge of the inquiry. Admittedly, Benítez, who claimed he possessed evidence of a plot through the involvement of another policeman, José Rivapalacio, had gained a reputation for being incorruptible by "cleansing" the Tijuana local police, firing 850 of the total force of 2,100. In Tijuana, while the border between Mexico and the United States is clearly visible at the end of the main street, the frontier separating corrupt police officers from the narcos who enjoy their protection is a lot harder to make out. In this context, the most plausible explanation for the Colosio murder is that there was a conspiracy involving some federal and local policemen, who may incidentally also belong to the *charola* cartel (*charola* is the Mexican word for a police badge) but who acted on orders from a superior interest group, of which the drug trade is merely one component.

The second major assassination, that of PRI General Secretary Francisco Ruiz Massieu, sheds some light on the dual nature of the passive and active alliances that have been woven over the years between big traffickers and corrupt politicians, which both now use to their own ends. The Ruiz Massieu family, an important economic player in Acapulco, where drug money—as in Cancun and Quintana Roo—penetrates deep into the local economy, found itself at the heart of the contradictions endured for a year by the hard core of the Salinas team—the "Harvard boys." The first, and strongest, such contradiction is that existing between Francisco's brother's job as head of counternarcotics at the Procuraduría General de la República (ministry of justice) and the protectors of the drug trade he turned to attack, after rubbing shoulders with them for a long time as a result of the rift between the PRI's "dinosaurs" and the party's new generation of technocrats. Another contradiction exists between the conservative motives for Colosio's murder and the increased blackmailing power of the traffickers who took advantage of the situation to assert, through bloody intimidation, how far the real or supposed reforms threatening their interests should go. Under such circumstances, ascertaining the identity of those who pulled the trigger, be they the Gulf cartel of Juan García Abrego or some other organization, is no longer so important. Searching for links between one or another PRI "heavyweight" and a local cartel is fairly easy, since those links are often notorious; but the result is a disillusioning, almost banal list of names. Decidedly, the best explanation seems to be a crack in Mexico's political system whose monolithic stature is no longer enough to ensure its automatic continuity. The search for a new "arrangement" between *narcos* and *politicos* is thus played out violently in the highest echelons of the state. Beyond the increasingly important role of drug money in the Mexican economy, the current crisis can be explained by the trouble caused by the traffickers and the elite that protects them. They could still sabotage any attempt to transform Mexico from an all-powerful bureaucracy into a pluralistic country open to social change.

Appendix One

Synthetic Drugs: A Revolution

A few years ago, a report assessing the likely state of medicine in Great Britain by the year 2000 predicted that "the frontier between narcotics and medicines is likely to become increasingly blurred, causing technical, ethical, moral, and political problems, the consequences of which remain difficult to assess even today." Today, a comprehensive review of drug abuse worldwide can no longer be limited to "natural" drugs (those derived from plants). Has the era of synthetic drugs, often forecast by the pundits, really begun? The importance these substances have assumed in the former communist countries could prove decisive.

A New Fashion

On June 11, 1994, the British weekly *The Economist* cited a Gallup poll carried out in Great Britain among fifteen- to twenty-four-year-olds showing that the proportion of those who had tried Ecstasy, alias MDMA (or its twin sister, MDEA or "Eve"), grew from 1 percent to 7 percent between 1989 and 1992. This proportion represents a market of about 500,000 regular users. In England, the three most widely consumed drugs are currently cannabis derivatives, amphetamines, and Ecstasy—in that order. Ecstasy, a stimulant with hallucinogenic properties, is wreaking havoc in Spain, Italy, Germany, and the Netherlands; these four countries absorb most of the drug's supply (80 percent of the amphetamine derivatives seized in Europe are manufactured in the Netherlands). Also produced by Dutch secret laboratories, LSD is making a dramatic comeback. Phenethylamine, amphetamine and mescaline analogs, of which no less than 179 derivatives have been identified, are all the rage in Florida and California. One of these new compounds, named "Nexus" (or 2C-B), appeared in Miami in 1993. It was probably manufactured by a laboratory located in Cape Town, South Africa. Nexus can also be found in London. Thus, in western Europe as well as in the United States, synthetic drugs are undeniably fashionable.

In the Footsteps of Crack

In the United States, forgotten or unknown substances appeared on the streets following the decline in the crack epidemic noted by the American authorities since the early 1990s. The current trend, illustrated by products such as "croke" (a cocktail containing 46 percent cocaine and 17 percent amphetamine), is the development of multidrug use. PCP (angel dust) is back in fashion in Canada (secret laboratories in Ontario specialize in it), in southern California, and in most major U.S. cities. The drug is marketed in suburbs and deprived neighborhoods by Los Angeles gangs and their affiliates throughout the United States (the same people who control crack distribution). Another stimulant, methcathinone, which appeared in 1991, is manufactured in the states of Colorado, Illinois, Indiana, Michigan, Missouri, Washington, and Wisconsin. Methamphetamine is essentially produced in the West and Southwest of the United States and in Mexico, as evidenced by the spectacular seizure at Mexico City airport in February 1994 of 2.4 tons of ephedrine (the main reagent for making methamphetamine) from Madras, India, on board an Air France flight. Distribution in the United States is in the hands of gangs of bikers or of Hispanic organizations. Ecstasy is manufactured on the East Coast and in Mexico. Fentanyl derivatives (powerful synthetic opiates that were briefly in vogue from 1983 to 1985) come from the Midwest and are sold as heroin (China White) in the big cities of the Northeast. Between 1991 and 1992, at least 126 deaths were attributed to fentanyl derivatives.

In 1993, 270 secret laboratories were destroyed in the United States, including 218 making methamphetamine, 22 producing methcathinone, 12 dedicated to amphetamine, and 6 manufacturing PCP. From a trafficker's point of view, synthetic drugs have two advantages: They can be manufactured close to the markets, and they are easily concealed. In 1986 Robert K. Sager, head of the DEA laboratory, estimated that for an investment of US$150 a chemist could produce 500 grams of 3-methyl-fentanyl (currently manufactured illegally in the Midwest of the United States, in Moscow and Kazan, Russia, as well as in Azerbaijan) in just four days. Since a dose of this substance is measured in micrograms (a postage stamp weighs 60,000 micrograms), a chemist who could sell 500 grams divided into 50 million doses, each for the price of a dose of heroin, would pocket a profit of about US$500 million.

Continually hampered by the appearance of new compounds (or "designer drugs"), law enforcement institutions readily admit that the only reason a boom in synthetic drugs has not yet occurred is the failure to suppress natural drugs—users still prefer the real thing to an "*ersatz*" product, even if it is a thousand times more powerful. This is especially the case now that the purity of the heroin and cocaine available on the street is constantly rising, while prices drop, probably as a result of overproduction worldwide.

Great Potential in the East

The entry, with a vengeance, of the former Soviet bloc countries into the drug market at the beginning of the 1990s may well have spectacular consequences. The choice open to criminal organizations there is either fostering the cultivation of drug plants or taking advantage of rundown chemical industries in order to produce synthetic drugs. Several factors tip the scales toward the second option: Basic chemical reagents are not subject to any serious form of control; highly qualified and underpaid chemists abound; and local users are not accustomed to natural drugs, hence they have no qualms about substitutes. Over the last few years clues that massive production is getting under way in the former Soviet bloc have been multiplying.

According to the German police, 20 to 25 percent of the amphetamine seized in Germany originate from Poland. The authorities in Warsaw estimate that their national amphetamine output supplies 10 percent of the European market. In Poland, university laboratories are under suspicion, and law enforcement officials stopped counting long ago how many smugglers they have arrested entering Germany and Sweden. The Czech Republic is hot on Poland's heels for the title of largest European producer of psychotropic substances after the Netherlands. Pervitine, a methamphetamine produced in liquid, injectable form and renamed Seco, is now consumed more widely than natural drugs in the Czech Republic. Rostoki, central Europe's biggest synthetic ephedrine manufacturing company, is based in a Prague suburb. At least 200 kilograms of ephedrine disappeared from a Rostoki plant there in the first six months of 1994. Furthermore, the 1994 report of the United Nations International Narcotics Control Board (INCB) mentions that 50 tons of that substance were diverted to Mexico via Switzerland, to be used to manufacture methamphetamine for the U.S. market. Moreover, Czech chemists are employed in laboratories located in neighboring Saxony, Germany.

Various cases that have occurred since 1992 have proved that Latvia and Hungary are favored by investors—especially German and Dutch—who bankroll the production of 3,4 methylenedioxyethilamphetamine (MDEA) and 3,4 methylenedioxymethamphetamine (MDMA) for the market of the European Union. Finally, the INCB expressed concern in April 1993 about the fact that Bulgarian state-owned firms (notably Sopharma and other chemical plants in the town of Doupnitsa) were exporting amphetamine and phenethylamine without permission under the brand name "Captagon" to Africa (Nigeria) and the Persian Gulf states via Turkey. On November 30, 1994, the Bulgarian police seized 16 tons of pharmaceuticals bound for the Netherlands with false documents. Sopharma's director and employees of a private company were arrested. Sopharma officials explained that the incriminating substances were a pharmaceutical thinner delivered by AEG, a German company. However, as far as the police are concerned, the state-owned company was acting as an intermediary in an illegal deal in synthetic drug reagents destined for secret Dutch facilities.

The former Soviet Union seems to be catching up with Poland and the former Czechoslovakia. Azerbaijan has specialized in the production of synthetic opiates (methadone, normorphine, 3-methyl-fentanyl) at Gyandzha and Baku. *Ephedra vulgaris,* the plant from which ephedrine is derived, grows in the wild in Kirghizistan and in Kazakhstan, around Almaty. In Kazakhstan, it seems, chemists have succeeded in manufacturing ephedrone (an analog of the infamous methcathinone made in the United States) from the plant. Elsewhere, in Russia, Belarus, the Ukraine, and the Baltic countries, synthetic ephedrine is isolated from pharmaceutical compounds and then turned into ephedrone. According to a report published on February 3, 1995, by the national association of Italian traders, *Confcommercio,* the Italian Camorra mob is exchanging billions in forged dollars for "great quantities of synthetic drugs that the

Russians now produce in enormous quantities." And in turn, these "goods generate considerable amounts of cash," which are then invested in the European economy.

China too is cashing in on its *ephedra* resources. Ephedrine and ICE (MDA hydrochloride, a very potent crystallized form of methamphetamine) laboratories are mushrooming in the Guangdong and Fujian provinces. As yet, their output is destined almost exclusively for the Southeast Asian market. The *yakuza,* who hold a monopoly over the Japanese market, have long ago set up methamphetamine (from ephedrine) production facilities in South Korea, Thailand, Taiwan, Hong Kong, and (since 1985) the Philippines. Since the end of the 1980s, Japan's annual consumption of amphetamine derivatives is estimated at 2 tons. But even this huge market can no longer absorb the whole of the output. ICE has now reached the United States via Hawaii, the West Coast, and Mexico. It also appeared in Paris for the first time in 1993, brought in by Filipino traffickers.

When the Dealers Are Rich Countries

The last notable, specific feature of the world market in synthetic drugs is that the usual direction of the narcotics trade is reversed. The industrial powers have no qualms about assuming the part of the dealer, while poor countries become consumers. Depressants of the central nervous system are the object of intense North-South trafficking. In most African countries, abuse of barbiturates (secobarbital) and benzodiazepines (diazepam, flunitrazepam), all manufactured by the European pharmaceutical industry and diverted from their therapeutic use, has become a major problem. Nigeria is a redistribution center—and also a production center—for fake medicines destined for the whole of Africa.

Methaqualone (Quaaludes) trafficking to South Africa has increased. Today, South Africa and the transit countries around it are the world's biggest market for the depressant. Known locally as Mandrax, it is mixed with marijuana before it is smoked. After licit methaqualone production stopped in India in 1984, secret laboratories cropped up in the Bombay region (under the control of groups organizing the heroin trade), in Madras, in Pakistan, and in eastern and southern Africa.

At a meeting held under the aegis of the Pompidou Group (a specialized body of the European Council) and the INCB in Strasbourg in March 1993, government experts confined themselves to noting that

Europe was playing an active part in the synthetic drug traffic. The information received since only confirms this disillusioning observation.

A Glossary of "Dangerous Drugs"

DANGEROUS DRUGS—a term used by the DEA to denote controlled substances other than cocaine, opiates, and cannabis derivatives. The category includes both substances produced by secret laboratories and diverted medicines.

DESIGNER DRUGS—chemical variants of controlled substances. Producers slightly modify the molecular structure of a banned substance in order to obtain the same effects without falling foul of the law, at least until the new drug is identified and recorded as a controlled substance by the authorities.

SYNTHETIC OPIATES—substances, generally derived from tar, coal, and oil by-products, possessing analgesic properties similar to those of morphine.

- *Methadone:* main heroin substitute, used for treating addiction.
- *Phenylpiperidines:* family comprising several thousands of synthetic opiates, notably including the following two groups:

  Pethidine or meperidine (ethyl-1-methyl-4-phenylpiperidine-4-carboxylate) and derivatives: marketed under various names, such as MPPP (or synthetic heroin), MPTP, PEPAP, etc. They have hallucinogenic effects.

  Fentanyl and derivatives: a powerful analgesic, discovered in Belgium in 1963. It appeared in the United States in the early 1970s. This is one of the basic precursors for designer drugs. 3-methyl-fentanyl is currently manufactured in the CIS.

AMPHETAMINE (AND DERIVATIVES)—a synthetic aminate with a chemical structure resembling that of adrenergic neurotransmitters. Amphetamine stimulates intellectual and verbal production and hides signs of tiredness, sleep, and hunger. It is also called "a working man's drug" or "poor man's cocaine."

- *Speed:* nickname of amphetamine sulphate, the simplest form of this type of drug; conditioned into pills.
- *Phenethylamines:* family of mescaline and methamphetamine analogs. Amphetamine and its derivatives are all phenethylamines. Some, like amphetamine and methamphetamine, have a purely stimulating effect; others, like DOM, have a marked hallucinogenic effect. Still others, like MDA and MDMA, are a combination of both.
- *Ephedrine:* main alkaloid present in *ephedra vulgaris,* a plant the Chinese have used for 5,000 years to treat asthma and as a stimulant. The main precursor for producing methamphetamine.
- *Methamphetamine:* an amphetamine derivative marketed legally under the name *Pervitine.* The simplest way to produce Pervitine is by chemically reducing ephedrine.
- *MDA* (3,4-methylenedioxyamphetamine): nicknamed Love Drug. In crystallized form it is called ICE and is smoked; 7 kilograms of ephedrine are necessary to manufacture 1 kg of ICE.
- *MDMA* (3,4-methylenedioxymethamphetamine): MDA analog known as Ecstasy. The synthesis of 179 variants of Ecstasy was published in the United States.
- *MDEA* (3,4-methylenedioxyethilamphetamine): a variant of Ecstasy produced in the Netherlands and known as Eve.
- *DOM* (2,5-dimethoxy-4-methylamphetamine) or *STP* (Security, Tranquility, Peace): one of the most powerful known hallucinogens.
- *Methcathinone* or *"cat"*: based on natural or synthetic ephedrine, with a chemical structure similar to methamphetamine and cathinone (the active principle of khat, or *Cathis edulis,* a shrub whose leaves are chewed for a mild stimulating effect in Yemen and the Horn of Africa) analog. It was discovered in the United States in the 1950s and began to be sold there in the 1990s as a powder that may be snorted, swallowed, injected, or smoked with marijuana. It is known as ephedrone in the former USSR, where it first appeared in Leningrad (now St. Petersburg) in 1982.

OTHER HALLUCINOGENS—these are former medicines declared illicit due to their dangerous side effects.

- *Phencyclidine (PCP):* a medical analgesic that appeared in 1957, belonging to the arylcycloalkylamines family. Also called angel dust, the medical use of PCP on human beings was stopped in 1965 due to its powerful hallucinogenic effects. It was subsequently used as a tranquilizer for animals before production was banned in 1978. Marketed under the form of cigarettes soaked in ether-diluted base. Piperidine (see above under **SYNTHETIC OPIATES**) is used as a precursor in the production of PCP.
- *LSD 25* (Lysergic Acid Diethylamide): lysergic acid derivative, an alkaloid derived from rye ergot. Usually nicknamed acid and marketed on blotters, each containing 20 to 80 micrograms of the substance.

DEPRESSANTS OF THE CENTRAL NERVOUS SYSTEM—these are tranquilizers, mood regulators, and sleeping drugs. They may sometimes be produced in secret facilities but are mostly diverted licit medicines.

- *Barbiturates:* substances used in medicine due to their sedative and hypnotic properties. Secobarbital, which is used to manufacture some barbiturates, is listed as a controlled substance and is the object of intense trafficking to Africa.
- *Benzodiazepines:* the main family of tranquilizers, including diazepam (*Valium*), chlorazepam (*Tranxen*), flunitrazepam (*Rohypnol*), temazepam (popular in the northeast of England and in London), etc.
- *Methaqualone:* nonbarbiturate sedative discovered in 1951, known in the United States as Quaalude and in South Africa as Mandrax.

Appendix Two

The Fight Against Money Laundering and Its Limits: The Case of Switzerland

1994 came as a rude awakening for those who believed that decisive advances were being made in the fight against money laundering. In the summer of 1993, an audit carried out by the FATF concluded that Swiss antilaundering legislation "could be seen as a model." Last year, however, some major cases demonstrated that Switzerland, as well as the United States and tax haven countries in Europe and the Caribbean, was still one of the main money-laundering centers in the world. Moreover, it came to light that Swiss banks had played a crucial part in major corruption cases that rocked Italy, France, Spain, and Brazil.

FATF Was Blind

In February 1994, Sheila Myriam Araña de Nasser, a Colombian national, was arrested near Geneva. She was the wife of Julio Nasser David of Barranquilla, one of Colombia's biggest drug traffickers. Sheila Araña's arrest led to the seizure of US$150 million that Nasser had accumulated since 1979 at the Zurich branch of Union de Banques Suisses (UBS), one of the three largest Swiss banks. Never before had such a huge amount of drug money been discovered in just one bank. Reflecting on the Colombian's unusual behavior—traffickers generally try to spread their funds among several establishments so as to minimize risks—a high American official with long experience in the fight against money laundering commented that Julio Nasser David must have felt "protected" at UBS. But the bank said it held Nasser to be a legitimate businessman, owning both ships and hotels, and it was never charged of any wrongdoing. However, UBS cannot escape the fact that Nasser had been indicted several times on drug-trafficking charges in the United States starting in 1986. Since 1991, he had been exposed as a major cocaine baron by a newspaper as widely read as the *Miami Herald.* Still, UBS kept him as a customer through 1994.

This UBS case also hurt FATF credibility. Before determining the "exemplary" nature of the Swiss antilaundering system, FATF experts had reviewed as a test the internal control mechanisms of one bank in particular. It happened to be UBS. After being criticized in the media, UBS argued that Nasser David's funds were left over from a time when there was no law against money laundering and when Swiss banks were not scrutinizing their customers as closely. The same point was made by the Swiss minister of justice, Arnold Koller, at the Naples world summit on international crime in November 1994. He added that the law against money laundering adopted in 1990 should prevent similar abuses in the future.

Cases Multiply

However, a money-laundering case tried in Texas in spring 1994 seemed to contradict Koller's optimism. At the conclusion of the trial, a federal jury found Antonio Giraldi, a senior executive with American Express Bank, guilty of having accepted funds from a money launderer employed by Juan Garcia Ábrego, the boss of the Matamoros cartel, one of Mexico's biggest trafficking organizations. He was sentenced to ten years in prison. To hide his tracks, Giraldi had moved Ábrego's funds through the Geneva branches of Bankers' Trust and American Express Bank. Part of the contentious transfers were made after August 1, 1990, the date on which the Swiss antilaundering law came into force.

In early September came Libertina Rizzuto's case. A grandmother and a member of the Rizzuto Italian-Canadian mafia family, she was arrested in Ticino as she prepared to withdraw funds obtained in part from drug trafficking at another of Switzerland's top three banks, Crédit Suisse. This arrest resulted from the Royal Canadian Mounted Police's largest undercover operation ever, and funds were seized not only in Switzerland but in Canada and other countries as well. A few weeks later, the Swiss public learned that Ecuador's biggest drug trafficker, Jorge Hugo Reyes Torres, had laundered significant amounts of money in Zurich banks, as well as in Germany and Liechtenstein. According to the DEA, the Reyes Torres family had been manufacturing several tons of cocaine every month since the early 1970s. It took a ceremony at the U.S. Embassy in Bern, where American officials solemnly handed over to Swiss counterparts some of the US$11 million of drug proceeds seized in Zurich, to make Swiss citizens realize that their banks had thus had the "honor" of being used by Ecuador's top cocaine boss, in addition to some of Colombia's and Mexico's biggest drug barons.

On November 30, Leon and Rachel Weinmann, a husband-and-wife team of Zurich accountants, were arrested in New York on charges of having laundered between US$60 million and $100 million for the Cali cartel in 1993 alone. The Weinmanns belonged to a laundering ring led by two New York lawyers. The drug proceeds were electronically transferred to their Zurich accounts from a Citibank branch in the Bronx. After this detour through Swiss bank secrecy, the funds were transferred to accounts in the United States or in Panama. The Weinmanns were caught simply because the telephones of their American accomplices had been tapped by the DEA and the FBI. Such apparent amateurism on the Weinmanns' part is a sure sign that launderers still feel secure in Switzerland.

Finally, on December 2, 1994, following an undercover investigation led by U.S. customs agents, a federal grand jury in Miami indicted on money-laundering charges Jean-Jacques Handali and Michael Ley, two executives at one of Geneva's largest private banks, Union Bancaire Privée CBI-TDB; Jeckiel Valero, a former executive at the same bank; and Albert Shammah, a customer of the bank. The indictment alleges that these four individuals and their American codefendants accepted for laundering at Union Bancaire Privée CBI-TDB monies described to them as drug proceeds by a trafficker's cousin. In reality, this trafficker never existed, and his "cousin" was a U.S. customs undercover agent.

Even before the indictments were issued, the case prompted a high-level American official to remark that progress made by Switzerland in the antilaundering fight has been "minimal" so far. The significance of the case lies in the fact that some of the financiers accused of laundering money were not outside intermediaries but executives at one of Geneva's largest banking establishments. (Union Bancaire Privée CBI-TDB has not been indicted and claims to have been deceived by its employee, Jean-Jacques Handali.)

The case is also significant because Albert Shammah is one of the defendants. (Albert Shammah says that he is innocent of the charges. So do most of the other defendants.) The indictment alleges that Shammah masterminded the transfer of the criminal funds from the United States to Switzerland, using a network of couriers and providing the same services to five or six other Swiss banks. According to a statement reputedly made by codefendant Handali, Shammah brought no less than 100 clients to Union Bancaire Privée CBI-TDB, which stems from the former Geneva Trade Development Bank.

A French national born in Aleppo in 1914, Shammah, who is well known in Geneva and in Israel, was indicted and arrested on similar charges in 1985. At the time, one of Italy's leading antimafia judges, Mario Vaudano, accused him of assisting in laundering funds for the Tirnovali-Soydan gang of Turkish heroin traffickers. He requested Shammah's extradition from Switzerland. But disregarding the separation of powers, the then prime minister of Italy, Socialist Bettino Craxi, as well as other prominent politicians and businessmen in Italy and Geneva, intervened and had Shammah released from jail. In a very controversial move, Swiss authorities then refused to grant Italy legal assistance in this case. In the end, Shammah was not extradited, and charges against him were dropped.

Apart from this case of drug money laundering, Union Bancaire Privée CBI-TDB has also been used by various individuals who were the target of investigations in corruption cases: Luis Roldán, the former head of the Spanish Guardia Civil; Giancarlo Rossi, a former stockbroker from Milan working on behalf of Italy's Christian Democrats; and Brazil's former president, Fernando Collor de Mello. In addition, in 1994 Swiss banks in general received a significant share of the funds fleeing Russia to the tune of $1 billion a month, at least some of which are of criminal origin.

Timid Judges Versus Stubborn Bankers

The number of laundering cases uncovered in Swiss banks in 1994 is ample proof that the law against money laundering has had only a mild deterrent effect, despite high hopes. The law's limited impact is partly due to a persistent weakness in Swiss law enforcement. Switzerland does not have a federal judiciary, except a supreme court of appeals. The responsibility for law enforcement is scattered among the twenty-six cantons. As a result, most of the above cases were raised by foreign authorities, mostly American. It took the intervention of an American undercover agent on Swiss soil, and inside the very premises of the bank, for the Handali-Shammah-CBI-TDB investigation to bear fruit. Such outside intervention demonstrates that the Geneva authorities cannot count on either the technical know-how or the political support required to carry out similar undercover operations within their own banks. Only the discovery of Julio Nasser David's funds at UBS can be credited to Swiss police. And this was mainly the work of a federal agent, Jacques-André Kaeslin, who had already almost singlehandedly, brought to light the well-known Shakarchi-Kopp affair seven years earlier.

Swiss judges and prosecutors have indeed improved the assistance they provide to their foreign counterparts. But they remain rather timid on their own soil. For instance, Ticino prosecutor Carla del Ponte (now prosecutor of the Swiss Confederation) did not spare her efforts in helping the team of Italian judges working on Operation Clean Hands. But she dropped her case against the FIMO financial company of Chiasso, Switzerland. FIMO was extensively used by the Milan financier Giuseppe Lottusi, who in the Big John freighter case was sentenced to twenty years for having laundered funds on behalf of the Medellin cartel and the Sicilian Madonia family. Silvio Berlusconi used this same FIMO company to make secret payments connected to his A.C. Milan soccer club.

Another reason for the timidity of Swiss judges and prosecutors when taking on Swiss banks without the support of foreign colleagues is the strong resistance of bankers and the all-powerful lawyers on whom they rely. Thus, Swiss bankers adamantly rejected an obligation to report suspicious transactions, such as that imposed on their European counterparts by a European Union directive. As a result, the Swiss Federal Council (executive branch) was forced to withdraw and rewrite a draft law including such a provision. More important, this new bill would also have made the whole financial sector subject to the law against money laundering—including assets managers, money exchange firms, accounting firms, insurance companies, and law firms. This expansion was advocated in the FATF's report on Switzerland because, FATF experts wrote, "such firms may either be controlled by launderers or be used for money-laundering activities." For example, the Weinmanns (see above) had an accounting firm in Zurich. Therefore, the financial sector opposes strengthening the measures against money laundering just as a continuing influx of drug money seems to call for tougher action.

One can detect a simultaneous desire to conceal and, when this proves impossible, to downplay the use of Swiss banks by money launderers. For instance, in 1994, one of Geneva's conservative parties, close to the private banking industry, attempted to pressure judges and prosecutors into not publicizing foreign requests for legal assistance, especially concerning financial matters, because, as a Geneva conservative state councillor (minister) said, the cumulative weight of these cases would add credence to the city's reputation as the "Capua of Europe."

In Zurich, after the discovery of the US$150 million of drug proceeds at UBS, the tendency has rather been to downplay the issue of laundering. Banking circles started to say that traffickers would always use Swiss banks because they are efficient. This attitude of resignation could pass for hard-nosed realism, but vested interests lie behind the bankers' benign acceptance of the status quo. Bankers claim that fighting money laundering is very difficult mainly because they think it is also too costly. With such a philosophy prevailing in Switzerland, it may be a long time before drug money starts avoiding Swiss vaults.

Appendix Three

The Legalization Debate in Europe

The blatant failure of the war on drugs, waged for a decade by the rich countries under the leadership of the United States, has reignited, with unprecedented intensity, a public debate on policies to fight drug addiction. A distinction needs to be drawn between the "decriminalization of drug use" and the "legalization of the drug trade." Decriminalization of use, whereby possession of a set quantity of drugs considered to be "for personal use" is not punished, is already in effect in most European countries (except France, Luxembourg, Belgium, and Portugal). The legalization of the drug trade, however, is a measure that can only be conceived of in global terms. If the drug trade were legalized in all the countries of the world at the same time, a dramatic fall in drug prices would occur, depriving international criminal organizations of a substantial share of their profits.

However, numerous criminal organizations, such as the various Italian mobs and the Chinese triads, have long ago diversified their activities, and legalization would affect them only in a minor way. Other organizations would probably switch to other sectors of illicit activity. The effect of legalization would in fact be felt most at the level of petty crime, which results from abusers' need somehow to find the money for their daily drug requirements. Therefore, what the debate is really about is what effect legalization would have on drug consumption. This is hard to predict, especially since there are no precedents (the end of alcohol prohibition in the United States represented in fact a return to an earlier situation) and because no prospective study has so far been undertaken.

Harm Reduction

Leaving aside the example of France, a remarkable caricature of political opposition to change, the crux of the debate in Europe is over the lack, on the one hand, of an alternative to the classic prohibition-dominated strategies (prohibition remaining a reference *faute de mieux*) and the growing relevance, on the other hand, of the implementation of measures aimed at "harm reduction" in AIDS-related matters. By addressing the problem in terms of treating drug abuse, whether by making substitutes more available or by distributing heroin, "harm reduction" advocates inescapably open up an ideological debate on the status of drugs and drug use in modern societies. After all, the proposed treatments go against the public dogma regarding abstinence as the necessary prerequisite to any sort of rehabilitation of drug abusers.

Thus, opinions everywhere fall into two opposing camps: those in favor of a lasting commitment by the authorities to a minimal program of harm reduction; and the upholders of the status quo, who fear that any softening of tough, repressive policies will clear the way for the advocates of pure and simple liberalization of the use of, and trade in, illicit drugs. This latter position is made stronger by the classic reluctance of any institution to question its role in society. Finally, the debate is further complicated by the repeated statements in favor of outright liberalization of the drug trade by such advocates of ultraliberal economics as the American Nobel Prize laureate Milton Friedman and the columnists of the serious British weekly *The Economist*.

The antagonism between both camps goes a long way toward explaining why a strange hesitancy was the hallmark of 1994. The well-known experiment in Liverpool, England, starting in 1985, in which heroin and syringes were distributed under medical supervision, was ended—administrative necessity was the excuse. Meanwhile, the Swiss federal authorities decided to extend the heroin and methadone distribution program they had started at the beginning of 1994 to 700 particularly dependent abusers. This action was taken to offset the blatant failure of the Zurich "open scene" experiment, the famous "drugs supermarket" of the Letten, which had itself replaced the Platzspitz Park experiment, terminated in 1992. The Letten, the scene of a dogged and bloody war for market control between gangs, was in turn closed in mid-February 1995. Swiss users were sent back to their towns of origin to enter the programs of their respective cantons, and foreigners were expelled from the country. In Rotterdam, the Netherlands, the Municipal Health Office is due to launch a program of heroin distribution in 1995, nearly free of charge, to about 100 abusers residing in the area. Ten years after a similar attempt was aborted in Amsterdam following an international outcry, the initiative was welcomed by the municipalities of Amsterdam, Heerlen, and Amersfoort, which declared themselves willing to follow suit.

Other countries of the world, which are usually less daring in such matters, are seriously considering harm reduction. Thus, in early 1995 a report by the provincial health authority of British Columbia, Canada, recommended decriminalizing heroin use and even distributing the drug in order to reduce deaths by overdose and the crime surrounding heroin abuse. In this part of Canada's west coast, an influx of very pure Asian heroin has now made drug abuse the leading cause of death among persons aged thirty-four to forty. The provincial government announced that a group would study the proposal and initiate discussions with other provinces and the federal authorities.

An Increasingly Isolated France

On November 29, 1994, France's National Advisory Committee on Ethics (CCNE) issued a report on drug abuse, a subject it decided to tackle of its own accord in April 1993. By choosing "to make their own contribution to the public debate," the experts triggered off a nice bit of controversy in France. The report first notes that "far from being rooted out, international drug trafficking has... exploded in spite of the considerable means employed to fight narcotics." As for France, "it chose to criminalize simple drug use, even in private, a measure not called for in international agreements." But "prohibition was not enough to stop the consumption of illicit drugs." The very concept of licit and illicit drugs "does not seem to be based on any coherent scientific evidence." How can "the nonabusing cannabis user" be considered "a criminal, when the alcoholic who is a danger to others is not," while "nonprohibited drugs (alcohol, tobacco, painkillers, neuropsychiatric medicines) are, on the whole, potentially as dangerous as prohibited drugs? Regarding the latter, it does not seem rational that the (moderate or abusive) consumption of all illicit substances should carry the same penalty, since their effects and toxicity vary widely." And the report, hammering the point home, notes that "public leniency regarding tobacco has fostered an unprecedented epidemic of cancers and heart diseases over the past fifty years," while the use of cannabis derivatives has become "quite common a practice among certain social groups, with its norms and its rites."

In conclusion, the CCNE advocates a "third path" between total suppression and the legalization of drugs, namely, specific legislation on each substance, "taking into account its toxicity, the risks of dependence and desocialization entailed by its use, and the risks it entails for other people." Moreover, the use of any drug "should only be punished when it occurs in public, or when evidence has been produced that it has a negative influence on others, especially the family circle." This amounts to little short of outright advocacy of the—at least partial—decriminalization of drug use. In May 1994, the doctors and psychiatrists who are members of the Association of Professionals Working on Drug Abuse (ANIT) issued a manifesto demanding that cannabis be dissociated "from 'the drug' problem" and that a study be undertaken on "a form of cannabis legalization that would confine prohibition, as in the case of alcohol, to the sale to under-age persons and permit control over marketing."

The opinion of the committee's wise men, even if it carries some moral weight, is by no means binding on the French government. In late 1993, Charles Pasqua, then the new minister of the interior, announced the launching of a major national debate on the decriminalization of drug use. In March 1994, Simone Veil, the minister for health and social affairs, established the Henrion Commission and gave it the task of engaging in large-scale consultation on the matter. The commission was to issue its conclusion by November of the same year. In January 1995, it was learned that commission members were still divided over a number of "too liberal" statements, lending credence to the feeling that the government's real objective was to stall the French debate over drugs rather than stimulate it. On February 3, the commission's report was finally made public. While they noted the imperfections of French law, the seventeen commission members were unable to settle the matter of the decriminalization of drug use. Refusing to adopt the distinction between soft and hard drugs ("it can... only be noted that some drugs are more harmful than others"), nine out of the seventeen experts nevertheless noted that the use of cannabis derivatives has become "commonplace and decriminalized in actual fact since the Peyrefitte [then minister of justice] circular of 1978, complemented by the Badinter [then minister of justice] circular of September 1984," and consequently that "the upholding of a penal sanction which is no longer enforced becomes derisory and discredits the justice system in the eyes of teenagers." The commission proposed a trial period during which cannabis prohibition would be confined to minors under sixteen years and to use in public places, following which, "in the absence of a deterioration in the situation in the following two years, a comprehensive regulation of the trade under strict state control could be contemplated." However, such boldness was immediately mitigated by the commission's conclusions that the use of "dangerous" drugs should continue to be punished.

The political context in France in early 1995 (the presidential election campaign) did not encourage consideration of these proposals. Indeed, the day before the Henrion Commission was to publicize its findings, the prime minister and presidential hopeful, Édouard Balladur, preemptively dismissed any notion of decriminalization. The French authorities are still holding tight to the dogma of prohibition, a fact that makes France almost a loner in the concert of European nations. Thus, while the United Kingdom, the Netherlands, Ireland, Italy, and Spain make a distinction between soft (cannabis-derived) and hard drugs, and while none of these countries (any more than Denmark or Greece) criminalizes simple use, according to a French law of December 31, 1970, the use of any drug still warrants two to twelve months in prison, and the possession of any amount of drugs is assimilated to trafficking and punishable by from two to ten years in prison. In 1994, even Germany moved closer to the position of the majority; in April, the Constitutional Court in Karlsruhe urged all *Länder* to stop criminalizing the acquisition and possession of hashish and marijuana for personal use.

The only visible evolution of the French position concerned the management of the risks of contamination of intravenous drug users by the AIDS virus. In 1990, while the Netherlands, Denmark, Italy, Spain, and the United Kingdom were offering programs for substituting heroin (which is injected and therefore riskier in terms of contamination) with methadone (which is swallowed) among thousands of drug abusers, only 50 places in similar programs were available in France. The result was that at least 30 percent of French abusers are contaminated by the AIDS virus and at least 70 percent are sick with hepatitis B and C. The corresponding proportion in both the United Kingdom and the Netherlands is 10 percent. In Germany, a country also behind in substitution opportunities, 5,000 places were made available to abusers in two years. France had 52 places in 1993. While 1,645 places were to be made available in France by the end of 1994, a mere 700 patients had been treated by that time. The reorientation of French health policy was implemented in haste, as a direct result of the trauma in public opinion caused by the "contaminated blood scandal" and the questions surrounding political responsibility in the transmission of the HIV virus. Thus, methadone was illegally distributed in France until January 1995, when the authorization to market the substance, thus far an experimental product in the country, was finally issued (the authorization for another substitute, buprenorphine, or Temgesic, will only be considered shortly).

The Netherlands: God's Work and the Devil's Share

Accused for years by fellow member-states of being the soft spot in the European Union's antidrug system, the Netherlands has recently engaged in a delicate exercise consisting, on the one hand, of providing its partners with guarantees in matters of the suppression of international trafficking and, on the other hand, of preserving the particularity of its own approach on local drug consumption. On January 19, 1995, Mrs. Winnie Sorgdrager, the minister of justice, declared that the Netherlands' policy of tolerance regarding soft drugs had "drifted" and announced her intention to "backpedal." Her main priority, she said, was the parliamentary debate due in May about a planned directive strengthening police and judicial control over the 1,500 coffee shops in the country that supply about one million regular and occasional Dutch cannabis users. In particular, this control would be implemented through a licensing system applicable to both the suppliers and operators of the coffee shops. "We must come back to the original mission" of the smoking rooms, the minister added, and that is to keep soft drug users away from the organized criminals who control the market in hard drugs. But, as the government itself admits, the coffee shops have become "places where soft and hard drugs mix, [they are] infiltrated by the underworld and managed by dishonest people who are only in it for the money." The average age of abusers, which rose steadily during the 1980s, was hailed as evidence that the Dutch policy was successful. However, in 1992 and 1993 it started declining.

The idea is to "reduce progressively the number" of coffee shops by closing down those that do not respect the rules prevailing at the time of their creation in 1976 (the *Opiumwet* law prohibits the sale of hard drugs, restricts the sale of soft drugs to 30 grams per adult, and condemns underworld interference, as well as advertising and inconveniences caused to surrounding areas). Furthermore, because of pressure from outside, the authorities are making efforts to fight the attraction of the Netherlands to users from neighboring countries. In Venlo, a town close to Germany, some coffee shops were closed down to curb "narco-tourism." The city of Arnhem is considering setting up "drive-ins" near the highway in order to keep German cannabis users from the city center. Finally, the Maastricht local council banned foreign clients from its coffee shops, before a court ruled that such a measure was unlawful.

Nevertheless, this evolution does not call the "Dutch model" into question. Rather, it is adapting it to the constraints of the moment and might in fact paradoxically represent a decisive step toward the legalization of soft drugs in the Kingdom of Orange. True, the minister "prefers to speak of regulation" rather than of legalization, but she insists she remains "totally convinced that it is necessary to separate the soft drug and hard drug markets." And, it should be added, to make a distinction, when it comes to soft drugs, between those that are locally produced and those that are imported. According to Adrien Jansen, a professor and researcher at the University of Amsterdam, 60 percent of Dutch users already smoke *niederwiet* (or Dutchweed), a hybrid with a high THC (the active ingredient of cannabis) content that is produced in the hothouses, gardens, and apartments of some 50,000 Dutchmen. With an annual harvest the police put at 40 tons, cannabis is allegedly now the country's sixth largest agricultural product in money terms, on a par with tomatoes. The Hague could be ready to legalize local production and only to fight imports of hashish and marijuana by the powerful criminal organizations that have turned the Netherlands into the hub of the European market. To allay neighbors' fears, Mrs. Sorgdrager says she is willing to prohibit *niederwiet* exports.

The question now is whether the European Union can live with the idea of harboring within its midst a country "legally" producing illicit substances. Anticipating the debate, Morocco, Europe's number-one hashish supplier, is already taking advantage of such ambiguity and adopting a wait-and-see policy in its negotiations with Brussels on the eradication of its own cannabis crops.

Index